AB

To my son

AB

THE AUTOBIOGRAPHY

MACMILLAN

First published 2016 by Pan Macmillan South Africa

First published in the UK 2016 by Macmillan
an imprint of Pan Macmillan
20 New Wharf Road, London N1 9RR
Associated companies throughout the world
www.panmacmillan.com

ISBN 978-1-5098-2257-7

9 8 7 6 5 4 3 2 1

A CIP catalogue record for this book is available from the British Library.

Printed and bound by CPI Group (UK) Ltd, Croydon, CR0 4YY

Visit www.panmacmillan.com to read more about all our books
and to buy them. You will also find features, author interviews and
news of any author events, and you can sign up for e-newsletters
so that you're always first to hear about our new releases.

CONTENTS

FOREWORD

Only a handful of international cricketers have seen their personal popularity extend beyond the boundaries of their homeland. AB de Villiers can be included in this very select group of globally acclaimed superstars.

It was during the 2015 Indian Premier League when, together with other members of the coaching staff of the Mumbai Indians, we watched AB destroy our bowling attack and win the game for Royal Challengers Bangalore. He was batting for the visiting side, but the Mumbai crowd – our supporters – chanted his name before every single delivery that he faced.

'ABD! ABD! ABD! ABD! ABD!'

The chant rang around the entire stadium. I had heard an Indian crowd chant before, but not like this. It was freaky.

AB's innings was extraordinary, full of amazing footwork, brilliant strokes and brilliant improvisation. I was sitting beside my fellow Mumbai coach Ricky Ponting, watching in awe, and when it was all over the former Australian captain turned to me and pointed out that each of AB's shots had been played into a gap.

'That's not luck,' he said. 'That is genius.'

I arrived back at our hotel, somewhat grumpy after our heavy defeat. My wife, Melanie, who had watched on TV, observed: 'Oh well, it must be a bit of a consolation that the game was won by your boy.'

She was right. AB was my boy, not because I played any significant part in developing his talent but because, ever since he had made his debut for the Proteas in 2004, his approach to the game – his positive batting and his energetic presence in the field – resembled the way I played during my international career, which ended the year before, in 2003.

At times, it felt as if AB had seized the torch from me and was taking it to an altogether higher and unimagined level.

His complete destruction of the West Indian attack in Sydney during the 2015 World Cup was so ruthless, so complete and so breathtaking that it left me feeling genuinely sorry for the bowlers.

It was incredible to watch. He was clearly loving the game, mastering the game and yet humbly respecting it at the same time.

AB's career achievements so far have honoured cricket wherever the game is played and Ricky Ponting was 100% correct – he's a genius. I am honoured that AB asked me to write this Foreword to his autobiography and I always feel privileged to be associated with him in any way.

Jonty Rhodes
March 2016

JONTY RHODES played 52 Tests and 245 one-day internationals for South Africa between 1992 and 2003, scoring more than 8 000 runs. Through his infectious energy and brilliant fielding, he became the most recognisable face in the Proteas team that emerged from isolation. He now works in the media and as a coach.

CHAPTER 1

GLORY

S omeone else should bat.

It is Sunday, 18 January 2015. South Africa are playing a one-day international at the Wanderers Stadium in Johannesburg and a capacity crowd is enjoying the warm sunshine. Sent in to bat, openers Hashim Amla and Rilee Rossouw are playing brilliantly, building the ideal plat-form for a winning total.

In the changing room, as our score passes 200 without loss, I approach Russell Domingo, our coach.

'Let Dave Miller go in next, coach,' I say. 'This is perfect for him.'

'No, Abbas, you're next,' he replies, firmly.

That doesn't make sense. Sulieman Benn still has two overs to bowl and, if somebody gets out, Miller should go in and have a full go at the left-arm spinner who typically turns the ball in to the left-hander. The situation is made for him. We're 1–0 up in the five-match series, and we're expected to win, but we need to take every opportunity.

Amla and Rossouw are still going well, dominating, taking the score past 220. It's worth another try.

'Coach, I'm serious. Dave should go next.'

'No, you're the best man for this situation.'

The scoreboard keeps moving as Hash strokes another boundary through extra cover.

I'm sitting on the physiotherapy bed in our dressing room. Dale Steyn, Faf du Plessis and Farhaan Behardien are around, and we're enjoying the buzz of another 'pink' Sunday at the Wanderers, the annual ODI when the Proteas and most of the spectators dress in pink to raise funds for and awareness of the fight against breast cancer. I'm nervous. This is my 177th one-day international but I feel as anxious as I did during my first.

'It will never change,' I say out loud, to nobody in particular.

'What?' Faf asks.

'The nerves – I always get so nervous before I bat.'

As I speak, Rilee is caught in the deep, out for 128. Our score is 247 for one. I'm up next. I grab my bat and make my way down the stairs. As I do, I trip and stumble. Faf and Dale burst out laughing.

Emerging from the long path leading down to the field, limbering up, loosening up, whirling my arms, for a moment, I become aware of the amazing stage ... a beautiful summer's day on the Highveld, the Bullring packed in pink, the Proteas going well, the crowd happy and excited. For an instant, I consider again how lucky I am to be playing this game for a living, to be representing my country and now to be captain of the national ODI team. That's enough emotion! I consciously snap back into the moment, block out the sentiment, the noise, the atmosphere and the bubbling anticipation. It's time to focus on the task, to find a way of getting back into the zone and settling into a rhythm, always respecting the opposition and the game, earning the right to express myself and play my game.

Hash has made 114 from 116 balls and he stands, waiting for me in the middle, so calm and controlled. We've been playing cricket with and against each other since we were teenagers, for school, province and country, and he's always been such a high-quality person and such a high-quality player.

'I'll have a look for one or two overs,' I tell him, 'and we'll go from there.'

The plan is simple: Hash bats through the innings and I settle as quickly as possible and try to inject momentum, going for everything, and hopefully getting our total to around 350, out of reach.

There are 69 deliveries left to be bowled.

Jerome Taylor runs in and bowls … a slower ball … straight and full … there to be hit. My drive is not perfectly timed, but it flies past mid-on and away to the boundary. That feels good. Sometimes in this complex game, for no apparent reason, everything just feels right. That imperfect shot feels right, no question.

The second ball is sliced, driven square for two, and the third is stunned down to third man for one, so I retain the strike for the 40th over, to be bowled by Andre Russell. I push a single to cover off the first ball and Hash takes a single off the second. Maybe this is the moment to accelerate.

FOUR, clubbed over mid-off, one bounce to the boundary … SIX, moving outside off, pulled over square leg and into the crowd … FOUR, a straight ball driven over extra cover, two bounces to the boundary … SIX, improvising, flicking over square leg, crouching on my right knee, losing balance but managing to get the ball away.

The scoreboard shows I've reached 28 from eight balls. Everything feels right. I don't normally play like this so early in an innings, but I feel I'm in a good place today. I'm not premeditating the shot. Before the ball is bowled, I look around, check the fielders, see the space and decide where I'm going to try to hit the ball. That usually leaves me with three or four shot options, and I pick one when I see the length.

So, for example, if I've decided to hit the ball on the leg side, I'll skip outside off, so a full delivery can be driven and a short ball can be pulled over mid-wicket; for anything pitched in between, I'll drop down on one knee and use my go-to lap shot, a flick over square leg, helping it on its way. That's the plan. It doesn't always work.

Taylor is back, and Hash glances a single from the first ball. As I look around the field, I see mid-off has been brought up to be one of the five fielders inside the circle, so I think I'll drive the next ball into that space. And that's what happens. It's a full toss and somehow the ball flies straight out of the middle and into the crowd for six.

Reality returns with a bottom-edge miscue and a dot ball, an inside edge for two and an ungainly swipe for two more. Taylor is bowling well. As I try to reverse sweep the last ball of the over, I miss completely and scurry a leg bye. The stroke feels awkward. Mental note: this is not the day for the reverse sweep; there's no need to force the situation because I am hitting the ball well, so I must stick to my strokes in the V and use the lap shot occasionally, always trusting my gut.

We've reached 288 for one from 41 overs, and remain on track for around 350. Jason Holder is leading the West Indies ODI side for only the second time and the 23-year-old seamer admirably takes responsibility and takes the ball to bowl next. I drive a single to deep mid-on from his first ball, and Hash takes one from the second.

It's time for full tonking mode again.

SIX, moving outside off, lapping a full toss into the crowd behind square ... SIX, opening the stance, creating room for a full swing of the bat and the ball goes over mid-off. The scoreboard announces I have reached 50 runs in 16 balls, setting a new world record in ODIs – but the records mean very little to me. Right now I'm enjoying myself, loving the pink bedlam and simply trying to hit every ball out of the ground.

SIX, another full-blooded, full swing of the bat, this time sending the ball a little too high and I watch anxiously as it just clears Marlon Samuels on the long-on boundary ... FOUR, on one knee, slapped away through the covers for another boundary. In the stands all around, everyone seems to be standing and clapping. I'm in the zone.

My mum and dad are somewhere at the Wanderers, watching with young Benjamin, the three-year-old son of my older brother Jan, but I have only a vague idea where they are. Danielle, my wife, is expecting our first child and not feeling too great, so she's watching on television at home in Pretoria. In crazy times like these, when I am out there in the middle, more than anything, I want my family, friends and teammates to feel proud.

We reach 312 for one with eight overs left, and my score is 61 from 18 balls. Hash says we can take the match away from the West Indians; we just need to keep going. He's right.

The 43rd over brings another six hooked into the roaring crowd at fine leg and a full toss guided to the third-man boundary, and the 44th brings two more boundaries, one edged past the keeper and one driven straight.

Things have changed so much since my Proteas debut in 2004; then it was about getting into line and my go-to shot was the drive through cover or square. Now I'm older and more experienced, and I'm improvising and trying to play the ball as late as possible, working to hit the ball to areas where there are no fielders or sometimes, like now, just going the aerial route, trying to hit the ball as hard and as high as possible.

The lap shot serves me well again, producing another six whipped over square leg in the 45th over, taking me to 88, and everything comes together again in the 46th over, bowled by Holder.

I'm constantly trying to work out what the bowler will do next. I watch the first two balls and, when I get on strike, for the third ball, the West Indies captain misses his length. I give myself some room and strike a drive straight back over his head for four. I'm working hard. But what now? He will probably try to correct himself and bowl perhaps a full-length yorker, bringing my lap shot into play, or maybe a slower ball dropped short, making me swing early and mistime my shot. Either way, I plan to send the ball into the leg side. Focus. Concentrate. What's he going to do?

SIX, he's opted for the yorker, but I step outside off, turn it into a full toss and flick the ball over fine leg ... SIX, he changes his angle, coming round the wicket, and it's another full-length delivery picked up as a half-volley and whipped over square leg. The electronic scoreboard announces I've reached 100 in 31 balls, creating a new world record for ODIs. The crowd roars and I raise my arms. It's a special moment, and I hug Hash in the middle of the wicket. OK, that's enough of that. I have learned over the years to contain my celebrations. Yes, I'm obviously happy but, first, there is always still work to be done and, second, it's important to show respect for the opponents and the game; so it's acknowledge teammates, family and friends as quickly as possible, and then get on with it. Holder is ready to bowl. Focus. SIX, swinging straight and the ball narrowly clears Russell at mid-on.

Our score reaches 383 for one, with four overs remaining. We're taking control.

Chris Gayle, the world-class West Indian batsman and my teammate at Royal Challengers Bangalore in the Indian Premier League, walks across and says: 'You're a legend.'

I feel embarrassed, awkward. I just laugh and reply: 'No, you're the legend.'

Sections of the crowd are chanting, in unison.

'A–B! A–B! A–B! A–B!'

This has happened before at the Wanderers. It's amazing. Never in my wildest dreams – and I dreamed a lot as a barefoot youngster growing up in a small town – did I ever imagine this could happen to me.

Block it out. Think about the next task.

The 47th over brings me a 12th six, backing away, driving over point, and Hash takes over in the 48th, crashing a fantastic drive to the extra-cover boundary and taking his own score to 152 from 139 balls.

Dwayne Smith bowls the 49th over of the innings and the magic carpet ride continues. SIX, driving a full toss over mid-wicket ... SIX, stepping outside off and pulling the ball just over Benn at mid-on ... FOUR, a yorker stunned and stabbed to the third-man boundary ... SIX, a short ball pulled into the crowd behind square leg ... SIX, a full swing of the bat sends the ball over the boundary at mid-off ... TWO, slog-swept to mid-wicket.

We've reached 436 for one, with one over left.

Russell is bowling and Hash drives a single off the first delivery. I swing the bat at the second, slicing the ball into the outfield. We run two. Russell moves to bowl around the wicket, firing the ball across me. I ought to respond, to take account of the new line and shift my stance to the off side, but I don't. Maybe I'm getting tired. I swing at the third ball, and miss completely. It's a dot. The fourth delivery is a half-volley outside off. I try to drive it above cover point but my timing is not great and Jonathan Carter takes a comfortable catch on the boundary.

I'm out, and there's a hush around the stadium. Then the noise resumes as I walk briskly towards the dressing room. I never feel comfortable in the limelight, the centre of attention, and I'm eager to reach the sanctuary of the dressing room, hoping the guys can finish the innings well.

I sit down in my place, and take a deep breath.

Did that just happen?

Did that really happen?

As the adrenalin subsides, I feel exhilarated and amazingly blessed.

Our innings ends at 439 for two in 50 overs. In response, the West Indians score a respectable 291 for seven, but never threaten to overhaul our total. We take a 2–0 lead in the five-match series.

It was an extraordinary day. But what *really* mattered?

It really mattered that the Proteas played well as a team; that we played cricket to excite people both at the Wanderers and watching on television, inspiring them to follow, enjoy and play the game. It really mattered that we delivered a performance to help persuade our supporters, and perhaps ourselves, that, as a squad, we really do have the ability to perform well at the imminent 2015 Cricket World Cup, and maybe even win it. For me, personally, it mattered that I had tried my best and made people proud.

The records and the statistics genuinely don't matter at all. They are flashed across the television screen during the broadcast or printed in the newspapers the following day, but they don't make much difference. Records really do come and go. True glory is measured in the memories, the human emotions that endure and enhance people's lives.

Even so, cricket does lend itself to stats and the one-day international on 18 January 2015 produced a few worth repeating:

Our total of 439 for two in 50 overs was a new record, passing the previous highest score by South Africa in a one-day international, the 438–9 when we reached a huge target to beat Australia in that famous match at the Wanderers in 2006; and our score was just four runs short of Sri Lanka's record 443–9 against Netherlands in 2006.

In my innings, I had managed to score 149 runs from 44 balls, including nine boundaries and 16 sixes. The 50 had been reached in 16 balls, a new ODI world record, beating the previous mark set by Sanath Jayasuriya, when he hit 50 from 17 balls for Sri Lanka against Pakistan in 1996; and the 100 had been reached in 31 balls, also setting a new ODI world record, beating Corey Anderson's 36-ball century against the West Indies in 2014.

The 16 sixes equalled the world record for the most sixes in an ODI innings, established by Rohit Sharma when he smashed that incredible 209 playing for India against Australia in 2013.

Hash and I had added 192 runs in 67 balls, scoring at a run rate of 17.2 runs per over, the highest run rate for a partnership in excess of 100 runs ever recorded against any Test-playing nation.

The 163 runs we scored in the last 10 overs of our innings were the most by any team in a one-day international since 2001.

This was also the first time three batsmen had scored centuries in the same innings in a one-day international.

The records made their way into the annals and history books.

I drove home.

For me, a major benefit of playing at the Wanderers is being able to drive home after the match and sleep in my own bed. On this occasion, after all that had happened on the pitch, amid all the friendly back-slapping and compliments after, I just wanted to get home and see Danielle. Straight after the usual team chat, I escaped from the noise and headed home to Pretoria.

My cellphone battery was dead, and I was feeling calm and quiet as I turned left down Corlett Drive and left onto the M1 north, listening to music as I drove towards Midrand, suddenly feeling close to God.

'Thank you,' I said out aloud.

I am a Christian, a child of God.

I strongly believe this book is not my story. It is the story of what God has planned and realised through me. I hope it can be read and understood as tales of His achievements, certainly not my personal achievements, and I would really like people to appreciate that whatever glory there may be needs to be clearly recognised as His glory, not mine.

These lines will make some people feel uncomfortable. I'm sorry. Religion can have that effect. I understand it is a personal and private matter, and I certainly do not wish to ram my convictions down anyone's throat. With that said, however, my faith and my relationship with God are incredibly important to me and, after long consideration, and plenty of prayer, understanding the downside, I am not afraid publicly to recognise God's role in my life.

This doesn't mean I see myself as better than anyone else. I am not. This doesn't mean I see myself as morally superior to anyone else. I certainly am not. What it does mean, however, is that I try very hard to be receptive to the teachings of the Bible, that I am sincerely committed to the Word of God and that I aspire to lead my life in that way.

Enjoying the peace of being alone in my car, driving home from the Wanderers to Pretoria that Sunday evening, I started to look at the trees and the clouds, and began to feel sentimental, emotional even.

Quietly, privately, I recalled the two moments in my life when God spoke directly to me, two specific moments I have not previously described to anyone, not even to my parents.

The first took place one evening in January 1995. We had been having a braai with our friends, the Erasmus family, at their farm, and we were heading home on the road from Settlers back to Warmbaths. My father was driving the Isuzu Frontier, with my mother in the passenger seat and my elder brothers Jan and Wessels in the back seat of the double cab. Aged 10, the youngest of three boys, I was alone, lying on a mattress in the back of the bakkie.

Thinking about nothing in particular, staring at the stars, I suddenly started sobbing and then properly crying. It felt very strange. We were all Christians and, as a family, we generally went to church on a Sunday, but all of a sudden, lying on my back, I was overcome with a sense of God's presence. Nothing like this had happened to me before.

What was He saying?

I tried to make sense of everything and decided He was telling me what sort of person He wanted me to be. He wanted me to stay humble and always to appreciate what I have. Maybe He saw me as a typical big-shot hero at primary school, selected for all the sports teams, strutting around the playground at break, thinking I was something special. But here, in the back of the bakkie, it felt as if I was being brought heavily down to earth.

The second moment took place 14 years later on a boat in Sydney Harbour when, aged 24, I was a member of the South African cricket team celebrating our first series victory in Australia in the modern era.

We had won the second Test in Melbourne by nine wickets, taking a decisive 2–0 lead in the series, and had immediately flown north to Sydney. The squad enjoyed what could be described as an unrestrained all-nighter, and some of us returned to our hotel around 6 am. For brothers Morné and Albie Morkel, Dale Steyn, Neil McKenzie and me, that meant only around 40 minutes' sleep before we needed to head out again, joining some Australians who had invited us on a fishing trip.

By 8 am, we were boarding the boat. It would be fair to say we were not exactly alert. The hangovers were universally severe. I was man down, and my condition soon deteriorated because I almost always suffer from motion sickness on boats. The organisers had originally said we would be staying in the harbour and conditions would be calm, but someone suggested the fishing would be better if we headed out to the open sea. My heart sank at the prospect but, ever willing to go with the flow and be the 'team man', I said nothing and resolved to suffer in silence.

Maybe I didn't look too healthy as the boat started to soar and dive on an ever-increasing swell.

'Are you sure you'll be all right?' Morné asked me.

'Yeah,' I replied, lying.

Before long, I made my way to an upper deck and found a place where I could lie down on my own. There was absolutely no protection from a burning sun, and I was severely dehydrated, feeling terrible and getting worse by the minute. One hour passed, then another, and another …

Morné popped up to check on me. 'You OK?'

'It's no problem. I'm fine,' I lied, again.

Then, all of a sudden, out of the blue, something hit me and I began crying uncontrollably. I lay there, distantly aware of the excited banter among the fishermen on the deck below, crying my eyes out, once again feeling as if my body was being filled with the Holy Spirit.

The core message seemed essentially the same as it had been on the back of the bakkie all those years before, just as blunt and just as uncompromising. He seemed to be saying: 'What on earth do you think you are doing? Who on earth do you think you are? Some kind of hot-shot international cricketer, scoring runs and winning Test series with the Proteas, thinking you are special, getting drunk too often, taking yourself too seriously? You need to stay humble. You need to make time for the people who are close to you – and you need to appreciate what you have been given.'

I lay there on that boat, alone, sobbing, stunned.

The boat eventually returned to harbour and I made my way back to the team hotel. As soon as I reached my room, I immediately phoned my mum and dad back in South Africa, and told them how much I loved them and appreciated everything they had done for me.

For a second time, He had spoken, and I had listened.

As my life continues to unfold, I know how fortunate I am to experience moments of glory, moments like the one-day international against the West Indies at the Wanderers on Sunday, 18 January 2015, moments when everything falls into place and when everything goes my way, moments when I am being showered with praise and compliments.

These are great moments. I am grateful, but I never need to be reminded that it's never my glory. It's all His glory. I think I understand.

CHAPTER 2

20 MENTZ AVENUE

'Take that cap off now. You're not worthy of wearing that cap.'

He was serious. I was shocked. All I had done was drop a catch off his bowling, but there was never going to be much of an argument. He was 22, and I was 11. So I did as I was told and removed my cap, my precious 'Jonty cap', the cap bought for me by my father when, on Friday, 17 November 1995, he took me to watch the second day of the first Test between South Africa and England at Centurion Park in Pretoria. For a young fast bowler named Shaun Pollock, it was his Test debut. For me, a boy in the crowd, it was my first ever experience of Test cricket.

The cap was my souvenir of a special occasion. It was green and had the name of my hero, Jonty Rhodes, in gold across the front; it instantly became my most prized possession.

'You don't deserve it,' repeated Gerrit Deist, the 22-year-old, a friend of my eldest brother Jan. As he spoke, he took the cap, threw it on the ground and trampled it into the dirt of our garden at 20 Mentz Avenue in Warmbaths.

I could feel the tears welling.

Don't cry, don't cry, I told myself, desperate not to look weak in front of Jan, 22, my middle brother Wessels, 17, and their friends, who had come to our house to play garden cricket, as they often did.

To be clear, I was working rather than truly participating and I was only allowed to be present as the 11-year-old younger brother who happened to be around. My friends were never invited to play, and my role was strictly limited to carrying drinks, fielding and, just maybe, to bat at the end of the day.

'You can continue fielding,' Gerrit said.

'OK, thanks,' I replied.

I understood my place, and scurried away to field on the square-leg boundary at Div Park, as we called the cricket ground we had created out of our garden, no longer wearing the Jonty cap.

This incident is as clear in my mind as if it happened yesterday. It was conducted in jest, of course – Gerrit Deist was and remains a great friend to me and my brothers – but it does reflect the uncompromising environment in which I learned to play the game. Ever since those days, I have been primarily motivated by the challenge of proving myself worthy ... worthy of just playing, worthy of being respected by the opposition.

In my mind, respect is never earned by a natural ability to hit the ball or field well. Respect is only ever earned by being a fighter. That's what I wanted to be. I wanted to be known as a fighter. There have been thousands of talented players, but there are only a handful of real fighters, and I wanted to be one of them.

This particular game of garden cricket ran well into the afternoon and evening, and I fielded and fielded and fielded until, as the sun was setting, I heard the words I had been waiting all day to hear.

'OK, AB, you can bat now.'

This was my chance. Gerrit was bowling. He paced out his run-up as far as he could go, right back into the rose bed. It had been a long day. Everyone wanted to get me out quickly. I had other plans.

Even now, whenever I'm asked to name the best bowler I have ever faced, the answer that springs most quickly to mind is Gerrit Deist. That's not the response I give in media interviews because it would need to be followed by a lengthy explanation but it's the truth. We later played club cricket together for Tukkies; I faced him in the nets on numerous occasions and he always caused me problems.

Back at Div Park, the odds were stacked against me.

He was 22, and I was 11. He was a tall, strong fast bowler playing senior club cricket in Johannesburg. I was a *laaitjie* playing barefoot at Warmbaths Primary School. We were playing on a kikuyu wicket measuring around 14 yards, rather than the usual 22 yards, and we were playing with a tennis ball, covered with insulation tape on one side, making it swing dramatically in both directions.

In fairness, Gerrit and the older boys did offer me one concession.

They said that, since I was so small and my bat was so heavy, as the bowler ran in, I was allowed to rest my bat on top of the rubbish bin that served as our stumps. It was a Duncan Fearnley bat handed down to me by Wessels, and it was three or four sizes too large, too heavy for me to lift and hold at the top of my backlift. More than 20 years later, there are a few echoes of this improvised backlift in my technique today.

I was ready. Focus, I told myself. Concentrate. Get into line. Fight. Don't give it away. Hit anything wide or short. Fight. Whatever you do, don't get out to the *oke* who trampled on your cap.

Gerrit ran in and bowled, again and again, but he couldn't get me out. It was well after sunset, and they couldn't get me out. Next my brother Jan came charging in off a 30-yard run with everyone else crowded around the bat, and they still couldn't get me out. I wanted to show them I was worthy of wearing the cap.

Fight. Get in line. Fight.

They started sledging. I ignored it. At one stage, while running a single, they physically blocked the middle of the wicket. Soon afterwards, I was actually lifted off my feet as I ran.

'That's not fair,' I protested. 'I'll tell Mom and Dad.'

'Do that and you'll never be allowed to play again,' came the reply.

No matter, I held my ground. I was fighting, loving every minute of the contest, intently watching every fast, seaming delivery. Concentrate, I urged myself. Focus, get into the line. Don't get out.

In the end, Jan decided enough was enough and hurled the ball at my back. I immediately burst into tears, and my mother emerged from the kitchen to call stumps at the end of an unforgettable day.

I retrieved the Jonty cap and put it on my head. The older boys left, oblivious to my emotions and excitement. I didn't care. I felt worthy and deserving, and that was all that mattered.

Div Park was special.

My brothers made it so.

Our family lived at 20 Mentz Avenue, on a large corner plot not far from the centre of Warmbaths, the town now known as Bela-Bela, an hour's drive north of Pretoria. The garden included large trees and an open lawn at least 30 metres long and 20 metres wide, the ideal location for what the three De Villiers boys considered a proper cricket ground in every respect.

Jan and Wessels thought of everything. They grew the kikuyu grass from seed. They 'borrowed' from the local high school a proper roller, which somehow remained in our garden for a few years. On one occasion, I was woken at 1 am in the morning and told to help roll the wicket for the next day's match.

The three of us were regular players, together with Gerrit Deist, another friend Gerald Pieterse and by far the best player in the group, Martin van Jaarsveld, a friend of my brother Jan.

Martin – or 'Jarre', as we called him – was an exceptionally talented cricketer, 10 years older than me, who played regularly in our garden and who advanced all the way through the Northern Transvaal and Titans provincial squads to make his Test debut for South Africa in 2002. He blazed a trail that I was proud to follow.

At Div Park, there were no rules about retiring when you reached a certain score and Jarre played many, many marathon innings. He would literally bat all day, over after over, and, hour after hour, fielders like me simply had to run to fetch the ball from every corner of the garden.

On one such occasion, when I was around 10 years old, I remember suggesting to Gerrit that we should try bowling fast, low full tosses at Martin in the hope that, with his apparently impeccable technique, he would play the ball straight back to the bowler and succumb caught-and-bowled to the local one-hand-one-bounce rule. It was a decent idea, but it didn't work and Jarre continued to write the record books at Div Park.

In the years that followed, Martin proved a constant source of support and encouragement to me. He was an established member of the Titans squad when I arrived as a nervy teenager and, taking me under his wing, he would tell the coaches how well I was doing, giving me confidence when I needed it most.

At one practice, he handed me one of those trimmed-down slim bats and said he would throw the ball for me. To my horror, he then called the coaches over to watch me bat.

'Oh my goodness, look at this *laaitjie*,' he would exclaim out loud, making sure everybody could hear what he was saying, as I somehow managed to hit every delivery in the middle.

We both attended Warmbaths Primary School, and today the school's A field is named the Martin van Jaarsveld field and the B field is named after me. That's the way it should be. I owe Jarre more than he knows.

In our young minds, 20 Mentz Avenue was not simply a cricket venue. It was a cricket complex.

Aside from the main field, with its carefully rolled turf wicket, there was also the B field, an enclosed, cemented back yard outside the kitchen measuring no more than eight metres square. For my mother, this was where our clothes were hung out to dry. For us, it was a spinner's paradise, a wicket with as much turn and bounce as any in the Indian subcontinent. If ever there was a place to learn how to play spin, this was it.

The matches were ferocious. Bowlers would tweak the ball hard and, bowling from no more than six metres, they would make each delivery spin and fizz, rear and bounce dramatically.

Batting seemed almost impossible.

Two or three fielders crowded the bat, taking advantage of the one-hand-one-bounce regulation, and they were 'supported' in the yard by a number of objects designated as additional fielders and deemed to have 'caught' the ball if it was struck against them on the full. There was one specific upright pole that held the clothes line and stood less than two metres from the batting crease. This pole was called Jonty because, in all those years of high-energy, frenetic back-yard cricket, he never, ever, ever dropped a catch.

Batsmen had to play with incredibly soft hands just to survive. If they wanted to score runs, and post any kind of total on the board, they had to be creative and to improvise, to guide the ball into vacant areas with all kinds of deft dabs, sweeps and glances. The back yard was a tough school, and a great school.

Jan and Wessels wrote the rules.

Anything hitting the kitchen door was out. Anything hitting any wall without bouncing was four.

This was not playtime.

Every game could scarcely have been more serious.

Each of us would select our own World XI, always fighting over who would have favourite players such as Jacques Kallis, Matthew Hayden and Adam Gilchrist. We would write down our teams on paper and each of us would bat through our entire order, walking away from the crease when you were out, writing down the score in the scorebook positioned just inside the kitchen door and then re-emerging as the next batsman.

Selection was often decisive. If you picked a left-hander, you would obviously have to bat left-handed when it was his turn to bat; that was a disadvantage, though not a bad training exercise.

The energy, the enthusiasm, the intensity were fantastic.

'Catch it! Catch it!'

Our anguished cries echoed from the yard through the house, famously waking my father, who worked hard as a GP in town and was accustomed to returning home for an early afternoon nap.

'Catch it! Catch it!'

'Keep quiet!' he would bellow from my parents' bedroom.

And we would keep quiet, at least until the next half-chance.

'Catch it! Catch it!'

Our lives revolved around sport, any sport, any time, any place.

Cricket? There was the A field at Div Park and the B field in the back yard, but there was also the driveway where the ball skidded nicely off the paving stones and there was occasionally the street outside our home, and we also spent hour after hour practising our slip catches in the swimming pool, hurling the ball at each other and diving around.

Golf? In decent weather, we played holes created around the garden, around that tree, over that bush. If it was raining, we played inside the house, using only a wedge and a putter on an improvised course that included a tricky Par 3 under the table in the living room and a demanding Par 5 running down the passage from our parents' bedroom, past our bedrooms, past the dining room and into the bar area; birdies were very rare on that hole, largely because you had to putt on the rugs and we used to place cushions underneath the rugs to change the contours of our 'greens'.

For swimming, there was of course the pool, but mere lengths from one end to the other were never going to fulfil our foolish quest for excitement and adrenalin, so we created a game that, looking back, was unbelievably dangerous but which at the time seemed just about the best imaginable source of fun.

We would climb onto the roof of the house and jump down from there into the pool below but, to land safely in the water, we had to jump out at least two metres to clear the paving around the pool. We executed simple 'bommies' most of the time, but some of my friends used to try somersaults as well. Looking back, it's difficult to understand how nobody ever hit their head on the side of the pool and suffered a serious injury.

My mother understood the risks all too well and unequivocally banned the game, which of course made it even more exciting to me and my friends.

'Is your mom home this afternoon?'

'She may be going out later. Why?'

'Well, maybe we can come round and play in the pool.'

So they would come to 20 Mentz Avenue and we would awkwardly hang around until my mother left the house, and then we would rush out, climb up onto the roof and start our forbidden games.

As a sports-mad youngster, this was an ideal environment. I could not have wished for anything more.

For facilities, beyond our adventure playground of a house, there was the Warmbaths Sports Club, where the De Villiers family would spend most Saturday mornings, playing golf or tennis, socialising. Everybody seemed to know everybody and, aged five or six, I was left to wander around as I liked, maybe hitting a few golf balls or finding an empty tennis court and playing with anyone who happened to be around.

For opposition, there were always my elder brothers.

Jan and Wessels always set the benchmark.

Both were talented sportsmen who played hard and generally fair, who pushed me to the limit and occasionally beyond, who treated me as an equal, who let me play with, who always found time to teach me how to play whatever they played, how to hold a bat, how to field, how to swing the ball, how to spin the ball, even how to oil my bat … and who, whatever happened, all these years unequivocally supported and loved me.

For so many years, growing up in their shadows, I lived in a constant state of over-excitement, forever looking forward to the next game with my *boets*, forever on the brink of bursting into tears, and loving every minute. At stages, it felt as if my only purpose in life was to prove that, no matter the odds, no matter what anybody said, I could do what Jan and Wessels could do.

In every single contest, I was stretching every sinew simply to reach their level.

If anybody ever conducts an academic study into the optimal childhood for an elite sports person, they will surely conclude that nothing beats growing up in the slipstream of talented, competitive older siblings.

I owe my brothers almost everything.

Jan is fully nine years older than me and, as a talented opening bowler in the Northern Transvaal Districts cricket team at Nuffield Week, he would have been absolutely entitled to ignore me as a pesky irritant, but he never did. On the contrary, he always engaged with me, motivated me and inspired me.

'Jan, I'll race you. Come on, Jan.'

'What?'

'I'll race you from this tree to that tree over there.'

'Really?'

'Come on!'

We were walking home from church on a Sunday morning in our smart clothes but, ever desperate to compete, I was challenging my eldest brother to an impromptu sprint. Most 20-year-olds would have told me to go away but Jan accepted the challenge. I won and, 20 years later, I'm still savouring the glow of victory.

Jan is now married to Karien, and they have two young children, Benjamin and Karli. He is now the owner of The Purple Trumpet, an outstanding boutique guesthouse in Waterkloof, Pretoria.

Wessels, our middle brother, is six years older than me and, for as long as I can remember, has been a source of comfort to me. As a boy, I remember often waking frightened in the middle of a stormy night and I would always make my way through to Wes' room and feel safe.

The substantial age difference could easily have been a barrier but, just like Jan, Wes was always happy to indulge his much younger brother, always willing to play, always willing to compete.

'Wes, let's play tag.'

'In a moment.'

'No, let's play now – just one game, please.'

'OK.'

The point of the game was to tag your opponent and run away so fast that he could not tag you back. In one game, I tagged Wes and set off in such blind haste that I ran straight into the knob of my bedroom door and knocked myself out. According to family legend, I was out cold for 30 minutes.

Wessels was also an outstanding young sportsman, a fine cricketer, a scratch golfer and, at one stage, the No. 1-ranked Under-14 swimmer in South Africa. Married to Carina and with two young boys, Jean and Josuah, he now owns four thriving Nando's restaurants located in the area north of Pretoria.

When the De Villiers brothers were not playing sport, we were watching sport.

We watched at the stadium when my father bundled us into the car and took us to the cricket at Centurion Park or the Wanderers, or to the rugby at Loftus Versfeld or Ellis Park in Johannesburg.

In 1995, when Allan Donald unleashed a barrage against Mike Atherton, the England captain, at the Wanderers, we were sitting on the old wooden benches at the Bullring, cheering wildly each time the heroic fast bowler completed an over and came to field on the fine-leg boundary right in front of us.

And we watched everything else on television.

In March 1992, my brothers and I were woken very early in the morning and allowed to sit bleary-eyed and watch Kepler Wessels' side beat

Pakistan in Brisbane; that was the first time South Africa played in the Cricket World Cup and that was the match made famous by Jonty Rhodes' diving run-out.

Did I sit there in the living room and dream of one day playing on that same stage?

No, in truth, that prospect seemed unimaginable.

In June 1995, while a newly, miraculously united country was becoming steadily more and more excited by the Springboks' progress in the Rugby World Cup hosted in our own country, my mother created our own 'executive box' in our living room, from where we watched all the Bok matches on television. With our faces painted in the colours of the new rainbow flag for the new rainbow nation, every game was a huge event.

More than 40 friends and family came to our house to watch the final against New Zealand. What a day! It was incredible to see how sport could bring so much joy to so many people.

I loved every minute of these big sporting occasions.

Almost without exception, I celebrated wildly whenever South Africa won. When South Africa lost, almost without exception, I cried.

The years passed. My brothers moved on to university and their careers. I found myself spending more and more time at home, alone, challenged to amuse myself. That was no problem.

If I wanted to play cricket, I put a ball in the bottom of a sock, hung it from the ceiling of the garage and played drive after drive, getting the feel of the ball in the middle of the bat, over and over again.

If I felt like playing tennis, there was a net marked out on the inside wall of the garage and I developed a game where I would play against 'the computer'. That meant serving as me, returning the rebounding ball as 'the computer', then playing as me and on and on until the point was won; the key, I soon learned, was to hit every stroke as hard as possible and to the very best of my ability. I never cheated.

For company, when my brothers were away, there was Boris, a Staffordshire bull terrier named after the German tennis player, Boris Becker. We became very tight, after a difficult start.

It was mid-morning at 20 Mentz Avenue. My mother was drying her hair and just a few metres away, aged five, I was sitting on the floor playing with my new canine friend Boris, pulling him, pushing him, wrestling with him. His tail fascinated me, so I turned it, twirled it, twisted it ... and broke it in three places.

Boris suddenly snapped and went for me, locking his jaw onto my head, sinking his teeth into my skull. My mother was oblivious to it all because she was looking in the mirror and could hear nothing against the whir of the hairdryer. It could easily have been over and out for the unfortunate five-year-old but, for some reason, my mother turned round and yelled. Boris let go and I escaped with a wound that required 15 stitches.

In such circumstances, dogs are usually earmarked as dangerous and quickly put down but my parents took the view that Boris had been provoked and assured us that he would remain our dog, a great decision.

He became my constant companion.

His favourite game was hide-and-seek. I would tell Boris to sit and wait, and he would stay unmoved while my friends and I ran off and found a place to hide somewhere in the garden.

'Boris,' I would shout, 'on your marks ... get ready ... go!'

At that moment, he would spring into action and start searching for us.

Beyond my brothers and Boris, I have been fortunate to have three great friends in my life. The four of us met in nursery school, have stayed close ever since, still see each other on a regular basis and, with modern technology, now remain connected on a WhatsApp group entitled 'Oerbuds', translated as 'ancient mates'. Johan Scheepers, Stoffel de Beer, Chris Swanepoel and me ... Skippy, Stof, Chris and AB.

We met on the climbing frames at Bosveldspruitjies, the nursery school across the road from Warmbaths Primary School, which we all attended; we were in the same rugby and cricket teams, constantly competing with each other, constantly chirping each other, and have remained pretty much as close and consistent ever since. Through all the twists and turns of our respective lives, we remain the same Skippy, Stof, Chris and AB.

The memories refuse to fade.

It is just another afternoon at primary school and four overactive boys are messing around in the playground, as ever throwing a rugby ball around. Disaster strikes when somebody kicks an over-ambitious up-and-under and the ball gets stuck in one of the thorn trees. Skip tries to shake the tree, but the ball doesn't move.

'Hey, AB,' says Stof. 'You've got a decent arm. Throw a brick at the ball. That will work.'

'Great idea,' I reply.

So we find half a brick. I take aim and manage to dislodge the ball with my first throw.

'Yeeeeeeeesssssssssss,' I yell, arms outstretched in triumph.

But it's pride before a fall. The rugby ball falls neatly from the tree. Moments later, so does the half-brick and it lands squarely on my head, leaving me lying stunned on the ground with blood gushing from a serious gash.

Stof stays and does what he can to stop the bleeding, while Chris and Skip run to get help from the principal's office. I sit for the next hour or so with a bag of ice on my head. I survive.

It is just another Saturday, but far from just another rugby match for Warmbaths Primary School. This is the Schools' semifinal, and we are playing away to Pietersburg East Primary School. This is David vs Goliath. We are a tiny school with no rugby pedigree. They are revered giants in our world, and they play in orange.

We appear to have no chance of winning but, under the guidance of Mr Swart, we have trained hard, and were still hardened by the training we endured with Mr du Plessis, our Under-9 coach, who told us to dive on our rugby field full of thorns, get up, sprint and then dive among the thorns again. Above all, with Chris at hooker, Stof at flank, me at scrum-half and Skippy at inside centre, we have a special plan.

The plan is called 'Quicksports' and, in our young minds, it is pure rugby genius.

I feed the ball into the scrum. Chris hooks the ball, flanker Stof takes the ball at the back of the scrum and runs straight at the orange fly-half. Just before he reaches him he flips a soft pass to me on his outside. I throw a dummy pass to my inside centre Skippy, cut inside and run through to score the try beneath the posts.

The move works perfectly in practice, and it works perfectly against Pietersburg East. 'Quicksports' yields our first try in what becomes a convincing victory – in our minds at least, the most sensational result in all the history of Rugby Union at Warmbaths Primary School. Many of the players' parents have driven to support the team in the far-northern town, and they are thrilled. Can life, we wonder, get any better than this?

Other memories do fade, strangely. We might have lost the final 24–0 to Pietersburg South Primary School. I do not precisely recall. It may have been a windy day with every bounce of the ball on a rock-hard field going against us, but I don't exactly remember. It is the vivid recollection of the semifinal that endures.

The four of us are back in the playground at break, and we have got hold of a cherry bomb, a spherical firework, and we are collectively yielding to the temptation of making some noise.

'I'm not sure that's a great idea,' says Chris.

'Come on, man,' the rest of us say, in unison. 'It'll be fun. Just do it.'

Chris is brave bordering on gullible, and he is eventually persuaded to place the cherry bomb in the corner of the playground, to strike a match and light the fuse, and then scamper away.

We wait for the blast, and wait, and wait. Has the fuse fizzled out?

No, it hasn't.

The firework goes off, and the massive explosion brings the entire playground to a standstill. All eyes turn toward the perpetrators and four 12-year-olds are soon standing before Principal Tom Beukes, trying hard to explain themselves. On this occasion, Stof and I get away with it. Chris and Skip take responsibility.

Stoffel de Beer has become a successful businessman, initially with South African Breweries and more recently with Toyota, but for the other three of us, he'll always be a kind-hearted softie; reputations earned at an early age have tended to stick.

'His parents have said Stof can come for a sleepover,' my mother announced one morning in 1990.

Stof and I were both six years old and, in our world, this was very big news. The De Beer family lived on a farm 10 kilometres outside Warmbaths, and we lived in town. I was excited.

Everything went well and the next morning I suggested we hit some golf balls around the garden. I had been given a nine-iron for my birthday – my Christmas and birthday presents were always sports equipment – and I was eager to show Stof. Unfortunately, he started crying; he was missing his mother.

'Come on, Stof, you'll be OK,' I said. 'It'll be fun.'

'Sorry, man,' he replied, 'I'm not going to make it.'

'So what do you want to do?'

'I want to go home.'

'Your mom is coming to collect you this afternoon.'

'I know, but I want to go home now. I want to walk home. Will you come with me?'

Disappointment instantly turned to excitement. Walking 10 kilometres to the De Beer farm sounded like a great adventure. I quickly agreed with the plan, realised we would need some food and ran to fetch a packet of Marie biscuits from the kitchen. My mother was not around, so there was no opportunity to say goodbye, and the two of us headed for the road that led out of town. After a couple of kilometres, we were joined by a Labrador. Neither of us knew the dog, but we were pleased to have company, so we continued our great trek.

'Where are you two going?'

The firm voice belonged to a policeman. We had been stopped.

'I'm going home to my mom,' said Stof, his courage evaporating, his voice faltering.

That was that, the end of our adventure. The two of us were bundled into the back of a van and taken to the police station, which was still exciting but we were starting to sense that the saga would not end well.

'We need to telephone your parents,' said the policeman.

'It is Warmbaths 2666,' I replied, pleased I could recite our number.

My mother came to collect us, and it is fair to say our parents made it abundantly clear to their respective sons that impromptu 10-kilometre walks were not to be tolerated in the future.

Chris Swanepoel has, like me, chosen to pursue a career in sport, becoming a professional golfer. He turned pro in 2004, and has won four tournaments on the Sunshine Tour, displaying all the energy, courage and determination that we admired in him when we were youngsters.

'So, Chris, what's the plan?'

It's 2001, we are 17 years old and, now at school in Pretoria, I am planning to spend the weekend back home in Warmbaths. Chris has recently been given a scooter by his father, as a reward for good marks at school, and it's difficult to imagine more fun than using the bikes to chase rabbits on the golf course.

'Well, Hannes van Staden and Jacques van Zyl are around,' he replies. 'Shall we take the bikes out?'

'Perfect.'

Jacques is the son of a colleague of my father's at the doctors' General Practice and he owns a bike as well, so late on Friday night the four of us make our way to the golf course. I am riding with Chris on his bike, and Hannes rides with Jacques. The game is simple: you spot the rabbits in the headlights and get as close as possible, so the guy on the back can jump off and catch a rabbit, hold it for a few seconds and then release it.

The team with the most 'captures' is declared the winner.

Chris and I were chasing one rabbit on the fourth fairway when Jacques and Hannes came flying past us at what, even by our standards, was exceptional speed. We were getting close enough to strike but we knew the course well and Chris started to slow down as we approached the dam on the famous fourth hole.

The fourth hole dam was, sadly, not famous enough for Jacques.

Everything happened incredibly quickly. The rabbit darted right. Jacques and Hannes, still travelling at top speed, hit the side of the ladies' tee, ramped at least two metres in the air and landed directly in the water. Jacques went down with his cherished bike, while Hannes was catapulted even further into the water.

Several anxious seconds passed until both finally bobbed to the surface and, when we saw that their injuries were nothing more serious than dented pride, the laughter began. Jacques spent two hours trying to retrieve his bike from the dam until my brother Wessels arrived with his bakkie at midnight and pulled the bike from the water.

Johan Scheepers, Skip, works for Telkom, and has remained the same tough, resourceful character. When his wife went into labour on the road from Warmbaths to Pretoria, he called my dad, who talked him through the entire process of delivering his child at the side of the road. All credit to him. He finished by tying the umbilical cord with his shoelace, helped his wife and baby into the car and completed the drive to Pretoria.

The four of us progressed through primary school together, barefoot until the age of 13. The younger boys never wore shoes at school, even in winter, and I was far from happy when the teachers forced me to wear shoes in my final year. I had been appointed head boy, and the head boy had to wear shoes.

The head boy also had to make a speech, standing in front of the school and welcoming everyone at the start of term. It was a Monday morning, as I recall, and the memory of that nightmare experience still makes me shiver. I was overwhelmed by nerves, and literally could not say more than a few words. It was horrendous.

In truth, I was much more at ease outdoors, playing sport, competing, getting into scrapes.

One afternoon all the Standard 5 pupils were swimming in the school pool and we were having a great time when an older boy called Allan arrived and told us to get out of the pool. It wasn't the first time this guy had given us a hard time, and I told him he was wrong and that we were allowed to be there.

'I said get out of the pool,' he repeated.

We had been throwing skidding catches at each other in the pool and, in a moment of madness, I took the wet tennis ball and hurled it at Allan, hitting him on the back, creating a red mark.

He turned round, instantly furious. We had one option. Run.

After scrambling to the entrance to the pool, we were soon sprinting along the narrow dirt path that led back to the sanctuary of the main school, but the older boys were too fast and soon caught up with us. We seemed set for a serious beating but, out of nowhere, Stof produced an amazing hand-off – I really couldn't believe my eyes – and I managed an inside-out sidestep and, somehow, we both got back to safety.

Allan was not going to let the matter rest there, and at the end of the day we saw him waiting for us outside the school gates. Unfortunately for him, in this particular week Stof and I were being collected by my elder brother Jan, who was on vacation from university in Potchefstroom. I explained to Jan what had happened, and he walked over to Allan and said: 'If you ever touch my little brother again, you will regret it.'

That was that.

We were never again bothered by Allan and his friends.

There was time for some formal education as well.

Warmbaths Primary School provided me, and many others, with an ideal start in life. There were many excellent teachers with strong values, a clear structure and proper discipline, all wrapped in the kindness and warmth typical of a small town where almost everyone knew almost everyone else.

The spirit of the school was most accurately reflected in the concept of the 'school patrol' where Standard 4 boys were designated to stand at the zebra crossing on the adjacent road at the start of each day and ensure their fellow pupils crossed safely. I was one of the boys given this responsibility in 1996 and, although it meant getting up early and being in position from 6.30 until 7.15 am every morning for a year, even in the freezing depths of winter, the school patrol taught me the importance of being organised and being on time.

Beyond my brothers, my friends and my school, the most significant influence on these formative years was, of course, my parents ... my endlessly giving and unconditionally loving parents.

AB and Millie married at a relatively young age and moved around what was then the Transvaal, eventually settling when AB took a position as a doctor in a general practice in Warmbaths.

My father has always been busy. Doctors always have patients who need to be seen and, when I was young, this commitment meant that, most of the time, he was unable to attend my matches. It followed that the days when he was standing on the touchline with the other parents, the rare occasions when he could get away from the practice, became huge occasions in my mind; these were precious opportunities to make him proud.

It is a perfect, sunny winter's afternoon in 1996 and I have been picked to play flyhalf for the Warmbaths Primary School 1st xv, selected to play among the older boys 'a year up'. I have previously played at scrumhalf and at centre, but this is the first time I have been given a chance in my favoured position, at No. 10.

We are playing Krugerpark Primary School – traditionally strong opponents from Potgietersrus and, in my time at least, the one school we never seemed able to beat – on our main field. The score is level at 5–5 and, with seconds left, we win a scrum on the Krugerpark 10-metre line. I glance across at the crowd of parents on the touchline and instantly spot my father, standing there in his gleaming white GP's suit, watching intently.

This is my moment. The ball comes back from the scrum. I steady myself and, playing barefoot, try to kick a 40-metre drop goal to win the game. The connection is good and the ball passes, if not quite soars, between the posts.

We win.

Amid all the celebrations and back-slapping excitement that followed, I heard only one voice.

'Well done, son.'

This memory is as crystal clear as if the match was played yesterday.

My father's family lived in Vryburg, where my grandfather – Oupa Jan, as we called him – was headmaster of Stellaland Primary. My grandmother passed away when my father was a teenager, but I saw Oupa Jan every time I went to play in a tennis tournament in Vryburg.

He had played fullback for Boland in his youth and, perhaps bearing in mind the pressures of competitive sport, he used to hide behind a bush when he came to watch me play tennis. I once asked him why. He said he thought that I might get nervous or feel extra pressure if I saw him standing beside the court.

We used to visit his house, where he would typically sit on the verandah reading the newspaper. Nobody was supposed to disturb him there but, as an indulged grandson, I was allowed to hit tennis balls against the wall behind him. As the ball passed inches from his head, over and again, he never moved or said a word.

My father has three sisters: Tannie Leens, who lives in Stellenbosch with her husband, WP Oosthuizen, and their three daughters, Anneke, Suzanne and Leentjie – I was always exceptionally close to Leentjie, because she was a fine tennis player and we spent a great deal of time together on the junior circuit; Tannie Gerbre, who lives in Mossel Bay with her husband, Harry Hill, and their children Vincent and Eleanor; and Tannie Suzanne, who still lives in Pretoria with her husband, Jurie van der Walt, and their four children, Jana, Riaan, who is my age and went to school with me, Eric and Jurie.

My mother's maiden name was Wessels and her family lived in Pretoria. Her father, Oupa Hans, was a bank manager at a number of Volkskas branches around the country before becoming head manager at the Volkskas head office; he and his wife Ramona had three daughters, Annette, my mum, then Wilna, and the three De Villiers boys were the only grandchildren.

When my Oupa Hans fell ill, he and Ramona moved to Bela-Bela to be closer to my mother. When he passed away he was buried in the town cemetery, and Ramona bought property in a retirement village and she is still going strong, still supporting her grandsons, enthusiastically watching the cricket on television with her friends.

Like many families in the northern part of the country, we drove to the coast each summer, spending the Christmas holidays moving from one family to the other. Oupa Hans and the Wessels family were usually based in Wilderness, while Oupa Jan and the De Villiers clan owned a holiday home in the Strand, near Cape Town.

Those were great days.

In Wilderness, we used to pitch a tent in the garden and play endless games of cricket on the beach – one year Gerrit Deist, 'the finest bowler I ever faced', came along and raised the standard of play. In the Strand, we would sit and listen in awesome admiration as Oupa Jan played 'Silent Night' on the harmonica.

'Shhhhh,' my mother would say.

Ah, yes, my mother, Millie de Villiers ... a force of nature, selfless, loving, as well as my tennis coach.

CHAPTER 3

ALL-ROUNDER

The Internet is a fantastic platform for information that has changed the world and empowered billions of people. It is also a place where complete falsehoods and exaggerations can be authoritatively presented as fact and repeated and repeated and repeated to a point where they effectively become 'facts'.

Sky Sports has rightly become one of the most respected sports news organisations and, on 28 February 2015, during the build-up to the 2015 Cricket World Cup, an online article was published on the Sky Sports website describing me as 'cricket's record-breaking all-rounder' listing various achievements.

It appeared – and still appears – on a trusted website, so it must be true.

Right?

'De Villiers was shortlisted for the South African national hockey squad,' the article says.

True or false?

False.

In truth, I played hockey for one year at high school and was a member of the Afrikaanse Hoër Seunskool Under-16A team that beat our near neighbours and rivals at Pretoria Boys' High for the first time, but I was never shortlisted for the national hockey squad, or ever came remotely close to that level.

'De Villiers was shortlisted for the South African national football squad,' the article says.

True or false?

False.

I have never played any organised football (soccer). We used to kick a ball around during break at school and the game has become part of the Proteas' warm-up routine. That is all.

'De Villiers was the captain of South Africa junior rugby,' the article says.

True or false?

False.

I played rugby at primary school and high school, and enjoyed every minute, but I never represented South Africa at any level, either at SA Schools or SA Under-20, and was never captain.

'De Villiers is still the holder of six national school swimming records,' the article says.

True or false?

False.

As far as I recall, I did set an Under-9 breaststroke record at Warmbaths Primary School but I have never held any national school swimming records, not even for a day.

'De Villiers has the record fastest 100 metres time among South African junior sprinters,' the article says.

True or false?

False.

I did not sprint at all at school. Elsewhere on the Internet, to my embarrassment, there are articles in which the great sprinter Usain Bolt is asked which cricketer could beat him in a sprint and he replies 'AB de Villiers'. Maybe, just maybe, I would beat him if I were riding a motorbike.

'De Villiers was a member of the national junior Davis Cup tennis team,' the article says.

True or false?

Almost true.

As far as I know, there was no such entity as the national junior Davis Cup team, but I did play tennis as a youngster, loved the game and was occasionally ranked as the national No. 1 in my age group.

'De Villiers was a national Under-19 badminton champion,' the article says.

True or false?

False.

I never played badminton at school. If my memory is correct, I have only ever played one game of badminton in my entire life, and that was just a fun game with Mark Boucher.

'De Villiers received a national medal from Nelson Mandela for a science project,' the article says.

True or false?

False.

I never undertook any science project of any significance, certainly nothing to attract the attention of the president. I was privileged to meet Madiba twice, both times as a member of the Proteas squad.

'De Villiers plays off a handicap of scratch in golf,' the article says.

True or false?

False.

I played golf often as a youngster with my brothers and with my friends, without ever receiving a formal lesson. I have always loved the game and enjoy driving the ball a reasonable distance. One of my proudest moments occurred when I hit a drive down the middle of the fairway, past my elder brother's drive, and overheard Wessels and my father debating my swing and trying to understand why the ball travelled so far.

In any event, as I recall, I did get my official handicap down to a respectable one when I was 15 but there's not much time to play golf these days and my handicap has drifted to nine.

These are the facts: decent at golf, useful at rugby and tennis when I was young, and enjoying cricket ever since. The errors will doubtless remain on the Internet and people will continue to believe I was some kind of prodigy at all those different sports, but the truth will hopefully somehow endure.

With all this said, I remain extremely grateful for the good fortune to be born with a natural ability to play sport, but ability only takes you so far. There are tens of thousands of talented sports people who never realise their full potential because it is ability plus opportunity that generally equals sporting success, and, for me, the opportunity to play sport, initially for fun and subsequently for a living, was presented by my parents.

They never interfered with coaches, never pushed me and never put pressure on me, but my father made substantial financial sacrifices that enabled me to play and my mother provided endless, selfless, unconditional support, driving me to so many training sessions and to so many matches and standing on touchlines; in tennis, she took on the responsibility of being my coach as well.

Millie de Villiers has always managed to find 25 hours in every day. Aside from taking care of her husband and her three sons and keeping the family home in order, she worked as an estate agent in Bela-Bela and still found the time to spend two or three afternoons each week coaching young tennis players.

Our entire family enjoyed tennis, playing at the local sports club – we called it 'the club at the end of the road' even though it was three kilometres from our home – and watching all the Grand Slam tournaments on TV. The stars of the game were our heroes. Steffi Graf, the German who won the Wimbledon women's singles title seven times between 1988 and 1996, was perhaps the greatest sweetheart in our house.

My older brothers, Jan and Wessels, played tennis and in June 1990 both were entered to play in a tournament known as the Lowveld Open in Nelspruit. My mother had seen me hit the ball while playing at the sports club and, after some discussion, decided she would put my name down for the Under-10 event. I was only six and still a few months from starting primary school, but she believed I could hold my own.

It would be my first experience of proper, organised competition in any sport and I could hardly have been more excited to see my name in the first of two groups of eight. We were going to play a round-robin format, with everyone playing against everyone else in each group. Every match would comprise nine games and the winner would be the player who finished with the highest aggregate number of games won.

I was drawn to play against the No. 1 seed in my opening match of the day and, perhaps understandably, the talented nine-year-old appeared slightly annoyed at being asked to play against the small, pesky six-year-old who was bouncing around and just couldn't wait to get started on the opposite side of the net.

There were some decent rallies and most of the games went to deuce, but I trailed 0–1, 0–2, 0–3 and then 0–4. I was not happy. When we passed at the net, changing ends between the fifth and sixth games, I deliberately bumped into him, even if I was not quite tall enough for my shoulder to connect with his shoulder.

He ignored my antics and eased to an 8–1 win. At the end, I refused to shake hands, burst into tears, stormed off court, climbed a tree and scrambled onto the roof of the clubhouse.

'AB, please come down,' my mother pleaded.

'No,' I said, sobbing.

'Come on, AB, please behave and come down.'

'No.'

The tantrum lasted for around 10 minutes until my increasingly embarrassed mother persuaded me to climb down from the roof by promising to buy me a remote-control electric car.

Tears dried, I pulled myself together and managed to win my second match 6–3 and, in my third match, worked to a position where I was leading 5–3 and 40–30 in the ninth and last game.

'I've got *balle de match*, Ma,' I yelled. 'I've got *balle de match*!'

My mother was helping to organise the tournament, sitting some distance away, but she heard my raised voice and came running to the courtside. I saw her arrive. This was fun.

My next forehand hit the net.

'Don't go, Ma,' I said, 'it's now *egalite*.'

It may seem odd that this highly excitable Afrikaans-speaking six-year-old boy should be competing in a tennis event in Nelspruit and speaking French but there was a simple explanation: only the previous week, we had been watching the French Open on television and I had learned to mimic the umpires at Roland Garros.

The next point was won, securing a 6–3 win and, somehow, I managed to win each of my remaining matches in the tournament. A very happy boy smiled throughout the long drive home.

Encouraged by this success, I started to spend more and more time playing tennis, walking to the sports club in town almost every day to hit some balls for an hour or so. I needed a training partner to hit the balls back and none of my friends were keen but, happily, my extraordinary mother almost always said yes.

A Canadian actor called Victor Webster has been quoted as saying: 'If you throw a pebble in the water on one side of the ocean, you can create a tidal wave on the other side.' The idea that a tiny and seemingly insignificant event can have enormous consequences may seem foolish but, in my experience, it is proven.

This is what happened.

A young and very small boy living in a small town in rural South Africa during the late 1980s starts to play tennis and appears able to hit the ball relatively well. So what? Not a lot, I suppose. There are literally millions of youngsters who show some degree of sporting ability at an early age.

A pebble is effectively thrown into the water when the youngster is introduced to a tennis coach named Danny Sullivan, a former professional player who just happens to be living in the same town. The boy's parents book and pay for two lessons per week and, completely unseen, a process is started.

'You need to hit 1 000 balls every day,' the coach tells the youngster, leaving him in no doubt that he will only realise his full potential if he is prepared to work hard and make sacrifices.

'You need to prepare correctly for every practice and every match,' he says, creating special routines for packing kit and equipment, and always remembering to bring a plastic bottle filled with water.

'You need to write brief notes for yourself, summarising your game plan, which you can read as you change ends between games,' the coach says, and so the seeds of lifelong habits are sown.

Danny Sullivan taught me basic lessons on the tennis court before my seventh birthday, and these basic lessons have remained with me ever since and become the foundations of my cricket career: hard work is non-negotiable, prepare properly for every practice and match, and create and stick to the game plan.

There is no doubt in my mind. The performances that appear to have pleased crowds in cricket grounds around South Africa, throughout India and elsewhere, originate from a tennis court in Warmbaths.

In fact, my coach seemed to have some idea of what could just possibly lie ahead for me. After another energetic training session, he told my parents: 'Well, this boy is certainly different – he'll either grow up to play for South Africa in one sport or another ... or he's going to end up in prison.'

Danny moved to Stellenbosch, embarking upon a distinguished coaching career that would include spells with Christo van Rensburg, Marcos Ondruska and Ivan Lendl, but he left me in the capable hands of an ideal replacement: his father, Derek Sullivan – Oom Derek, as I called him.

'AB has great potential,' Oom Derek would tell my parents, 'and he ought to train every day, but he must never stop enjoying the game. There should always be time for an ice cream.'

The advice made sense then, and it still makes sense all these years later. However high the stakes, sport must always retain an element of enjoyment – even if, in time, the ice creams did become beers.

When Oom Derek retired as a coach, my mother started to take me and a few other young players to attend a one-week tennis clinic run by Theuns van Rensburg in the town of Bethlehem in the Free State. It was a demanding schedule, with tennis starting at 7 am every morning and running through until 5 pm in the evening. Oom Theuns had introduced the Nick Bollettieri method of coaching to South Africa and, at one stage, the renowned American coach actually attended the course in Bethlehem.

So, after playing in the Lowveld Open in 1990, aged six, I joined the year-round programme of age-group tennis tournaments played throughout South Africa. The Northern Transvaal Open was our 'home' event, played at Groenkloof in Pretoria, and we invariably drove to compete in both the Southern Transvaal Open in Johannesburg and the Eastern Transvaal Open in Benoni. December and January brought even longer car journeys to compete on the so-called Sugar Circuit, incorporating the Free State Open in Bloemfontein, the Natal Open in Durban, the Border Open in East London, the Eastern Province Open in Port Elizabeth and the Western Province Open in Cape Town.

Endless hours on the road brought two challenges: car sickness, which I simply needed to bear, and what became an intense fear of getting stuck in traffic, arriving late and being disqualified.

'How long till we get there?' I used to whine *ad nauseam*.

On one occasion, we were severely delayed by a traffic jam on the N1 between Pretoria and Johannesburg and, somewhat flustered, we arrived at the Ellis Park courts to hear my name being called on the public-address system. I was seconds away from being disqualified, but the organisers let me play. The scare served me well. From that day, I have always tried to leave enough time and to avoid being late.

Players tried to enter all the events nationwide because they all offered points that counted towards the national rankings, constantly updated in every age group through Under-10, U12, U14, U16 and U18.

I enjoyed the experience, enjoyed the competition and enjoyed some success, designated as No. 1 or No. 2 seed in most tournaments and generally ranked No. 1 or No. 2 in the country in my age group.

As the years passed, and as I played in more and more matches and tournaments, I gradually learned to manage the nerves that regularly threatened to overwhelm me every time I played ('stick to all the same routines'), to cope with opponents who returned the ball with no pace, tempting me to try to hit too hard ('stay patient') and even to behave properly when I lost a match ('it is fine for you to be upset but don't show it').

After the sit-down strike on the roof of the clubhouse, my parents showed zero tolerance.

'Throw your racket once and you will be pulled off court,' I was told. I never did.

'Disrespect the referee once and you will be pulled off court,' I was told. I never did.

'Disrespect your opponent once and you will be pulled off court,' I was told. I never did.

Tennis became a huge part of my life. There was training almost every afternoon. Club, provincial and national tournaments were held throughout the year; they were generally scheduled during the school holidays, but when there was a clash with cricket or rugby, it was usually tennis that took priority.

Were people suggesting I would one day become a professional tennis player?

I think so. My forehand was decent but I remember that there was concern about my serve because it was difficult to inject any genuine power when I was relatively short for my age. At one point, I was coached to serve like Boris Becker, throwing the ball high and leaping into the air as I served. I suppose, if I had been able to serve like the great German, I would have continued to develop and might have played at Wimbledon, Flushing Meadows and the rest.

Several of my rivals on the junior circuit did turn professional.

Izak van der Merwe was an outstanding player from Stellenbosch who grew up to win three professional titles, compete at Wimbledon and represent South Africa in the Davis Cup. Kevin Anderson is a couple of years younger than me, though somewhat taller at 6' 8", and we had some close matches all those years ago. I have enjoyed following his career, through the quarterfinals at the 2015 US Open and into the world's top ten.

There were others, giants in my memory.

Christopher Westerhof, a left-hander from Durban, was my most difficult opponent. We seemed to play each other in semifinals and finals all over the country. The matches were invariably tight and there were many tie-breakers but, somehow, he was generally able to win the points that mattered. He had the edge.

Michael Shapiro was another fine player. I remember playing a semifinal against him at Groenkloof in Pretoria when he was 14 years old and I was a year younger, and everything went my way. Every serve, every passing shot and every volley came off the racket perfectly and the tennis coach from Waterkloof High School approached my parents and offered me a bursary to attend his school. It was exciting to be scouted and I recall thinking that maybe I could turn pro and play at Wimbledon, but one swallow doesn't make a summer.

Danie van der Walt, from Witbank, was another top performer, and I was fortunate to have him on my side of the net when we were ranked as the No. 1 Under-14 doubles pair in the country.

I continued to play tennis when I moved to Afrikaanse Hoër Seunskool,

'Affies', representing the school in matches against rivals such as Grey College, Bloemfontein and Pretoria Boys' High, but the schedule became complex on the big sporting days when tennis clashed with either the rugby or the cricket.

A choice had to be made, and I decided to stop playing tennis.

Why?

I wanted to play team sports. At Affies, I saw the special spirit and camaraderie within a team, whether it was rugby or cricket. I felt the intensity of a group of people pulling together under pressure, celebrating together in victory and feeling sad together in defeat, and I loved every minute of it. For me, there was nothing more exhilarating, nothing more worthwhile than being part of a team, setting the team above everything.

Looking back, I learned a lot from tennis. I will always remember the advice given to me by Danny Sullivan and his father Oom Derek, and I eventually learned to control my nerves, to conceal my utter devastation when I lost and, ultimately, to take responsibility for my performance.

It was not an easy decision and, in some respects, I felt as though I was letting down my parents, specifically my mother who had committed so much time and effort to my tennis and who would have so much enjoyed seeing me go further in the game, maybe even to Wimbledon, but she understood my reasons. I clearly remember her telling me she agreed with my choice – and, as ever, she offered unconditional support.

CHAPTER 4

'LET THERE BE LIGHT'

More than 240 new boys have gathered in the school hall, each wearing the school uniform of white shirt, grey trousers and the distinctive red, green and yellow blazer. It is January 1998, the start of the school year, and the hordes of nervous 13-year-olds wait quietly for instruction.

One of the matrics, starting his last year at school, appears and starts to explain how each new boy will be allocated to an older boy and be mentored through the year; in return, the new boy will assist the older in carrying his bag, writing out his homework and other tasks.

'And you will call the older boy "Master",' he adds, 'but, first, you must learn the school Honour Code. It's important you learn these words so you can live by these words. Write them out 100 times.'

The boys pick up their pens and write the code once, twice, three times, four times ...

In our school, we give honour to God and His Word and we strive to live by Christian principles. We are grateful for the talents we have received from God, and we use these talents in His honour. We strive to be helpful and to serve. We respect and honour our parents and teachers and behave considerately towards all people, particularly women and superiors. Our

*word is our honour. We believe in self-control, self-discipline,
humility and loyalty. We serve our school and protect its good
name in word and deed. We keep ourselves and our environment immaculate and clean. We stand for our Language, our
Nation and our Country.*

Ninety-eight times, 99 times … 100.

I was one of those new and nervous boys and, as we completed the
task, I looked across the hall and happened to catch the eye of a friend
I had first met two years earlier at the South African primary schools
cricket week, where he was playing for Northern Transvaal and I was a
member of the Northern Province side. He nodded at me and smiled in
unspoken acknowledgement of a job well done.

It was not the first time we had risen to a challenge together, nor would
it be the last.

My friend in the school hall was Francois du Plessis, or 'Faf', as he was
and is universally known. He was in the same year as me at high school,
most often in the same class, usually in the same sports team and always
in the same boarding house; from those days through all these years, we
have been teammates at Affies, teammates in the Titans provincial side
and teammates in the South African national team.

Faf and I have walked a long road together. Through countless
training sessions and matches, countless trips and tours, scrapes and
adventures, we have got to know each other extremely well and have
become close friends and eager rivals, forever spurring each other to
greater achievements.

Looking back, the image of us that endures in my mind is of two
excited high-school boys fielding side by side in the covers, prowling like
hungry wild animals, literally pouncing on the ball at every opportunity, supporting each other, challenging each other to be faster and more
agile, to concentrate harder.

Of course we have combined in moments that have attracted far wider attention – most notably batting to save the second Test against Australia in Adelaide in 2012 and adding 206 for the third wicket in a one-day international against Australia in August 2014 – but, for me, we were exceptional at high school.

That might seem odd, but Tiger Woods might understand.

I recently read an interview the great American golfer gave to *Time* magazine to mark his 40th birthday and he was quoted as saying: 'I peaked at 11, to be honest with you. I played 36 tournaments that year, all in California, and won them all, never lost. I probably had the cutest girlfriend in all of sixth grade. And I had straight As, no A-minuses. They were all perfect As. I've been trying to get back to that ever since.'

It might be stretching reality to suggest that Faf and I peaked at 16, but those really were the days at Affies. We relished every match, embraced every challenge and loved every minute.

We were fortunate to attend a great high school.

Everyone has their own concept of an ideal school. For me, it would be a place with outstanding facilities in an inspiring location, with plenty of importance attached to sport throughout the year, a clear identity and a strong sense of belonging, a place where nothing is more valued than a fighting spirit.

Happily for me, and for tens of thousands of others, a member of parliament named Jan Joubert and a pastor called Chris Neethling founded precisely such a school in Pretoria.

At a time when Dutch and English were the country's two official languages, Joubert and Neethling recognised a growing push to replace Dutch with Afrikaans and created the first purely Afrikaans-medium school in South Africa. The Afrikaanse Hoër Seunskool duly opened on 28 January 1920, with 44 pupils and three teachers in a house belonging to General Piet Joubert. The school soon moved east to larger premises and, in 1929, settled on its current site at No. 1 Lynnwood Road, across the street from what would become Loftus Versfeld, one of the world's most famous rugby grounds, home of the Bulls and the site of many Springbok triumphs.

For me, Affies is everything.

I am massively proud to be an Affies old boy and hugely privileged to be associated with the school; and I will always be grateful for the values instilled in me during my formative years, between 1998 and 2002.

From that scary day at the start of our first year when the matric boy asked us to write out the Honour Code 100 times to being introduced to my 'mentor', an older boy named Anton Swanepoel (I called him 'Meester Swannies' and he used to call me BA), through all the traditions to instil discipline, humility and respect, I loved the spirit.

Believe me, it's a special place.

This simple fact first dawned on me one bright, bracing Highveld winter's day in 1992. Under clear blue skies, in perfect sunshine, 12 000 people had gathered at the school to watch Affies play an Administrator's Cup rugby match on the A field. My brother Wessels had started at Affies at the beginning of that year and my parents reckoned this was an ideal opportunity for us all to drive from Warmbaths to Pretoria to see him.

As an eight-year-old younger brother, I looked around in awe. The sheer number of assembled parents, families, friends and old boys was impressive, but I couldn't take my eyes off the packed bank of white-shirted Affies boys filling the stand on the eastern side of the ground, packed shoulder to shoulder, singing their school songs from start to finish.

It was a great day.

'I want to go to Affies,' I told my mother as we drove home.

She smiled.

'I'm serious,' I said.

I was fascinated by anything and everything associated with Affies, and I started to take a particular interest in my older brother's school uniform, generally returning home from Warmbaths Primary School, nipping into his room, borrowing one of his Affies jerseys and wearing it for the rest of the day.

On one occasion, feeling brave, I nipped into his room at the start of the day and turned up at my primary school wearing the Affies jersey – grey with the famous red, green and yellow trim.

Our primary school headmaster was not pleased.

'De Villiers, you need to take that off,' he told me.

'Why?'

'It's the uniform of another school.'

'I'm wearing this jersey because it is so cold today,' I protested gamely.

'Take it off now.'

'Please, sir.'

'Now.'

The years could not pass quickly enough and, in January 1998, I duly arrived at Afrikaanse Hoër Seunskool as an excited new boy, and obediently wrote out the school's Honour Code 100 times. I missed my parents and home back in Warmbaths, but few boys could have been so eager to start boarding school.

For me, it was the start of a special time in my life ... take the N1 south towards Pretoria, turn off the highway at the Lynnwood Road off-ramp, head towards the city, past Menlo Park High School on your left, past the University of Pretoria hostels on your right, on until the soaring floodlights of Loftus Versfeld rise ahead of you. Then, at the roundabout, with the Pretoria East NG church ahead, look to your left and see the school gates, and note the school crest attached to the central post and read the visible motto ... '*Laat daar lig wees*' (Let there be light).

Welcome to Affies.

Our sister school, the Afrikaanse Hoër Meisieskool, stood beyond the church, and if you followed Jorissen Street round to the left past our A field, turned left on Walton Jameson Avenue and headed up the hill, you

LET THERE BE LIGHT

would find the fine, expansive grounds of Pretoria Boys' High School, our neighbours and rivals, generally known as 'Boys' High', with alumni such as Springbok rugby captain John Smit and cricketer Eddie Barlow.

As far as we were concerned, Boys' High was OK but the fates had granted Affies the prime location in Pretoria, on the main road, in the lap of Loftus, front and centre, impossible to miss.

Arriving at the main gate, you see Huis Pannevis, the red-brick boarding house for new boys, away to your left, and Huis Frank le Roux, the boarding house for Standard 7 (Grade 9) and Standard 8 (Grade 10), much further to the right. The grounds are compact but intimate, a home away from home.

The buildings are impressive but Affies is distinguished, above all, by its spirit … something we used to call 'Affie guts', that special fighting spirit that runs through the entire school community, fuelling the energy of the boys at work and at play, driving the whole-hearted commitment of the teachers and staff. In my experience, in my time, it was the people who made the school.

It was people such as Jacques Rudolph, whom I so admired. He was three years ahead of me and, when I was 14, I remember feeling so privileged to carry his cricket bag for him. Jacques went on to play 48 Tests for South Africa between 2003 and 2012, and it was a thrill for me to be his teammate.

It was people such as Fourie du Preez, two years ahead of me at school, who shone in our 1st XV rugby team and advanced to play 164 matches for the Bulls and 74 Tests for the Springboks. In October 2015, when the Proteas were on tour in India, the players gathered in a hotel room to watch the Boks play Wales in a Rugby World Cup quarterfinal at Twickenham, and nobody cheered louder than me when Fourie scored the winning try.

It was people such as Francois Swart, Fourie's close friend and half-back partner at school, whom everybody expected would play for South

Africa but who tragically passed away in a car accident. Francois was two years older than me and yet, when I was first chosen to play in the school cricket 1st XI, he always found time to encourage me. Such acts of kindness seem insignificant but they could not have been more important to a 15-year-old amongst older boys.

I remember one occasion when the whole team went to lunch at the Swart home before we played in a schools semifinal at the Technikon ground and his mother cooked for us. All these years later, I am still in contact with Tannie Sally, and she often sends me a text message when I am lucky enough to score runs.

It was people such as Francois Geldenhuys, also two years ahead of me at school and a fine cricketer who backed me when I was most in need. 'French', as we called him, was captain of the Northern Transvaal team at the Coca-Cola High Schools cricket week in 2000, and when our coach planned to put me at seven in the batting order, it was French who spoke up and insisted I be given the chance to open the innings.

Fortunately, I was able to take the opportunity; I scored a century that week, and went on to be included in the South African Colts team and then the South African schools team a year later, and so on. Would I have made that kind of progress if French had said nothing and I had been left to languish down the order? Nobody knows.

What is known is that there are thousands of exceptionally talented young sportsmen and -women all around the world who never realise their full potential simply because they get lost in the system, simply because they never have the chance to show what they can do at the crucial time. It is a simple fact that I got my chance because, at the crucial time for me, French Geldenhuys spoke up and insisted I open the innings.

And, in a school that offered much more than competitive sports teams, it was about people such as Gunther Bender, from Secunda, who was my roommate in the boarding house and who used to study the Bible with me. He invariably came top in History and grew up to be a success-ful political speechwriter.

These were the great people who made a great school.

In my first year at Affies, there was a general expectation that I would focus on tennis and follow in the footsteps of old boys such as Danie Visser and Johan Kriek, both of whom had enjoyed successful careers on the professional circuit. Johan had risen to No. 7 in the world in 1984 and Danie was ranked as the No. 1 doubles player in the world in 1990. Our excellent coach, Oom Theuns van Rensburg, wanted to steer me in the same direction.

Ever eager to please, I played for Affies in a tennis match against Grey College, Bloemfontein, but even by then my focus had started to shift towards the broader appeal of team sports, to the boys who were walk-ing past the tennis courts, laughing and joking with each other on the way to rugby training.

They seemed to be having so much more fun.

I decided to stop playing tennis and turned to rugby, believing my suc-cess at primary school would continue.

Following extensive trials, the Under-14 rugby teams were listed and pinned to a noticeboard.

What? Really?

Surely there is a mistake?

There is a De Villiers in the Under-14F team ... the F team! Is that me? Could it be another De Villiers? I checked all the lists. There was no De Villiers in a higher team. That De Villiers was me ... in the F team.

I did manage to play a few matches for the Under-15E team the follow-ing year but I was disappointed and, in my Under-16 year, I chose to play hockey instead of rugby. That decision might not sound like the greatest example of 'Affie guts', but I was not getting anywhere on the rugby field and so I sought another option. Apparently stuck in a traffic jam in one sport, I decided to take a detour and seek another route to success.

Hockey was a new sport to me but I was included in the B side, learned the rules, scored a few goals and, three weeks later, was selected for the Under-16A side. We had a strong team and a successful season, including a first-ever win by an Affies hockey team over an equivalent side at Pretoria Boys' High. Our near neighbours were traditionally stronger in hockey but, after many years when our A side was considered only good enough to play their B or C sides, our Under-16As were given the opportunity to play As against As, and we won.

One year of hockey was great, but one year of hockey was also enough. For my last two years at Affies, I decided to return to rugby and try again to succeed in the sport that mattered most at our school.

Nothing would come easy. I trained hard and tried to impress but, when the 1st teams of the season were put up on the noticeboard, I was chosen to play flyhalf for the 5th XV. Fair enough, I thought. Then, out of the blue, midway through the year, a couple of guys were injured and I was invited to play at 10 for the 3rd XV. Mr Potgieter, the 2nd XV coach, happened to see me play and liked what he saw.

'De Villiers,' he said, 'I would like you to join the 2nd XV training squad.'

At last, this was the break.

Our next fixture was the derby against Boys' High. It felt like the most important match of my entire life and, catapulted into playing flyhalf for the 2nd XV, I managed to make a few decent breaks and to kick seven out of seven attempts at the posts. It was a great day, and we stormed to a wonderful 40–0 victory.

'How did the first team get on?'

'They won ... just,' came the reply.

People were saying that Sarel Potgieter, one of our star players, was playing out of position at 10 and wanted to move to centre, but there was no obvious alternative at flyhalf. The whispering and speculation started. Literally, in the space of three weeks, I had been brought in from the wilderness of the 5th xv to the brink of playing for the school's 1st xv, the celebrated Wit Bulle (White Bulls), so named in reference to our white jerseys and the Blue Bulls who played across the road at Loftus. The unthinkable had suddenly become possible.

Everything was going my way ... or so it seemed.

'AB, the head wants to see you in his office.'

What now?

Our headmaster was Dr Pierre Edwards, a former Northern Transvaal and Springbok fullback in his own right, and the expression on his face suggested this was not going to be a positive conversation.

'Please tell me about this radio station,' he said.

My heart sank.

'It was just a bit of fun, sir.'

'Did you say fun? I understand you and a few other boys have created a radio station broadcasting around 500 metres that is being listened to at the girls' school. Is that correct?'

I nodded.

'And I am told you have been speaking nonsense on this radio station.'

I nodded again, assuming he knew everything about our 'pirate radio', and confessed.

Two older boys had created the station and a group of us created the content, a mix of music and light-hearted interviews in which we spoke about how we were going to **** up Boys' High, for instance. Somebody also remarked on air that the daughter of one of the Affies teachers had exceptionally attractive legs. It was meant to be fun but, sitting in the head's office, it became clear we had crossed the line.

'This is unacceptable behaviour,' he concluded, 'and we will decide your punishment later.'

Six other boys from my year were called to see Dr Edwards about the radio station, and they successfully covered their tracks, persuading the head they had done nothing wrong. I became the fall guy.

A few days later, my mother was summoned to the school to be told what had been decided, and she duly walked in to see one of the senior masters while I sat in the car and awaited my fate.

She emerged 10 minutes later, in tears.

'They've expelled you from the boarding house for the rest of term,' she said, sobbing. 'I don't know what we are going to do now. We live so far away. You may have to go to another school.'

I remember that my main concern at the time was that someone would walk past us, in the school car park, and see my mother in this distressed state, but the scale of the punishment did surprise me.

Everything was happening so fast.

My mother was still extremely upset and Carel Kriek, one of the most widely respected teachers at Affies, was suddenly standing beside our car. He was the 1st team rugby coach, and had also coached our Under-15 cricket side; he was almost my mentor at school and he tried to calm the situation.

'Look, the decision has been made,' Dr Kriek said, 'and we must respect that, but you must not even think about moving to Waterkloof or any other school. You might soon be chosen for the 1st XV and everybody wants you to stay at Affies. We'll make a plan about your accommodation for the rest of this term.'

I felt better, and my mother managed to drive our car the short distance to the Waterkloof Glen shopping centre, although she was still crying when we parked outside the Nando's restaurant.

'Ma, please stop crying,' I said. 'Everything will be OK.'

She was obviously concerned for me, and I loved her for that, but Dr Kriek was right ... we did make a plan. In the end, it was arranged that I would stay in Brooklyn with the family of my father's sister, Suzanne. She had married Jurie van der Walt, a former hurdles champion, and they welcomed me into their home. Riaan, their son and my cousin, was also at Affies and, each and every day, we took a bus to and from school together.

This new hardship did me no harm at all and may even have forced me to grow up a little. Every morning, Riaan and I would make our special Bovril sandwiches, perfecting the art of spreading the Bovril and the butter on the hot toast so quickly that they would melt together; any other way affected the taste and was unacceptable. And the entire Van der Walt family could not have made me feel more at home. I was even able to sleep in my father's old bed, which had been moved from my grandparents' old house; his initials were engraved in the headboard.

My routine changed, but my burning ambition to play for the Wit Bulle remained the same and, just a week after being thrown out of the boarding house, I was named among the 1st XV substitutes for what would be a tough match against Die Brandwag from Humansdorp, ranked as the No. 4 school team in the country.

I was excited, nervous and relieved to see Danie Opperman would be playing at centre. This was the same Danie Opperman who had grown up with me in Warmbaths, the same Danie Opperman who had been my teammate at primary school, who had suggested to the coach that he move to centre so that I could play at flyhalf, who had applauded when I kicked the drop goal. Now, five years later, the same Danie Opperman was one of my teammates in the Affies 1st team, and he was still backing me.

With little more than 10 minutes to play, we were leading 21–9 and I was finally told to warm up and get ready to come on as a substitute flyhalf. I could not have been more thrilled and excited. With the entire school watching, I sprinted out to join the game and Danie Opperman gave me the thumbs-up.

My first pass was a skip pass, past Danie, into the hands of Deon Venter, our captain and outside centre, and my first place kick was a touchline conversion that sailed between the posts to secure the 28–9 win. What a day! The whole school was singing in full voice at the final whistle, and I could not have been happier.

A few more appearances as a substitute were followed by a couple of starts and I was included in the Affies squad that set off on tour to Jeffreys Bay. I was earmarked for the traditional initiation while on tour, some slapping on the back, but the same Danie Opperman was there as well, looking after me.

The 2002 season, the following year, unfolded as unquestionably the highlight of my rugby life and, to be frank, one of my greatest experiences ever. To be the starting flyhalf for the Wit Bulle through all 23 matches, to play in an Affies 1st XV that lost only one of those games, was an incredible experience.

We had a decent team.

Sarel Potgieter, outside centre and captain, went on to play for Western Province and the Stormers. Pierre Spies, our tall, quick and powerful eighthman, was a year younger than most of us but advanced to play 136 matches for the Bulls and 53 Tests for the Springboks. Derick Kuün, flanker and vice-captain, played for the Bulls and later the Kings, and captained the Eastern Cape side against the British and Irish Lions in 2009.

Heino Kühn, our scrumhalf, was also a fine cricketer: just as we were the halfback pairing on the rugby field for Affies in 2002, so we were destined to team up again to open the batting for South Africa in a T20 international against England at SuperSport Park in Centurion only seven years later, in 2009.

Jacques-Louis Potgieter, fullback, went on to play for the Bulls, Cheetahs and Sharks in Super Rugby, and then to enjoy a successful professional career in France with Bayonne, Dax and Lyon. Weber van Wyk, flanker, would become a leading cricket agent working for the Essentially Group, representing Protea players such as Faf du Plessis and Morné Morkel and always willing to assist me. Steven Botha, an outstandingly gifted wing, scored 49 tries, more than anyone had ever scored in a single season for the Affies 1st XV.

Dr Kriek was our coach and his assistants were the legendary Sakkie van der Walt and Johan van Graan, a young coach destined to become the forwards coach for both the Bulls and the Springboks.

In fact, it was more than a decent team; it was an exceptional team.

The Affies A field was our home ground, bordered by the grandstand where the entire school stood shoulder to shoulder, another grandstand for the Club 600 for old boys and parents, and the Frank le Roux boarding house, where I stayed for a few years and where we spent many happy evenings socialising in the most sought-after room overlooking the rugby field, the room allocated in 2001 to Wynand Olivier, the centre who later played for the Bulls and the Boks.

We wanted the A field to be a genuine fortress and we started the season with emphatic victories over Wynberg Boys' High School and Pietersburg, as well as a couple of hard-fought wins over tough opponents such as HTS Middelburg and Paarl Gimnasium. In fact, we had managed to win 12 out of 12 by the time we prepared to play Grey College, Bloemfontein, traditionally one of our greatest rivals, at home on Saturday, 25 May 2002.

The day dawned bright and sunny, and the sense of excitement was extraordinary.

Grey Bloem and Affies were widely recognised as the two outstanding school teams in the country at the time and, with three draws between the teams in the previous five seasons, most people were suggesting that the winner of this particular match would earn the right to call themselves the No. 1 school side in South Africa.

The stakes were high, and my parents decided to drive from Warmbaths to Pretoria to watch the game – in fact, they would not miss an Affies match all season – and were having a late breakfast nearby when they saw Hansie Cronjé, the former South African cricket captain, eating at the same restaurant.

As an enthusiastic Old Grey himself, Hansie had travelled to watch the big match and would have felt reasonably optimistic about the outcome. The visiting team included promising young players such as hooker Bismarck du Plessis and scrumhalf Ruan Pienaar, both destined to become Springboks and global stars of the game.

More than 14 000 spectators occupied every available space around the A field and we started in a blur, scoring early, dominating every phase of the game. Our crowd was delighted, roaring approval of every move, every break and every tackle. Life could not get any better than this.

We led 21–0 towards the end of the first half; then we won a scrum on our 22-metre line. Heino Kühn whipped the ball back to me and I aimed to punt the ball into touch ... but Ruan Pienaar managed to charge down my kick, collected and scampered clear to score a try. I have always insisted that Ruan was at least two metres offside – that's my story, and I'm sticking to it – but the referee awarded the try, our lead was reduced to 21–7 and, on the stroke of half-time, the tide had turned.

There is a Grey legend that Hansie telephoned his father Ewie during the break, relayed the score and said he thought Grey could still fight back and win the game.

So it proved. Grey mounted attack after attack. In one move, Bismarck du Plessis literally ran straight over me. Then they scored again. We called an intricate move deep inside our own half in which I was meant to dummy both centres before popping the ball inside to the wing, but only succeeded in being crunched by their inside centre, Rieel de Kock. They scored again. I think it's true to say I touched the ball three times in those last 20 minutes.

Final score: Affies 21, Grey College Bloemfontein 46.

Our only consolation was that, for the fifth year in succession, adding up the results of all the age-group matches played between the schools on the same day, we won more matches than Grey.

The following weekend, we travelled to play Maritzburg College in Pietermaritzburg and scored an outstanding try late in the game to secure a 20–19 win. However, the match – like every match played in South Africa on Saturday, 1 June 2002 – was overshadowed by the shocking news that Hansie Cronjé had died earlier that morning in an air crash in the Outeniqua Mountains near George. He was only 32.

Hansie erred in communicating with betting syndicates and his mistakes were well publicised, but these should not obscure his immense contribution to South African cricket between 1992 and 2000, scoring more than 9 000 runs and captaining the national team to no fewer than 27 Test victories and 99 ODI wins, effectively building the stage upon which so many other Protea cricketers, including me, have been able to perform.

Our season continued with an important 21–6 victory over Boys' High and a free-flowing 37–28 win at Waterkloof, when we played some enjoyable, fast, attacking rugby, and made steady progress in the Beeld Trophy, winning a quarterfinal and semifinal, and so securing our place in the final.

Another perfect sunny day, another huge crowd, another massive occasion: our final opponents were Waterkloof, again, but this was a much tighter game and, although we dominated territory in the opening 20 minutes, we needed to start building a score. We won a lineout on the right-hand side of the field and, impulsively departing from the game plan, I decided to attempt a drop goal. Thankfully, the kick passed between the posts.

We scored a try in the corner soon afterwards, but midway through the second half I fell awkwardly in a tackle and dislocated my elbow. It was agony. The bone literally popped out of the socket. The medic calmly stretched my arm and popped it back but, for a scary moment, my sporting career had hung in the balance.

I was forced to leave the field but my teammates went on to secure a 19–16 win, claiming the Beeld Trophy and ensuring we finished the 2002 season with a record of played 23, won 22 and lost one. Our average number of points per match was 32 and our average margin of victory was 17.5 – not bad, not bad at all.

Beyond playing high-school rugby for Affies, there were also opportunities to play representative rugby and I was fortunate to be selected for the Blue Bulls Under-18 team, and later the Under-19 team, wearing the famous light-blue jersey, playing at Loftus Versfeld, and still always dreaming of playing at a higher level.

I was also selected to play in the Blue Bulls high-school team competing in the 2002 Craven Week at Woodburn Stadium in Pietermaritzburg. We had a strong squad, including Pierre Spies and Derick Kuün from Affies, as well as Chiliboy Ralepelle from Boys' High, but my oldest friend at the tournament was captain of the KwaZulu-Natal team, playing at home and our opponents in the last match of the opening day.

Antonie Claassen is the son of Wynand Claassen, Springbok captain on the famous 'demo' tour to New Zealand in 1981 and one of my father's oldest and closest friends from their days at Tukkies. Our families have been friends for as long as I can remember, and a photograph of me and Antonie when we were four years old shows us wearing our respective Bulls and Natal rugby jerseys. Fourteen years on, an identical photograph was taken of the two of us wearing larger Bulls and Natal jerseys before the match at the Craven Week.

Antonie would eventually move to France, settle there, and enjoy a fine professional career, playing club rugby for Brive, Castres and Racing Metro, and win six caps for the French national team.

The Bulls-Natal match at Woodburn Stadium attracted plenty of media attention, with reports covering a full page in the *Beeld* newspaper, and we started strongly, taking an early lead. However, Peter Grant was playing flyhalf for KwaZulu-Natal and, showing the talent he would subsequently take to Western Province and the Stormers, he seized control all on his own, scoring two tries and guiding the home side to a 36–32 comeback win.

That dramatic defeat at the 2002 Craven Week would be the pinnacle of my career in rugby.

By then, it had become clear that my future lay on the cricket field.

It's a simple fact that cricket at Affies did not engage the same scale of emotions or draw the same crowds as rugby, but it's also true that the school excelled at the summer game, leading the extraordinary development of cricket in Afrikaans schools across the country since the mid-1990s.

Most of the credit for this remarkable progress should go to Deon Botes, who coached the Under-15A team when he arrived at Affies in 1998 and has been guiding the 1st XI since 1999. Knowledgeable and dedicated, he has encouraged and inspired generations of young cricketers. It was he who ensured we were regularly invited by Maritzburg College to play at the highly rated Michaelmas cricket week and it was he who, season after season, organised fixtures for us against the likes of Hilton College, Durban High School, Michaelhouse and Grey College, Bloemfontein.

The opportunities to play these schools, to be tested at this level, as much as anything, made it possible for the likes of Jacques Rudolph, Faf du Plessis, Heino Kühn and me to realise our potential.

Carel Kriek was also involved in cricket at the school; it was he who had the foresight to bring in top-quality professional coaches such as Dennis Lindsay, the famously agile South African wicketkeeper between 1963 and 1970 and the man who, among all those who have ever kept wicket in 10 or more Test matches, conceded the fewest byes per Test.

'Hey, Du Plessis and De Villiers, what do you think you're doing?'

An afternoon cricket practice at Affies had just started, and it was Mr Lindsay shouting at us.

'Nothing, sir,' Faf and I replied in unison, as we continued jogging around the field in the warm-up.

'Nothing? That's not what I call nothing. You came late for practice. Now you're tripping each other. You're throwing stones at each other. You're fooling around. Go away. Leave immediately.'

'But sir ...'

'Just go away, now.'

Somewhat stunned, Faf and I left the group and headed towards the nets in the corner of the cricket field. We reckoned we would hang around there and throw a ball at each other; no such luck.

'I said go away,' Mr Lindsay shouted across the field at us. 'That means go away. If you don't want to practise seriously, you are wasting your time and you're wasting my time, so please disappear.'

The lesson was learned.

Faf was our star player at school, selected for the 1st XI when he was only 14 years old. I joined him in the school team midway through the following season, when we were both 15, and we played together in the Affies side for the better part of four years, generally winning ... and completing most practices.

As ever in cricket, the statistics don't lie.

We won 20 out of 29 matches in 1999 and, in 2000, won 23 out of 25 matches, losing only to Grey College when we were destroyed by the bowling of Ryan McLaren, who would later play for South Africa.

Our standards slipped slightly in 2001, when we won 21 of our 24 matches, losing three out of four matches early in the season, including a painful defeat to Boys' High and further losses against St Alban's and to St John's from Johannesburg. I suffered a minor slump in batting form early in the season, and might have been dropped if I had not been keeping wicket, scoring 578 runs in total; Faf scored 751 runs.

I missed a large part of our final season at school, in 2002, recovering from the dislocated elbow suffered on the rugby field, but returned to the team and scored 425 runs in nine matches, including 113 against Tygerberg. Faf again played brilliantly, leading by example and scoring 994 runs at an average of 58.

We had won 21 out of 23 matches, losing to St Alban's and drawing with Maritzburg College, when we prepared to play our last two matches of the season: at home to Pretoria Boys' High and then away at King

Edward VII School (KES) in Johannesburg. For Faf, me and a few others, these would be our last matches for Affies.

'AB, you may have to miss the next two matches.'

Deon Botes had called me aside and explained that the Northerns selectors had chosen me to play in the provincial B team final against Western Province B in Cape Town. That was exciting news, but I was torn.

'To be honest, sir,' I replied, 'I would rather finish our season with my friends.'

'Are you sure? This is a great opportunity.'

'I know, sir, but I don't want to miss the matches against Boys' High and KES.'

The Northerns selectors were duly informed I was unavailable for the B team final but my decision didn't look so great when, in the match against Boys' High, I was out for a duck before the rain began to fall. Play was abandoned but Mr Botes and his counterpart agreed that the match would be replayed a week later.

So we travelled to play KES. They had a talented team that included captain Blake Snijman and Vaughn van Jaarsveld, both of whom would later play provincial cricket, and a tight match came down to the last over, with KES needing three runs to win with one wicket standing and two balls remaining. The batsman swung, sending the ball high in the air. I started running away from the wicket, getting under the ball to take the catch and win the match ... watching the ball over my shoulder, running hard ... watching the ball, stretching out my arms ... and dropping the catch.

My heart sank. The moment still ranks among the greatest disappointments of my career. The batsmen had run two and, off the last ball, the KES batsman tapped and ran the single required for victory.

The replayed match against Boys' High followed a few days later and I was determined to make amends. After anxiously surviving an early

LBW appeal, I set about the bowling attack with purpose and managed to score 196 runs with one ball of our 50-over innings remaining. One more six would bring up my double hundred but I was caught on the boundary; even so, we won the game and the 196 remains an Affies record.

Over a four-year period, Affies played 103 matches and lost 11 – not bad. I had scored a total of 1 839 runs, but largely played second fiddle to Faf, who had scored a remarkable 3 190 runs.

Deon Botes was the first coach to make me think about my batting technique, about how to hold the bat, how to stand at the crease and how to play my strokes; until then, having learned the game playing with my brothers at Mentz Avenue in Warmbaths, I was simply content to hit the ball as hard as possible.

At the same time, my parents felt I would benefit from additional one-to-one coaching and they arranged for me to work with Shane Gouldie, who was the Youth Director at the Titans. Every Friday afternoon, my mother would drive to Pretoria, collect me from Affies, drive me to Centurion Park for the practice with Shane, wait around, drive me back to Affies and then drive for another hour or so back home.

Shane certainly helped me with my batting, as well as with my wicketkeeping but, above all, he gave me confidence in my ability to play the game. It appears to me that, whatever the challenge, whatever the circumstances, everyone benefits from having someone who unequivocally believes in them. In my life, through my teens, as I was growing up and contemplating cricket as a career, Shane Gouldie filled that role for me.

So, in December 2002, almost five years after arriving and writing the Honour Code 100 times, I left Affies with a real sense of sadness. A group of us wanted to mark the milestone in our lives.

'What can we do?' one of my friends asked.

My brother Wessels had told me about a tradition of buying a trunk, filling it with various souvenirs of our time at Affies and then burying the trunk somewhere in the school grounds. I explained the plan to my friends, and they loved it. So that's precisely what we did.

We bought a large trunk and filled it with various items. I put inside my Affies blazer and tie, and a long letter, as well as a bottle of wine and a bottle of Champagne. Then, in the middle of the night in our last week, we crept outside, dug a large hole in the lawn just to the left of the school gates, buried the trunk and carefully replaced the turf.

Our original plan was to exhume our trunk in 2012, on the 10th anniversary of leaving Affies, but some of us could not get to the school on that date, so we agreed to delay the ceremony until the 20th anniversary of our leaving, in December 2022. It goes without saying the existence of the trunk remains a closely guarded secret.

So please don't tell anyone.

The Afrikaanse Hoër Seunskool continues to go from strength to strength and I take every opportunity to go back and visit the school – in fact, I wish I had the time to visit more often than I do. In 2015, after watching a rugby match on the A field, one of those special days, I was asked by the 1st XV captain to join his players in singing the school song with the rest of the boys all joining in. It was at that exact moment that I realised that once you have attended Affies, you never really leave.

CHAPTER 5

FAST LANE

It would be wonderful to reflect on the two years between December 2002 when I left high school, and December 2004 when I made my Test debut for South Africa, as an exciting time of swift progress, the purposeful and planned transformation of a school boy into an international cricketer.

It would be wonderful ... but it would be untrue.

In reality, this was a frenetic, stressful and at times frightening period of my life when I was very largely living from day to day, from practice to practice, from match to match, from party to party; it was a period when things ultimately went well for me but it was also a period when things might have gone spectacularly wrong.

Batting? As far as I was concerned, batting amounted to not much more than trying to hit almost every ball for four. Planning? Planning rarely extended beyond phoning around and organising the bar where my friends would meet that evening.

Far from being impeccably organised and marching towards my destiny, I often felt as though I was being carried along by a wave, at the mercy of fate, able to do little more than work hard in the nets, do as I was told by the coaches and hope for the best.

Deep down, I did always believe there was a destiny, always retained an unspoken confidence that, whatever happened, somehow, one way or another, I would be successful in cricket … somehow. There was, how-ever, no clear way forward; there was never a grand plan. Most of the time, I did not have much idea what would happen next.

In effect, after leaving school, my career moved into the fast lane, and cars travelling at higher speeds are far more likely to crash because driv-ers have less time to identify what is happening around them and less time to react to danger. The safety margin is removed and what might normally have been a near miss can become a serious accident. Somehow, in 2003 and 2004, I managed to stay on the road.

There are many talented 18-year-olds who leave school with dreams of playing international sport, but few realise that ambition.

What separates the few from the many?

Some will say that, in almost every case, it is luck … the luck of being selected for the right team at the right time, of performing well when it really matters, of being noticed by the people whose opinion really counts. No matter how gifted you may be, the argument runs, you need at least a little luck to get the breaks and reach the top.

Others will say it is hard work … being prepared to practise harder and longer than others, to make more sacrifices, to get an early night when your friends are out and about so you can be fitter and sharper at practice the next morning, essentially to want the prize more desperately than other talented youngsters vying for the same place.

There were certainly one or two moments when luck played its part, when the breaks went my way, and it's also true that I have always enjoyed, even relished, the hard work and long practices, although, to be absolutely honest, in the first few years of my career, there were not many times when I felt it was necessary to miss the party.

Everything just happened.

After leaving high school at Affies, I followed the well-trodden path across Lynnwood Road to the University of Pretoria, to study Sports Science. The course included an Anatomy module, which I particularly enjoyed because it meant I could learn about the human body in lectures and then go home at the weekend and discuss the subject on equal terms with my father, a medical doctor. I remember feeling very proud.

Even so, in February 2003, my university studies would have scored around four out of 10 on the excitement scale, while the 2003 ICC Cricket World Cup that was about to start in South Africa rated 9.5.

The telephone was ringing.

'Hello.'

'AB, it's Dave Nosworthy here. We would like you to play for the Titans against Canada on Tuesday, 4 February, at Centurion Park. It's a warm-up match for them before the World Cup.'

'Er ... sorry ... did you say play for the Titans?'

I was stunned. Dave had watched me play for Affies a few months earlier and been kind enough to encourage me, but I never expected a call from the Titans coach just a few weeks after leaving school.

Arriving at the stadium on the morning of the game, literally as a boy among men, it was good to see some familiar faces in the home dressing room. There was Jacques Rudolph, whose cricket bag I had carried when I arrived at Affies, and there was Martin van Jaarsveld, who had so often played garden cricket at our home in Warmbaths.

My excitement levels were raised even further when I saw the cameras and realised the match was being broadcast live on SuperSport, and it turned out to be a special day. I shared an opening stand of 105 with Jacques and then, batting with Martin, took the score to 223 before I was bowled by off-spinner John Davison for 109. The Titans eventually made 365 for two in 50 overs, and then dismissed Canada for 148.

To score a century on my Titans debut, live on television, was an exhilarating experience but I was brought down to earth the following Saturday when I was selected to play in the Tukkies 2nd team, not the 1st team ... the 2nd team. This seemed odd. I was bemused. One moment,

I was up. Next moment, I was down. To repeat, through this period, I really didn't have a clear idea what was going on.

Colin Dettmer, the Tukkies coach, was adamant that he paid no attention to schoolboy reputations or provincial selection; as far as he was concerned, youngsters just out of school needed to prove themselves before playing in the university 1st team. That was his policy and he stuck to it. That was fair enough.

'Where are we meeting tonight?'
'News Café at nine?'
'OK, I'll see you there.'

So the student life continued, interspersed with sporadic moments when I would see or hear something on the cricket field that made me stop and think. On one occasion, playing for the Northerns B team, I arrived at the Technikon ground to find Quentin Still, a senior player, reading a newspaper. I sat beside him and tried to engage this experienced player in conversation … without success. He eventually turned to me and said gravely: 'Young man, we score our runs after lunch.'

Barely out of school, I was far too scared to ask what on earth he meant. It took me some time – perhaps too much time – to understand his point that, in cricket, it's usually wise to keep things tight in the morning and the runs will flow more easily as you become more settled.

'Menlyn is going to be quiet, so let's go to the DropZone?'
'In Hatfield? No problem, I'll be there.'

The telephone was ringing for a second time.
'AB, it's Dave Nosworthy here. I'm calling to let you know you have been selected for the South African Under-19 tour to England in June.'
'Thanks.'

In addition to being Titans coach, Dave was also head coach of the national Under-19 side, a stroke of good fortune for me. I was excited, and an eager and talented squad gathered for eight days of careful preparation at the new High Performance Centre in Pretoria. We were all aware that the previous South African Under-19 team to tour England had been 'whitewashed' in 2000, and we were fiercely determined to play well.

The senior Proteas squad was also playing England and, in the very same week Graeme Smith's side were beating England at Lord's (with Graeme scoring 259 and Makhaya Ntini taking 10 wickets), we set about the task of playing the first of three unofficial Tests against the England Under-19 team at Headingley in Leeds.

Our match turned when a fast bowler from Bellville in the Cape named Vernon Philander took five for 50 in the English second innings. Chasing 228 in the fourth innings to win, we lost early wickets but Rieel de Kock and I managed to build a partnership and both scored half-centuries; we won by six wickets. He was, incidentally, the selfsame Rieel de Kock who had flattened me with the perfect tackle when playing for Grey College against Affies a year before.

England called up a young opening batsman called Alastair Cook for the second unofficial Test played at New Road, Worcester, and he made 51 in their first innings total of 523. Batting under pressure, we collapsed to 28 for four and followed on. Defeat seemed inevitable.

However, by now, a talented left-handed batsman from Cape Town was emerging as the star of our squad. His name was JP Duminy and, coming together in desperate trouble at 54 for three midway through the third day, he and I set about the task of saving the match; we concentrated, worked hard and reached stumps at 166 for three. The partnership continued on the final morning, and by the time JP was finally dismissed we had added 220 runs for the fourth wicket. The middle order and tail continued to fight through a nervous afternoon and evening, and, with two wickets standing at the end of play, we salvaged a notable draw.

'That was a brilliant and courageous effort,' said coach Dave Nosworthy in the changing room afterwards, 'and one day, AB and JP, I reckon you will do that again for the national team.' He was right.

This was my first overseas tour and I was loving every minute, enjoying the tough cricket against strong opponents, relishing the challenge posed by different conditions, enjoying the experience of playing in a country where 'summer' sometimes felt like an Antarctic winter.

Faf du Plessis, my friend from school and ever-present teammate, was on tour as well and I remember us being so determined to do well, speaking so often about how much we wanted to win the series. With each run and each practice session in the nets, we were evolving from schoolboys into professionals. It's difficult to exaggerate the value of national age-group overseas tours for youngsters making this transition.

The third and final match of the series, played in Chelmsford, was magnificently dominated by Faf. He made 177 in our innings of 646 and then took three wickets for 39 runs as England were beaten by an innings and 163 runs. The 'Test' series was won 2–0, but celebrations were postponed until after the one-day series that followed.

The opening ODI was played at Arundel and, chasing 268 to win, we appeared to have done enough when, in the penultimate over, I was caught behind off Liam Plunkett for 143 from 153 balls. Yet seven runs were still required and, after losing another wicket and allowing a few dot balls to slip by, we needed four from the last two balls. Aaron Phangiso, the slow left-arm bowler from Ga-Rankuwa, was facing; using a bat he had borrowed from me at the last minute, he struck the winning boundary.

Rain washed out the second and third one-day matches but we didn't mind and the squad could not have been happier as we flew home, with series wins in both the 'Tests' and the ODIs.

Life was good and it soon got even better. I was selected to play for Tukkies at the National Club Championships and Gerrit Deist, my friend and the outstanding bowler in our boyhood games of garden cricket, was in our side, still swinging the ball after all these years. I remember how, in a pool match against the Sparkport Delta club team from Durban, he bowled three perfect away-swingers to Dale Benkenstein and then clean bowled him with an in-swinger. We had a strong team and won the title in 2003, beating the University of Port Elizabeth in the final.

The telephone was ringing yet again.

And, again, it was Dave Nosworthy.

'AB,' he said, 'we'd like to offer you a Northerns contract for the 2003/04 season.'

It was a junior contract, worth R5 000 per month for six months. I was thrilled and contacted my uncle Chris, my mother's brother-in-law, because he was a radiologist and, I reckoned, was best qualified to advise me on how I should manage and invest my new-found wealth.

It had become clear that my future lay in professional cricket and, since I was not especially enjoying my Sports Science course, I decided to withdraw from my studies to focus on the game. It was not an easy decision, but I discussed the matter at length with my parents and they agreed I should focus all my energies on the game.

Northerns began their 2003/04 SuperSport Series campaign with a four-day match against Western Province, starting in Centurion on 17 October. It would be a significant day for two young cricketers, both of whom were included in the team because senior players were away on tour with the Proteas, both of whom would be making their first-class debut – one a young batsman from Warmbaths called De Villiers and the other a talented, long-haired fast bowler from Phalaborwa by the name of Dale Steyn.

Side by side, one as nervous and apprehensive as the other, we started a journey that would take us to every major cricketing stadium in the world, to unimagined places and experiences. That morning, playing for Northerns in front of a few hundred people at SuperSport Park, the limit of our ambition was to look decent.

The fates were kind. Dale picked up a couple of wickets in the Western Province first innings, and I managed to score a couple of half-centuries, making 58 in an opening partnership of 122 with Alviro Petersen in our first innings and then contributing 61 to a second-wicket stand of 114 with Martin van Jaarsveld in our second. In each innings, I was out caught off the slow left-arm orthodox bowling of Claude Henderson. The match was drawn and, to their relief, the two unknown debutants had managed to look decent.

A week later, we drove 45 minutes down the N1 to Johannesburg to play Gauteng at the Wanderers, and again I managed to get some runs, scoring 62 and then 54 as we won the game by 223 runs. Justin Kemp and Paul Harris, with six for 59 in their second innings, were our heroes but I was pleased to have played my part and to have launched my first-class career with four consecutive 50s in my first four innings.

Did I know what was going on?

Not really; I was simply trying to survive and not look stupid.

The inevitable bump back down to earth came quickly. I scored 0 and 17 when we lost at home to Border, and was left out of the side when senior players returned for the match against North West.

What was next?

Living from week to week, playing from match to match, I was selected for the South African Under-19 squad to participate in the Commonwealth Under-19 Championships, but not in Durban or Cape Town ... in India. So we headed overseas again and spent three weeks in the subcontinent, far from home over Christmas and New Year.

Faf du Plessis and JP Duminy were in that team, and I remember we used to go for early morning jogs through the chilly streets of Lucknow. Eight teams were divided into two groups for the 50-over tournament and we continued our form from England, played well and reached the final at the Nahar Singh Stadium in Faridabad. Things were running my way again and, still believing that almost every ball was there to be hit, I managed to score 193 runs from 143 balls in the final. More importantly, as a team of eager 19-year-olds, we secured a notable tournament win in India.

Were we hailed as stars of the future?

Did we feel like stars of the future?

If that was the case, I was blissfully unaware of such expectations. In my mind, I just wanted to play for Northerns. The 2003/04 season hurried towards its conclusion, but our hopes of winning a trophy were dashed as we were defeated by Gauteng in a Standard Bank Cup semifinal at the Wanderers.

Then the telephone rang yet again.

'AB,' said Dave Nosworthy, 'would you like to play in Northern Ireland?'

'Where?'

'Northern Ireland … there's a club called Carrickfergus and they're looking for an overseas player.'

I told my parents. They encouraged me to go.

Why not?

I was scarcely 20 years old, eager to gain experience, eager to play cricket, eager to hit the ball. So I flew from Johannesburg to London and on to Belfast, and was met at the airport by someone apparently in a rush. There was no time to lose, he said, so we drove up the M5, on to the A2, on towards 'Carrick' on the northern shore of the Belfast Lough, barely 30 kilometres across the water from Scotland.

'What's the hurry?' I asked.

'The match has already started,' he replied.

We drove straight to the ground where Carrickfergus CC had won the toss and decided to bat against Belfast Harlequins. I was told to change, get padded up and be ready to bat at No. 3. The first wicket fell a few minutes later and, two hours after arriving in the country, I walked out to bat for my new club and introduced myself to my teammate in the middle.

'Hello, my name is Barry Cooper,' he said, in a New Zealand accent.

'Hello,' I replied, working hard to look relaxed.

'It's a tricky wicket out here,' Barry continued, barely pausing for breath. 'Take it easy. Don't try anything flashy. Let's push the ball around; if we can get somewhere near 200, it'll be enough.'

'OK,' I said.

'And watch out for the off-spinner,' he added. 'That's Ijaz Ahmed, but it's not the famous one. This one played a couple of Tests and ODIs for Pakistan a few years ago. We'll take 20 or so from his 10 overs.'

The instructions passed in my left ear, and straight out of my right ear. Ijaz bowled. I aimed to drive him back over his head but miscued. The ball looped up in the air and fell just wide of mid-off. I survived, but Barry was not happy and, at the end of the over, he walked down the wicket and told me: 'I think I said you'll struggle to drive on this pitch.'

Again, I couldn't resist the challenge. In Ijaz's next over, I walked down the wicket and managed to drive a straight six, and then repeated the act off the next delivery and eventually scored 82 runs from 85 balls. I was enjoying myself – and continued to enjoy myself throughout the three months spent living among the wonderful people of Northern Ireland.

Barry was my friend, teammate and landlord, providing me with a room in his house, and I survived what was for me the new experience of cooking my own food and washing my own clothes. It was good to be taken out of my comfort zone and dropped into a whole new world. I tried to make myself useful during the week, but lived from weekend to weekend, from match to match, and was relieved that I could score runs under the burden of being the 'overseas player' at the club, against North Down, Donemana, Lisburn and Logan, and against Waringstown, Bangor and Downpatrick.

Against Cliftonville in mid-July, I scored 233 not out and became the first Carrick player to score a double century and, a week later, opening the batting against Instonians, I scored an unbeaten 208 in our total of

312. These performances in Ireland gave me valuable confidence.

The telephone was ringing … again.

This time, during a pivotal period of my career, Dave Nosworthy told me to travel home immediately because Ray Jennings wanted me to join the South Africa A team tour to Zimbabwe. I said a rushed farewell to Barry and my teammates in Carrick and flew from Belfast to London to Harare and then on to Bulawayo, where I joined an A team squad that included the likes of captain Ashwell Prince, Albie Morkel, Hashim Amla, Neil McKenzie and Paul Adams.

Ray Jennings was a hardcore coach, and I enjoyed the way he challenged us. One of the finest wicketkeepers ever produced by South Africa and a key member of the great 'Mean Machine' Transvaal team of the 1980s, he left no one in any doubt that he wanted players to be tough in everything they did and to show some guts in tough times. Ray used to wield the bat during endless fielding drills, literally smashing the ball at our shins and expecting us to get something – anything – in the way. It didn't matter to him as long as the ball was stopped. I dared not flinch. Some players said the coach was crazy, but I loved every minute.

The first unofficial Test at Queens Club went well. Replying to Zimbabwe A's 186 in the first innings, I contributed 91 to our first-innings total of 307. Eventually set 168 to win, I managed to score 84 as we eased to victory by seven wickets.

A second unofficial Test started three days later at the same venue and, after Albie Morkel and Neil McKenzie scored runs, we pushed hard for a second win – but, as you would expect, the Zimbabweans fought hard, and had two wickets standing when the match ended in a draw.

I was pleased. Things had gone well. I was up, but I was soon down again when I was left out of the A team to play three one-day matches against Zimbabwe A. My prospects suddenly seemed uncertain. To some, it seemed, I was a talented young dasher who lacked the patience and technique to be consistently successful at the highest level.

The South African A team flew home and prepared to play two four-day matches against New Zealand A, with the first starting at SuperSport Park in Centurion on Wednesday, 8 September 2004. The touring side won the toss and reached 241 for seven by stumps at the end of an unremarkable first day. The Kiwi tail wagged on the second morning and they were eventually bowled out for 328 just before lunch.

I had kept wicket during their innings and then quickly switched pads to open our innings with Andrew Puttick, from Western Province. Eager to play some strokes, I hit four boundaries and raced to 30 from 25 balls. It was fun until, in the ninth over, I was out, caught behind off the medium-paced bowling of Chris Martin with our total at 43 for one. We reached 136 for four by the close of the second day, and appeared well placed.

All seemed well when the players started to arrive at the ground on the third morning of the match, on Friday, 10 September.

But very soon all was not well.

'AB de Villiers, you will never play in a team coached by me again!'

Ray Jennings had called a team meeting before we went out to warm up, and it quickly became clear that the coach was extremely angry and that there was one subject on his mind … me.

He was going ballistic.

'Who the hell do you think you are, De Villiers? You walk in and you are so loose. You don't respect the opposition and you don't respect the game. That attitude is going to cost us. It's not good enough for this team and I promise you won't play in my team again.'

He was not finished. There was no discussion about the game or our plan for the day.

He continued: 'It's just not acceptable …'

Ashwell Prince, our captain, eventually intervened. 'Ray, it's fine,' he said. 'Ray, let's focus on the game now.'

I was shocked, speechless. Several teammates came over afterwards and told me not to worry, but I was stunned by the ferocity of the criticism from someone I respected so much. Ray had a point, of course, and, looking back, I understand that he was so disappointed and so angry precisely because he recognised I could achieve something in the game and he didn't want me to waste that potential.

Ray remains one of the outstanding coaches of my career and a man who has my complete respect; as the years went by, I did play for him again and we were destined to enjoy many great days together, with him as the coach and me as a player, with the Proteas and then with Royal Challengers Bangalore in the Indian Premier League.

Back at SuperSport Park, Zander de Bruyn and Hashim Amla scored excellent centuries and the A team 'Test' meandered to a draw. A second match followed at Willowmoore Park in Benoni and, having managed to keep my place in the side, we dismissed New Zealand A for 127 and were left only 39 runs to win. Under no pressure, opening the batting again, it seemed reasonable to attack the bowling, so I played some shots and scored a brisk 32 runs from 20 balls, including five boundaries.

Then the experienced Boeta Dippenaar was recalled to take his place in the third 'Test' in Potchefstroom, replacing me and opening the batting with Puttick ... and Boeta scored a century.

What now?

Returning to the relative safety of the Titans squad, my fortunes did not improve as we opened our SuperSport Series campaign by losing at home to the Eagles. I kept wicket again, which was fine because it kept me involved in the game, but scored four when batting at No. 6 in the first innings, and then managed only 12 runs, albeit including a four and a six, when batting even further down at No. 8 in our second innings.

I was down, but I was up again the following week when we played Western Province in Benoni, scoring 151 in a really enjoyable second-wicket partnership of 317 with Martin van Jaarsveld. Graeme Smith, the South African captain, was playing for Western Province, and I remember hoping he had been impressed by the batting of the boys from Warmbaths, now known as Bela-Bela.

Dale Steyn took four wickets as we dismissed Province once, and then again, having asked them to follow on, and I scored a quick, unbeaten 40 in the last innings as we won by nine wickets.

Confidence returned and Northerns then travelled to Port Elizabeth to play a Warriors team that included the likes of Mark Boucher and Makhaya Ntini. Dale took another five wickets as we bowled them out for 165, and I scored 124 as we posted a first-innings score of 365, laying the foundation for what turned out to be an encouraging win by eight wickets.

Meanwhile, clouds were gathering above the Proteas. Following disappointing results on tours to New Zealand and then Sri Lanka, Eric Simons had stepped down as coach, and was replaced by Ray Jennings, promoted from the A team until at least the end of the season.

The combination of my decent early season form for the Titans and the problems endured by the national side, who then set off on a brief tour of India and lost the Test series 0–1, prompted some speculation … but, in the middle of November 2004, as far as I was concerned, the chances of me being picked for South Africa were between very low and zero.

On Thursday, 2 December 2004, the telephone rang again.

It wasn't Dave Nosworthy.

It was Haroon Lorgat, then convenor of the national selectors.

He introduced himself and said: 'AB, we would like you to open the batting for the Proteas in the first Test match against England at St George's Park in Port Elizabeth, starting in two weeks.'

I could not believe what I had heard. Haroon continued and said I had to join the squad a few days later at a training camp to be held at the High Performance Centre at the University of Pretoria.

'Is that OK?'

'Yes, thank you very much, Mr Lorgat.'

After the call ended, I immediately phoned home to relay the news to my parents. Two years after leaving Affies, nine months after playing in the Tuks second team ... it was almost unbelievable.

Arriving at the first day of camp, I was a wreck.

'Hello, Mr Kallis.'

'Good morning, Mr Smith.'

'Hello, Mr Pollock.'

'Good morning, Mr Hall.'

'Hello, Mr Ntini.'

Everyone was kind, and I decided I would keep my head down, say as little as possible and try as hard as possible.

It was both exciting and terrifying to find myself suddenly included among this squad of heroes and legends, to be eating and training alongside players I had so much admired on television. I was suddenly painfully self-aware, worried about saying the wrong thing at the wrong time, fretting about who might happen to be standing in the lift when it opened in front of me, concerned about where I would sit at the table ... the opposite of the apparently self-confident, carefree Tukkies student who had spent so many happy hours, literally, in the bars half a kilometre from the High Performance Centre, cheerfully chatting to girls and ordering beers for my mates.

Now and then, I started to wonder what these established international cricketers thought of me. Did they notice me at all? Had they been told I was a cocky youngster who had no respect for the game? But time spent wondering is usually time wasted.

In that first week with the Proteas, I wanted to be nothing more and nothing less than myself, the product of my upbringing. Whether I stayed in the team for one Test or 100 Tests, I wanted to earn respect as a fighter, as a guy who never ducks a challenge, who always puts the team first and who is respectful to players and coaches, who always,

always gives everything. I wanted to be the tough little *boereseun*.

What did this mean?

It meant giving every ounce of energy to every task at every oppor-tunity, and, more than that, being *seen* to give every ounce of energy to every task at every opportunity. It meant getting hit painfully on the end of the finger during a fielding practice and not wincing, not complain-ing, not missing a moment before diving for the next catch.

It meant being happy to face the fast bowlers in the nets, where the bounce was unpredictable and where the ball would usually be whistling past your ears or crunching into your ribs; it meant never dodging the challenge, saying I would bat the next day or saying I would rather take some throw-downs in the middle.

Being tough, being brave, being determined, always coming back for more, always finishing the session, never complaining, getting hurt and carrying on, getting hurt again and carrying on again – through these actions, I wanted to earn the respect of senior players such as Smith, Kallis and Boucher ... and, in the years to come, this was how any talented youngster coming into the Proteas squad would earn respect from me.

So the squad flew down to Port Elizabeth and, early on the morning of Friday, 17 December 2004, drove from the hotel to St George's Park to play the first day of the first Test against England. The South African selectors had picked two young players to make their Test debuts – one a young batter from Bela-Bela called De Villiers, the other a long-haired fast bowler from Phalaborwa by the name of Dale Steyn.

Just as we had played our first-class debuts together 14 months before, so Dale and I made our Test debuts on the same day. It was going to be another special occasion, particularly because my parents had travelled all the way from home and were sitting in the main grandstand alongside Derick Kuün, my friend from school who was keeping a promise we had made to each other.

One evening at Affies three years earlier, when we were both prefects keeping watch over Standard 6 boys while they were supposed to be studying, Derick and I sat down, set some targets for ourselves and wrote them in a little book: one was to play for an Affies team that won the Beeld Trophy, which we did (although we predicted we would play Middelburg in the final and we actually played Waterkloof), and another was that we would one day play for South Africa in rugby or cricket; it didn't matter which.

That night we made a pact that, if either of us ever did play for South Africa at either sport, the other would make sure he was there, in the stands, watching the debut.

Derick proved as good as his word and took his place at St George's Park alongside my parents. I am just sad that, though he had a fantastic rugby career, captaining the Bulls at every level, playing more than 100 provincial matches, captaining South African schools, playing for the South African Under-19, Under-21 and Sevens teams, he was never given the chance to play for the Springboks. If he had, I would have been sitting there in the stands.

My first Test was a blur ...

It's a hot day in Port Elizabeth and the warm-up feels especially tough. Ray is cracking the whip as usual, and I am enjoying the intensity, working hard. My shirt is drenched. Captain Graeme Smith wins the toss and we will open our innings together. I am still sweating from the warm-up.

Matthew Hoggard bowls the first over. Second ball of the match, Graeme fends outside off stump, finds the edge and Andrew Strauss takes a decent catch at third slip. We are zero for one and Jacques Rudolph comes out to join me in the middle, two old Affies side by side under pressure. Steve Harmison, then ranked as the No. 1 bowler in the world, bowls the second over. I am focused on surviving.

In the ninth over, Harmison offers some width outside off stump and

I manage to drive the ball through the covers to the boundary. That feels OK. Next ball, he bowls shorter and still a little too wide. I manage to rock back and cut the ball for four behind square wicket. In a moment of youthful innocence, I think to myself: 'Is this really Test cricket? Batting against the No. 1 bowler in the world? It's got to be tougher than this.'

Jacques and I take the score to 63 for one in the 16th over. I am facing Andrew Flintoff and the sixth ball of the over nips back and clatters into my pad. English voices scream in unison for LBW and, as my heart sinks, umpire Simon Taufel raises his finger. Wasn't it going high? I think it was, but that doesn't count for much. I am out for 28.

The Test flashes past. We eventually make 337 in our first innings, but England respond well and reach 238 for one when Andrew Strauss, on 126, executes a powerful square cut. The ball is coming straight at me, but I manage to hold the catch.

I am working hard in the field, chasing everything, diving at every opportunity, sprinting between overs to fetch a cap from the bowler and take it to the umpire, chattering, encouraging my teammates. Someone says I am fielding like Jonty Rhodes. Somebody actually says that! There is no greater compliment. All these years after that humiliating afternoon in the garden at 20 Mentz Avenue, when I was told to remove my Jonty cap because I didn't deserve to wear it, maybe I have earned the right.

We are playing under constant pressure. I score 14 in the second innings, and we are dismissed for 229. Set only 142 to win, England ease to victory for the loss of only three wickets.

The second Test starts on Boxing Day at Kingsmead in Durban, and I am told that (a) I will be keeping wicket, and (b) I will be dropped down the order to bat at No. 7. No problem – I do as I'm told. Whatever is good for the team is good for me, and if that's what the selectors say, that's how it will be. I enjoy keeping wicket because it keeps me busy.

We bowl out England for 139 and Jacques Kallis scores a classy 162 in our first innings of 332, but England respond well in their second innings and reach 273 without loss when Marcus Trescothick finally edges the ball. My feet are going one way, the ball is going another way, but I hold the catch and am soon submerged by celebrating teammates.

England's mammoth second-innings score means that, after dominating the first two days, we suddenly find ourselves under pressure and batting to save the Test on the last day. I come to the crease at 173 for six after debutant Hashim Amla is out. Martin van Jaarsveld goes soon afterwards. England are hunting for the win but, in fading light, Shaun Pollock and I fight hard for 27 overs. We survive. The Test is drawn and I finish on 52 not out.

Playing strokes and scoring runs is great but, first and foremost, I want to be known as a fighter, so the rearguard action feels good.

The series moves to Cape Town for the third Test, and Kallis leads the way again, scoring 149. I am keeping wicket again and score only 21 when batting at seven in the first innings and just 10 when batting at eight in the second innings. Amid these failures, Test cricket is starting to feel a little more challenging than seemed the case in Port Elizabeth.

England are eventually set 501 to win and, after I manage to stump Robert Key off the bowling of Nicky Boje, they are dismissed for 304. We win the third Test by 196 runs and level the series at 1–1.

Heading to the Highveld for the fourth Test at the Wanderers, Mark Boucher is rightly recalled to keep wicket and I remain in the middle order, batting at six. I start reasonably well in the first innings and bat for an hour, reaching 19, including three boundaries, but then Hoggard bowls a bouncer; I can't resist the temptation to hook and am caught at fine leg.

The Test continues and we are ultimately set 325 to win in the fourth innings. I am promoted to open with Herschelle Gibbs after Graeme Smith is concussed during the warm-up but I am dismissed for three, LBW to Hoggard, falling forward again, getting my weight distribution wrong again, and we are bowled out for 247, defeated by 77 runs.

Times are tough. We trail 2–1 in the series, with only the fifth and final Test to be played at Centurion, and I am feeling the pressure. Called up as a 20-year-old stroke-player, for all my energy and efforts in the field, I have been moved around the order and produced underwhelming scores of 28, 14, 14, 52*, 21, 10, 19 and 3. It's not good enough and I sense that more low scores at SuperSport Park will result in me being dropped.

Have I ever been so nervous?

I don't think so.

The first day is rained out, but my parents and brothers are watching on the second morning as Michael Vaughan wins the toss and decides to field. I am told I will open the innings with Herschelle, with Graeme batting lower down at five. That's fine with me because I enjoy the new ball coming on to the bat. This is sink or swim and, in tough batting conditions, I manage to swim, working hard to reach 50 and then moving into the 90s.

Ashley Giles, the left-arm spinner, is bowling accurately. I thrive until I am eight runs from completing my first Test century, but I am impatient to reach the landmark and decide to execute a lap sweep for four. The foolish premeditation proves fatal. I'm struck on the pad, the English voices are appealing again and I am out, LBW for 92.

We scramble to 247 all out, which is about par on a tricky two-paced pitch, and England make 359 in reply, taking time out of the game and making it difficult for us to force a win and square the series. We lose two quick wickets in our second innings and, on the back foot and unavoidably focused on surviving when we are really looking for an opportunity to attack and win, Jacques Kallis and I come together at 29 for two.

I start to settle, still feeling as if I am batting to save my place, and, increasingly confident batting in my home ground, start to build a partnership with Jacques. Runs start to flow from my two favourite shots – the square cut to anything fractionally short on or outside the off stump, slashed away past point, and the slog pull to mid-wicket off anything fractionally short. Over by over, run by run, I reach the 90s.

Hoggard runs in to bowl, and the ball is short and inviting. I manage to pull over mid-wicket for six, taking my score to 98; sitting in the stands, my father is particularly pleased with the stroke.

Two runs needed for a Test century. An over passes. Another over passes. I try to force the ball into the leg side for two, but succeed only in getting a leading edge that thankfully lands safely. Jacques is watching sympathetically and he walks down the pitch between overs. 'Keep calm, youngster,' he says. 'It will come, it will come.'

And it does come. Simon Jones bowls wide of off stump. I get into position and play the square cut, sending the ball speeding to the boundary, taking my score into three figures. I am eventually out for 109 in just over four and a half hours of careful batting.

The century feels good, but when England bat again there is no time to take the 10 wickets required to force the win. They do lose four wickets, but the fifth Test ends in a draw and the series is lost 2–1.

Our changing room is quiet after the match. We are disappointed by the defeat. However, sitting at SuperSport Park, among the Proteas, all these senior players, these heroes and legends, I feel personally satisfied and relieved, I feel as though I have made a decent contribution to the side, as though I'm worth my place – as though I belong.

CHAPTER 6

JOINING THE CLUB

Feeling as though I belonged in the Proteas team was never going to be enough.

The experience of being selected to play for South Africa and scoring a century in the last Test of my first home series was fantastic, but I worked hard to see this event – albeit the realisation of a boyhood dream – not as the end of anything but as the beginning of a new and even greater challenge.

That's the nature of sport: you work hard to climb the mountain, eyes fixed resolutely on the peak, and then, just when you think you've reached the top, another higher peak comes into view and there's no option but to keep working and continue climbing … and if and when you scale that peak, another peak appears. There's always another peak, always another challenge. The job is never done.

It soon became clear to me that I would have to work hard to keep my place in the side. For a 20-year-old youngster joining a consistently successful team, driven by a core group of outstanding and established players, absolutely nothing could be taken for granted, and the Proteas continued to thrive.

During the 26 months between my first series at home against England in December 2004 and the ICC Cricket World Cup held in the Caribbean in March 2007, the South African national team won no fewer than seven out of 10 Test series and triumphed in eight out of 11 one-day international series.

That's a decent record. We were a decent side, a talented team that prided itself, above all, on being intensely competitive, on fighting for every wicket and scrapping for every run. It didn't matter whether we were playing at home or in front of hostile crowds on tour on the subcontinent or in Australia, we wanted to be known as the national side that never gave up, that trained the hardest and played the hardest, on and off the field.

Our team was built around three mighty pillars, three of the greatest cricketers ever to play for South Africa: Graeme Smith, Jacques Kallis and Mark Boucher. I was privileged to be their teammate.

Graeme – or 'Biff', as he became known – made his Test debut against Australia at Newlands on 8 March 2002, and played his last Test 12 years later, almost to the day, against the same opponents at the same venue. In his 117 Tests, he scored 9 265 runs at an average of 48.25 and, in 197 one-day internationals, he scored 6 989 runs at an average of 37.98.

He was appointed Test captain at the age of only 23, asked to inspire a new side, and he proceeded to lead his country in no fewer than 109 Test matches, many more than anyone else in the history of the game, with Allan Border, of Australia, second on 93 and Stephen Fleming, of New Zealand, third on 80.

Of all Graeme's statistics, perhaps the most telling is that he scored 27 Test centuries and, whenever he reached three figures, the Proteas simply did not lose the Test. At Lord's and at Edgbaston in 2003, and again at Edgbaston and at Perth in 2008, he produced magnificent epic innings that effectively won the match.

I respected him because he was tough and uncompromising, because he believed in what he said and did, and because he backed his words with actions. Through the sheer force of his physical presence and personality, he transformed South Africa from talented underperformers into steely, consistent winners, and he was not too concerned if lesser men were upset along the way.

Graeme was easy to follow because he led from the front. He could be severe, not hesitating to let us know when our performance fell below required standards, but he could also be gentle and encouraging. On a personal level, he always backed me and believed in me. I can't explain how much that meant to me. In tough times, when many were ready to dismiss me as too loose, his unwavering support helped me bounce back.

Biff wasn't tough in every respect; in fact, he was and probably remains terrified of ghosts, a reality that prompted me to have some fun at his expense during the days when we were preparing to play the third Test match against India in Kanpur during November 2008.

We were both staying on the third floor of the hotel but I was allocated a standard room while, as captain, he was given a luxury suite that included his own living room and bedroom. Looking around one evening, I realised it would be only slightly dangerous to climb out of my window, step onto the narrow ledge and then climb through the window of his living room and so gain access to his suite.

I attempted to execute this manoeuvre, only to discover the latch of his window was firmly locked. Undeterred, I climbed back to my room, knocked on his door and pretended to be making a social call, asking him how he was doing, complimenting him on the suite, and discreetly loosening the latch on the window.

The stage was set and, later that same night, when I was sure he was in bed, I set off again, climbed out my window and in through his, and successfully reached his living room. I proceeded to move a few pictures around on the wall and to switch on the television, turning the volume up high, and then hid behind a curtain. Graeme leapt up and rushed through from his bedroom to look around. Seeing nothing, he switched off the TV and returned to bed. When all was clear, I climbed back out of the window and silently returned to my room.

An hour later, I repeated the same routine and managed to sneak safely back to my room. Another hour later – really enjoying myself by this stage – I set off again, turned on the TV and rushed back to my room.

The next morning at breakfast, I was sitting quietly when Graeme spoke up.

'I swear there's a ghost in my room,' he said, telling us how his television had kept turning itself on the previous night and how he had to keep getting up to turn it off. I could not resist repeating the entire procedure that night, but enough was enough, and the identity of the 'ghost' was eventually revealed.

In my opinion, Jacques Kallis is the greatest Test cricketer of all time. In the entire history of our game, there has never been a player who has remotely matched his achievements.

'Jakes' could run in, bowl at 140 kilometres per hour, and produce great deliveries to dismiss great batsmen at crucial moments in the game, and then he would go out and score 150 runs. Nobody else has ever done that. He was so much more than just an outstanding jack-of-all-trades all-rounder ... he was a frontline bowler as well as a frontline batsman, and he was an exceptional slip fielder, too, with brilliant hands and movement.

The statistics leave no room for discussion.

Longevity? He played in 166 Test matches between 1995 and 2013, a career spanning 18 years. Batting? He scored 13 289 runs in Tests, including 45 centuries and 58 half-centuries; only Sachin Tendulkar and Ricky Ponting have scored more runs. Bowling? He took 292 Test wickets in 3 372 overs, ranking 29th in the list of all-time wicket takers. Fielding? He held precisely 200 catches in Test matches.

Consider that, in addition to these feats, he scored another 11 579 runs and claimed another 273 wickets in 328 one-day internationals, plus another 666 runs and 12 wickets in 25 T20 internationals, and it becomes abundantly clear why, for so many of us who played alongside him, Kallis will always be king. Innings after innings, tour after tour, season after season, he was a model of consistent brilliance.

Beyond the numbers, he was quiet, relaxed and always approachable. Never the kind of person who would walk up to you and presume to tell you what you were doing wrong, he was always open, receptive and sympathetic to anyone who sought his help and advice.

Jacques became my fixer. In tough times, when it felt as though I couldn't score a run and I couldn't understand what I was doing wrong, in those lonely and confusing times, I would seek his advice and he would always respond, giving me the benefit of his time, his knowledge and his experience.

It is June 2007 ... and the South African team is playing against India and Ireland in a triangular tournament called the Future Cup in Northern Ireland. We are playing an Indian team depleted by illness and led by Rahul Dravid at the Civil Service ground near Stormont, and I am not in a good place at all.

With only two half-centuries in my previous 14 ODI innings, I am opening the innings with Morné van Wyk and, to be blunt, I feel completely out of touch. Zaheer Khan opens the bowling with a maiden to Morné, leaving me to face the second over from RP Singh. A mistimed glance, a rushed block deep in the crease, left alone, an inside edge squirting to square leg, a tame drive played and missed, a block ... another maiden over; we are 0–0 after two.

It's difficult to exaggerate the agony of a batsman who is out of touch, hard to explain how the art of batting – which can seem so easy and natural when everything is going well – can suddenly be transformed into something that is not just challenging but feels truly impossible. You stand there, concentrating on your stance, your grip, your backlift, focusing on everything and nothing, and every ball looks like a hand grenade.

Zaheer bowls another maiden to Morné. The total is o–o after three overs, and I am starting to become aware of a knot in my stomach, an ache of anxiety deep within me.

RP Singh is bowling the fourth over. I am facing and his first delivery swings away far down leg side. MS Dhoni parries the ball towards fine leg and, as the umpire signals a wide, we take the single. I reach the non-striker's end and breathe deeply. This is no fun at all but, at last, we're off the mark at two runs for no wicket.

Next ball, RP bowls short of a length on leg stump and Morné fends the ball towards midwicket. There is nobody there, so I call for the single and start running ... but the ball hasn't travelled far and RP is following through and fielding it himself. Morné sees the danger and shouts, 'No', sending me back. I turn and dash back to the non-striker's end but RP throws the ball to Dravid, who takes off the bails. I dive and stretch ... and I'm out.

AB de Villiers run out 0 (14m, 6b, 0x4, 0x6) SR: 0.00

Worst of all, as I walk slowly back to the pavilion, getting out almost feels like a relief.

'Jakes, do you have a moment to speak?'

'Sure.'

So we spoke, and spoke, and spoke about my general concerns, about my batting technique, about getting the distribution of my weight correct so I didn't lose balance; and that afternoon we went to the nets, just the two of us, to put into practice what we had discussed – and we went again the next day, and the day after that.

Confidence slowly returned and, after scoring 63 and 107 in ODIs against Zimbabwe, I managed to make 77, 45 and 103 not out in consecutive innings against Pakistan. Cricket quickly seemed fun again but I will always remember that, in one of my darkest hours, Jacques Kallis had taken time to show me the light. I will always admire him for his knowledge and his achievements, and I will always love him for his kindness.

When he spoke, I listened. I have always responded well when a friend or a coach really believed in me, and when Jacques encouraged me I instantly felt upbeat and confident.

In the first few years of my international career, while waiting to bat, I used to sit on the balcony of the changing room and watch the match because I thought it was important to be seen to be supporting the team. One day, I mentioned this to Jacques, and told him I would prefer to watch the game on television.

'Just do what you feel is right,' he told me. 'Back your instincts and you'll be fine.'

'Thanks, Oupa,' I replied.

Everybody in the squad tends to get a nickname. Shaun Pollock was 'Oupa' ('Granddad') on account of his many years of service to the team and, when Shaun retired, I worked hard to ensure the name was seamlessly transferred to Jacques Kallis; and, happily, the nickname stuck.

Oupa had spoken and that was all I needed to hear. Ever since, nine times out of 10, before going out to bat, I sit quietly in the changing room, watching TV coverage of the match, with the commentary turned down. The live broadcast is usually delayed by a few seconds, which means significant events, such as the fall of a wicket or a boundary, are signalled by the noise of the crowd outside before we see them on the screen.

This small change in routine may seem relatively insignificant but it has helped me walk out to bat in a calmer frame of mind, and it would not have happened if Jacques had not said it was OK.

The third pillar of the Proteas team was Mark Boucher, the model South African battler, brave, combative and courageous. Within the squad, he was my big brother, always looking out for me.

'Bouch' played in 147 Test matches in 14 seasons as South Africa's first-choice Test wicketkeeper. He claimed a remarkable 555 Test dismissals, including 532 catches and 23 stumpings, more than any other keeper in the history of the game – 139 ahead of Adam Gilchrist, of Australia, who is second on the all-time list. As a batsman who generally came in at No. 7 or No. 8, he scored 5 515 Test runs, most of them made under pressure as, seemingly again and again, he rose to the challenge of digging his team out of trouble.

The quality of his performances over such a long period was astonishing and, on a personal level, I recall so many moments when he went out of his way to look after me.

When I was a nervous 20-year-old at my very first Proteas training camp in Pretoria, he invited me to join him and a few others for a drink at DropZone in Hatfield, and he took me aside and told me I should relax because he was sure I would do well. Better than anyone, he understood how an apprehensive youngster can be boosted when a senior player takes just a moment to say the right things at the right time.

That week and through all the weeks that followed, he was always beside me, the first to praise me when things went well and the first to console me when things went wrong. He taught me the importance of working hard – come on, he would say, let's go to the gym and train. And he taught me the importance of taking time to unwind in what was always a demanding schedule – come on, he would say, let's go play golf or let's go for a run or let's go swim or let's take the guys out for a drink.

Professional sport is often portrayed as a ruthless, selfish, competitive environment where veterans warn younger players to look after themselves because nobody else will look after them. That's just how it is, they would say, because there's always somebody wanting to take your place and threaten your livelihood.

Through his words and actions, Mark Boucher proved that the opposite can be true. He has always been incredibly giving, offering his time, encouragement and advice. 'Hey, Bunk,' he would say to me at the end of a long day's play, as ever thinking of somebody else, 'that was a great cover drive when you were on 42.'

He used to call me Bunk and I used to called him Trunk; I have no idea why.

Most remarkably, he continued to give time and support under the most trying circumstances, even when his own place in the team was being threatened. At various times, the national selectors were tempted to ask me to keep wicket instead of him, creating a space to include another specialist batsman or bowler. This was rarely a good idea because he was a world-class wicketkeeper and I was not; and, in every form of the game, picking the best available keeper generally makes sense. But even in these times when we were cast as direct rivals, he remained my greatest supporter, my role model and my big brother.

It is Monday, 9 July 2012, a warm summer's afternoon in England, and the Proteas are fielding against Somerset at Taunton in a warm-up match before the first Test at The Oval.

Bouch is keeping wicket and, at the age of 35, he seems as fit, eager and motivated as ever, determined to do well in what he has already announced will be his last Test series before retirement. Imran Tahir's googly clean bowls the batsman, Gemaal Hussain – and one of the bails flies freakishly into the keeper's eye.

I am fielding at cover and I rush in to celebrate the fall of the wicket with the rest of the team but, as I run, I see Bouch fall to the ground. I instantly know something is seriously wrong because, if I have learned anything in the past eight seasons, it is that he never goes down …

The legendary wicketkeeper is helped off the field by our physiotherapist and, that evening, undergoes surgery on his lacerated eye. We visit him in hospital and I remember how, even in these most terrible circumstances, he was still thinking of others, wishing us well.

It seemed so unfair. If he had not been injured in Taunton, if he had not been forced to retire, if he had been able to play in the three-Test series against England, he would have (a) played his 150th Test at Lord's, and become the first wicketkeeper to reach that milestone, (b) almost certainly have scored the 56 more runs he needed to become the highest run-scorer among wicketkeepers in Tests, passing Gilchrist's record, and (c) completed the two dismissals he required to reach 1 000 in his international career and so become the first to reach that mark.

In fact, Bouch maintains he did reach 1 000 dismissals for South Africa, even if his catches and stumpings add up to 998. 'People sometimes forget the two Test wickets I took as a bowler,' he says.

In the end, however, the records and statistics don't count for much. Mark Boucher's legacy confirms him as one of the greatest wicketkeepers of all time and as an incredible human being; and it is completely in character that he should now be directing so much time and energy to preserving the rhino population.

Smith, Kallis and Boucher were the three pillars.

I respected them and admired them. But more than anything, I wanted to impress them and wanted them to like me.

So when they trained hard in the nets, I trained hard and was the last to leave the practice. When they said it was time to relax, get out of the hotel and have a few drinks, I would follow them out of the hotel and have a few drinks and would usually be the last to leave the bar.

In effect, they were the leaders of the Proteas club and I wanted to become a member.

It's true some resented the trio's continuing dominance and success, and it's also true that, perhaps eager to create a headline or sell a book, some have claimed they operated as a clique, looking after their own interests ahead of the team.

This is nonsense. As the saying goes, tall trees catch the most wind, and as far as I am concerned, Smith, Kallis and Boucher deserve nothing but unequivocal praise, admiration and respect.

So the roller-coaster ride began ...

2005

After the Test series against England, my highest score in the five ODIs that follow is 20. I need runs. The first Test in Zimbabwe presents an opportunity to play a decent innings and secure my place on the forthcoming tour to the West Indies. I open our innings with Graeme Smith and, together, we take the score to 217 without loss before I lose patience, try to slog the left-spinner over mid-wicket and get myself out for 98.

The tour to the Caribbean is special, even if the public-address announcer in the drawn first Test in Georgetown, Guyana, can't pronounce my name. He attempts to introduce me as I walk out to open with Graeme but stumbles over his words, amusing the fielders and the crowd.

The Proteas are invited to attend a sponsor's function before the second Test in Port of Spain, Trinidad, and, while standing to one side, trying to keep my head down, I look up and see Brian Lara walking towards me. What could the celebrated West Indian batsman want with me? I start to panic.

'Hello,' he says.

'Er, hello,' I reply, scared, barely able to look him in the eye.

'I see they have trouble pronouncing your name, youngster,' he says, 'but I don't have a problem. It's A. B. D. E. V. I. L. L. I. E. R. S. You see, I can spell your name. You can play the game.'

With that, he turns and walks away, disappearing into the mass of people. I am stunned and excited at the same time, and immediately start looking for Mark Boucher in the crowd to tell him what has just happened, to tell him that one of the greatest batsmen of all time not only knows my name but says I can play.

We win the Test in Trinidad but the West Indies win the toss and elect to bat first in the third Test at Bridgetown, Barbados. Lara scores an imperious 176 in their total of 296 but, feeling confident and comfortable, I manage to score 178 in our reply. We win by an innings and 86 runs, and take a 2–0 lead in the series.

Life is great. The Caribbean is such a fun place that, for all our hard work, there are times when the tour almost feels like a holiday, happy times when we mess around on jet skis, or relax at the beach or play golf. I am beginning to believe this is the best tour ever: I'm scoring runs, the weather is great and the West Indian fans are knowledgeable and upbeat, dancing in the stands and having a good time even when their team is losing.

Graeme and I combine to produce another successful opening stand in the fourth Test at St John's on the island of Antigua, and we reach 245 without loss before I am dismissed for 114. The home team replies with an epic innings of 747 all out, a batting marathon during which all 11 members of our team have a chance to bowl.

With the match destined to end in a draw, I am asked to bowl 11 overs of 'baby seamers' before lunch and, to my horror, am then told to continue bowling into the afternoon, sending down another 10 overs. The experience of bowling no fewer than 21 overs in a row would leave me feeling sore and stiff for days afterwards, but I'm enjoying myself and, in a moment of pure delight, I am convinced I have trapped Dwayne Bravo LBW.

'Hoooooooooowzaaaaaaaaaaaaaat!' I roar.

The ball seems to be hitting the middle of middle stump but the umpire says: 'Not out.'

Dismissing an established batsman like Bravo would have been memorable, but there is consolation when I take the wickets of two tail-enders, bowling Daren Powell for 12 and having Tino Best caught by Herschelle Gibbs for five. In the final analysis, my figures are 21 overs, six maidens, two wickets for 49 runs.

Soon afterwards, I am asked to take the wicketkeeping gloves, so Mark Boucher can have a chance to bowl and, annoyingly, he claims the wicket of Bravo, caught by Ashwell Prince for 107. It must be rare for a wicket-keeper to bowl and take a Test wicket, but in this Test two wicketkeepers bowl and both take wickets.

But as the roller-coaster soars, so the roller-coaster dips …

In and out of the ODI side, selected one week, left out the next, selected again, I get a few starts in the one-day international series against the West Indies, then playing for an Africa XI against an Asia XI, then in a home series against New Zealand, and then on a short tour to India, but I can't get past 39 in nine innings and I'm almost relieved when, in December, we revert to playing five-day Test cricket on tour in Australia.

The Aussies are a powerful team that includes Justin Langer, Matthew Hayden, Ricky Ponting, Mike Hussey, Adam Gilchrist, Shane Warne, Brett Lee and Glenn McGrath, but we hold our own in the first Test in Perth. I feel in decent form and reach 68 in our first innings before being bowled by a straight ball from Warne. We battle hard through five days and Jacques Rudolph's unbeaten century secures a creditable draw.

Moving on to Melbourne, we prepare for the Test at the MCG starting on Boxing Day.

The Australians bat first and two of their stars score centuries in the first innings. This is a tough and relentless contest, although the renowned sledging of the Australians seems relatively mild compared to what I experienced from my older brothers and their friends in our back garden. Yet, amid the hustle and excitement of a full house at the MCG, I remain a largely innocent 21-year-old in awe of our celebrated opponents.

I bump into one of the leading Australian batsmen during the lunch interval.

'Well batted today,' I say instinctively, without really thinking. 'That was a great knock.'

He looks at me, says nothing and slowly shakes his head as if he simply can't believe this insignificant youngster from Pretoria has dared speak to him. I feel six inches tall, blush and walk away.

Glenn McGrath has witnessed the exchange; he follows me into the corridor and taps me on the shoulder. 'Don't worry about him,' he says. 'He's always grumpy. You're doing well. Keep going.'

In 20 seconds, the great fast bowler makes me feel fully five feet ten-and-a-half inches again and shows why he is revered as one of the sport's true gentlemen, respected wherever the game is played.

Encouraged, I score 61 in our first innings before falling LBW to the selfsame McGrath, even though I reckon the ball struck me outside the line. We fight hard, as usual, but subside to McGrath and Warne in the second innings, lose at the MCG and are then defeated in the third Test at Sydney. Australia win the series 2–0.

Nobody likes losing but I feel positive about my performance. Then Haroon Lorgat, convener of selectors, calls me aside and tells me they have decided to leave me out of the squad for the triangular ODI series with Australia and Sri Lanka. I am distraught. I want to stay with the team but, instead, I must fly home.

2006

The best response to being dropped is to say nothing and score loads of runs. I find some form while playing for the Titans in the domestic T20 series and, when the Proteas arrive home in mid-February, I am recalled to the side for the home leg of the series against Australia: a T20 international, five one-day internationals and three Tests.

We win the T20 by two runs and take a 2–0 lead in the ODI series, but are then pegged back by the Australians and stand level at 2–2 when we head to the fifth and deciding ODI in Johannesburg. It is 12 March 2006, and a full house at the Bullring witnesses maybe the most memorable one-day international ever played.

Australia bat first and set what seems an unassailable target. Ricky Ponting thrashes 164 in 105 balls, including nine sixes. The tourists post a mammoth 434 for four in 50 overs. That should be that.

It isn't. To the amazement of an increasingly thrilled Wanderers crowd, Herschelle Gibbs leads the charge, batting at his brilliant best and cracking 175 runs from 111 balls. Wickets keep falling but the 'impossible' chase continues and, amid amazing scenes, Mark Boucher leads us to victory with one ball left and one wicket remaining.

The Test series that follows is almost an anticlimax, as the Australians prove too strong, winning comfortably in the Cape, and then in Durban, and finally in Johannesburg. We are humbled, whitewashed 0–3 at home, but there are no excuses. The touring side dominates. Sometimes you just say: 'Well done.'

But there's no time to rest.

As the Aussies fly home, the New Zealand team arrives and, within days, we are fighting hard on an up-and-down wicket at SuperSport Park in Centurion. It's a tight match and, dropped down the order to bat at No. 6, I fight hard and manage to score 97, the top score in our second innings. We are grafting.

'Who wants to watch Robbie Williams at Loftus tonight?'

It's an unusual offer in the middle of a Test but I love my music and, with a few others, accept the offer to attend the concert. The following day, we dismiss the Kiwis for 120 and win the Test.

There's a great vibe in the changing room after the match. These are special moments, when you sit with your teammates – and generally the opposition as well – celebrating a tough win with a few beers. Amid all the travel and the pressure, all the time spent away from home, these are the good times.

Jacques Kallis and Shaun Pollock have reached the milestone of their 100th Tests in the same match. Polly looks happy. He's talented, competitive and smart, and has the ability to extract movement out of any pitch. Above all, he's got a great heart. On the night before my first Test, I found a handwritten message of encouragement pushed under the door of my hotel room. It was written by Shaun Pollock, and I still have it today.

Makhaya Ntini also looks pleased with the win. Always so full of energy and enthusiasm, he has given everything yet again, running in hard and taking another five wickets as he helps secure another Test victory. We draw the second Test in Cape Town, but a win at the Wanderers wraps up a solid 2–0 series win.

The next stop is Sri Lanka. Graeme is rested for a tough two-Test tour and we struggle, losing heavily in the first Test and narrowly in the second. The feel-good factor evaporates in the heat.

As the roller-coaster soars, so the roller-coaster dips …

We turn our attention to the ICC Champions Trophy tournament in India. A foot injury keeps me out of our three warm-up wins against Zimbabwe and, although fit again, I am left out of the team that loses our opening match, against New Zealand. I am impatient. I want to play, and am recalled for the second game, against Sri Lanka. We win, and then overcome Pakistan and, suddenly, we're heading for a semifinal.

The venue is Jaipur. The opposition is the West Indies. We bat first and suffer an early collapse, but I play what seems to be an important knock and we reach what appears to be a competitive total, 258 for eight in our 50 overs. But appearances can be deceiving. Chris Gayle strides out to the crease and, in his inimitable way, crashes an unbeaten 133, taking his team to victory with no fewer than six overs to spare.

We're disappointed to see our high hopes of winning an ICC one-day tournament dashed again, but there's never any time to mope, and we fly home for another summer of cricket. India are the visitors and, as we win the ODI series 4–1, I find some form and finally start to feel reasonably established in the Proteas' one-day side. It's taken two years of being in the side and out of the side, but there are plenty of fine players around.

The Test series follows. India win comfortably in Johannesburg. We win comfortably in Durban. It's an excellent contest but, quietly, I am beginning to struggle. With scores of six and 17 while batting at No. 6 at the Wanderers, and then nine and 47 while opening at Kingsmead, everything feels a little up and down.

2007

Victory in the New Year Test at Newlands secures a 2–1 series win over India, but I manage to score only one in the first innings and 22 in the second. Nobody is saying too much but, as a batsman, you can never run away from the numbers after your name. My numbers are undeniably low and I'm worried.

There's no time to rest, reflect and recover and, barely a week later, we are playing the first Test against Pakistan at Centurion. Mohammad Asif, a fine fast bowler, is not helping my situation. He nips the ball around in both directions and, still opening, I am still struggling. In the first innings, I am dismissed by Asif for four. In the second innings, I am dismissed by Asif for 12 and, immediately after getting out, I head straight for the showers at SuperSport Park. There is no one else around. And nobody notices as, in despair, I stand under the water and cry – properly cry.

Pull yourself together, I tell myself, and I do; I dry off, go back to the changing room, and work hard to make sure that, even in poor form, I bring energy and enthusiasm to the group. It's not about me. It's about the team, and the only stat that matters is that we win the series 2–1.

That said, there is no respite for me. Even while the team is thriving, I manage only two and 15 in the second Test in Port Elizabeth, and, in the third Test at Newlands, I score just 11 and four.

This is beginning to feel like the most difficult period of my entire international career, and well-meaning advice flows from every side. Some say it's my backlift. Some reckon it's my balance. Some say I'm trying to play too many strokes too early in my innings. Becoming increasingly desperate and increasingly confused, in seeking a solution I start to dig in every area of my game, but as I dig the hole just gets deeper and deeper.

'Just take it one ball at a time,' Jonty Rhodes tells me when we meet in Cape Town. It is sound advice.

'Write down on paper how things felt when you were getting runs,' Jacques Rudolph tells me, 'so you can get back into that same mindset when things go badly.' That seems to make sense as well and, alone, I find a piece of paper and write: 'Watch the ball, clear mind, strong feet' ... 'Watch the ball, clear mind, strong feet.'

I work hard in practice. I stay positive. I am backing myself and I know I am going to come out on the other side of this bad run and yet, even as I keep smiling, I know I am running out of chances.

Mickey Arthur is the Proteas' coach. He's a good man and an honest man and, on the morning before the first ODI against Pakistan in Centurion, he sits me down and tells me bluntly that I need to score runs if I am going to keep my place and be included in the Proteas squad for the 2007 ICC Cricket World Cup in the West Indies.

With no more credits left, this is the time to deliver, or to disappear.

Mercifully, I find some form, and score 67 in the first ODI at Centurion and 43 in the second ODI at Kingsmead, and then 50 not out at Newlands and 71 not out at the Wanderers. We win the series impressively and, two weeks later, I take my place in the Proteas squad that flies to the Caribbean, determined to win the World Cup, and resolved to set aside our history of misfiring and misfortune in this showpiece event.

I look around the plane. There is no doubt we have the firepower. Graeme Smith, Jacques Kallis, Ashwell Prince, the big-hitting Justin Kemp, Herschelle Gibbs, Mark Boucher and me: it's a fine batting line-up. Shaun Pollock, Makhaya Ntini, Charl Langeveldt, Andrew Hall and the ever-gutsy and combative André Nel are our bowlers.

The tournament is going to be a marathon rather than a sprint, with the pool phase being followed by a Super Eight phase followed by semi-finals and the final. The drawn-out format appears to suit the needs of television rather than the game, providing endless broadcast hours but lacking focus and intensity.

We are based at Basseterre on the beautiful island of St Kitts, and start our campaign with emphatic victories over the Netherlands and Scotland. The tragic and untimely death of Bob Woolmer, who was coaching Pakistan and had just seen his team lose to Ireland, casts a shadow over the World Cup but the cricket continues and we lose to Australia by 83 runs in our third match, although both teams have already qualified for the Super Eights.

More than three weeks into the trip, the cricket is finally becoming meaningful and we squeak home against Sri Lanka, reaching a target of 210 with one wicket and 10 balls to spare. I am dismissed for nought, on my way to setting a new record of four ducks in a World Cup, and yet I would still manage to average over 40 in the tournament. For me, the 2007 World Cup would be a story of either zero or hero, with very little in between.

We defeat Ireland next but then lose to Bangladesh in Guyana and suddenly find ourselves under pressure when we play the hosts West Indies in Grenada. Batting first, at 36 for the loss of Graeme after 10 overs, we are getting ourselves into a tight corner, but Jacques Kallis and I steady the innings and add 170 runs in 29 overs.

My hamstrings are sore and I start to cramp repeatedly. As running becomes more and more painful, I resort to hitting boundaries and eventually finish with 146 from 130 balls. Herschelle and Bouch continue to attack and, when it really counts, we post an imposing total of 356 for four in 50 overs. Once Gayle is run out by Ashwell Prince and Lara is bowled by Jacques Kallis, the home team subsides and bows out of their own tournament.

In contrast, we are starting to believe. At last, could the World Cup dice finally be starting to fall our way?

Needing one more win to secure a place in the semifinals, we fall short against New Zealand in Grenada, but once again respond well to a must-win situation and overcome England in Barbados, bowling them out for just 154 and then reaching the target with only one wicket down and more than 30 overs to spare.

We look and feel strong as we prepare to play Australia in the semifinal in St Lucia.

Graeme wins the toss and we bat first at the Beauséjour Stadium. Our game plan is to attack, to knock the powerful Australians off their stride and quickly get on top. The plan fails.

Graeme goes first, then Jacques, then me, and then Ashwell and Mark in successive deliveries from McGrath. On a big day, on a day when so many South Africans are sitting in front of their televisions and pinning their hopes on us, we collapsed to 27 for five in the 10th over, and there is no way back. We battle to 149 all out, but the chase is a cruise for the Australians and they coast to victory and yet another World Cup final.

Defeat prompts huge disappointment within the team and back home, and inevitably leads to recriminations.

People suggest the squad is unhappy, divided and run by a clique known as the 'The Big Five': Graeme, Jacques, Mark, Justin Kemp and me. The suggestion is nonsense. I am not aware of any clique, and I have never heard of any group called 'The Big Five'.

Others say our inconsistent performances, alternating between excellent and average, are caused by a drinking culture within the squad. This is more nonsense. We did go out now and then, but no more than any other team in the tournament and no more than was reasonable during such a long tour. In fact, in my view, the reality that we can have a good time together increases, rather than hinders, our chance of success.

Somebody within our own management even went so far as to suggest that the cramp I suffered while batting against the West Indies, and scoring 146 runs, was caused by alcohol; he is clearly unaware I have suffered from cramps during long innings throughout my career, but the baseless rumour duly does the rounds.

Why did we lose so heavily in the semifinal?

In my view, we simply tried too hard. We wanted so badly to overcome South Africa's historic World Cup jinx that we departed from our carefully developed plans and went for the Australians too hard and too soon. We needed to stay calm and to play our normal game.

In a World Cup semifinal, that is much easier said than done.

CHAPTER 7

CROSSROADS

It wasn't going to be enough.

It simply wasn't going to be enough for me to play cricket for South Africa and to play a big innings now and then and then to endure some poor form and then to make some runs again. It wasn't going to be enough for me to be just another run-of-the-mill international batsman with an average in the mid-30s.

I wanted to be much better than that. I didn't say anything to anyone – there was no point boasting or bragging. But, quietly and privately, I promised myself I would become the best batsman in the world. That was my goal. Nothing less would suffice. I believed I had the potential, and I wanted to be No. 1.

And yet, as the 2007 season unfolded, it started to become clear that significant changes would need to be made in two specific areas if there was to be any chance of this goal being realised.

First, I needed to improve my batting technique, specifically to develop a correct and solid defence. Just playing strokes and attacking almost every delivery was not going to be enough.

Second, I needed to become much more disciplined, more organised and more professional, on and off the field; I needed to create a trusted support system that would enable me to focus exclusively on the cricket. Living from match to match, from deal to deal, from party to party was not going to be enough.

As the year wore on, it began to feel as if I was reaching a crossroads in my cricket career, as if there was a high road and a low road stretching ahead of me. It was time to choose.

In the world of international cricket, time is a precious commodity. Usually, there is no time to plan and to reflect, no time to make changes in technique and no time to create new structures. The calendar is packed and there is rarely any significant amount of time between the end of one series and the start of the next.

We returned home from the 2007 ICC Cricket World Cup in the Caribbean and had to endure both the expected criticism and the usual claims that, in losing so heavily to Australia in the semifinal, we had once again choked on the big occasion. Being beaten by a stronger side never seems an adequate explanation.

There followed two of the more obscure events in the schedule.

The Afro-Asian Cup involved composite teams from Asia and Africa playing three 50-over matches in India, a concept that may have seemed reasonable on paper but generally failed to set any pulses racing. Eight South Africans combined with three Kenyans in the African XI, and we lost the series 3–0. My inconsistent form continued. I was bowled by Mohammad Asif (him again) in the first game, and scored 70 in the third match.

The next stop was Belfast, where South Africa joined hosts Ireland and India in a triangular one-day tournament known as the Future Cup. As it turned out, the Future Cup did not have much of a future, even though there was some decent cricket played and a strong Indian side deservedly claimed the title.

I continued to struggle with the bat and, during the fortnight in Northern Ireland, leaned heavily on the generous support and knowledge of Jacques Kallis as I finally started to address the issue of my defensive technique. In the past, I had struggled but then scored runs and assumed everything would be fine, and carried on, and effectively dodged the core issue. In Belfast, at long last, helped by Jacques, I confronted the problem.

Even though I had been playing international cricket for two-and-a-half years, even though I had scored centuries in Tests and one-day internationals, I did not really know how to defend.

From my school days at Affies through my debut for South Africa and on to a life on the treadmill of international cricket, there had never seemed any time to learn, never time to undertake any formal education in the basic skills of the game. For as long as I could remember, it had seemed enough for me to try to hit almost every ball either to or over the boundary, seemed enough for me to attack and play strokes.

In Belfast, in June 2007, it was no longer enough.

Working with Kallis, one on one in the nets, we looked at my grip and my backlift. We looked at the position of my head and studied the transfer of my weight when I played back or forward. Hour after hour, as he threw balls at me and offered advice, we began to construct a proper defensive technique.

The Proteas played three one-day internationals in Zimbabwe during August 2007 and the hard work began to pay dividends as I scored 63, 0 not out and 107 in an encouraging 3–0 series win. The transformation was not complete but a process had been started, and at least now there was hope of better times to come.

We returned home to compete as the host team in the inaugural ICC World Twenty20 tournament, hopeful that, with a little luck, we could finally win an official ICC limited-overs event. Twelve national teams arrived in the country, providing plenty of entertainment in a frenetic 13-day schedule ...

The Wanderers is packed for the opening match between South Africa and the West Indies, and very soon it looks as though Chris Gayle is going to steal our show. He crashes 117 runs in 57 balls, and helps his team reach 205 for six in 20 overs. Are we really going to fall at the very first hurdle?

The first ball of our innings is a searing Daren Powell bouncer and it crashes into Graeme Smith's finger. He is hurt and the physio rushes to his side but, after swallowing a few painkillers, he carries on and continues his innings. He's not going anywhere. That's proper leadership, I say to myself. That's a fighting spirit.

Herschelle Gibbs emerges as our hero, thrilling the crowd with an array of drives and pulls, scoring 90 runs from just 55 balls, and powering us to our target with two overs to spare. More than 26 000 spectators go wild. I contribute 16 runs from nine balls, including a six and a four, a bit-part player again ...

Our place in the Super Eight has already been secured when we prepare to play Bangladesh at Newlands, but another win sustains our momentum and we progress to a group alongside India, England and New Zealand from which two teams will advance to the semifinals. Maybe this is our time.

We defeat England at Newlands as the outstanding Albie Morkel excels with bat and ball, and we overcome New Zealand at Kingsmead, with Justin Kemp scoring 89 and Morné Morkel taking four wickets. I score only 18 and then one in these two matches, but the team is winning and that is what matters. Amid a growing sense of excitement around the country, at last, everything seems to be going our way ...

It is our third and final Super Eight match and, still unbeaten in the tournament, we are playing India in Durban. They bat first and are reduced to 33 for three in the sixth over. We're buzzing. We're on our way. Rohit Sharma and MS Dhoni recover, but our eventual target of 154 in 20 overs seems within range.

Kingsmead is a cauldron of anticipation. Let's get this done. There are two routes for us to reach the last four: if we score 154 and win, we knock out India and, according to the maths, if we reach just 126, we will lose the game but we will still advance because we will have a better run rate than New Zealand.

Let's get this done. Shanthakumaran Sreesanth bowls the first over and sprays the first delivery down the leg side for five wides. Graeme confidently clips the fourth ball for four and we're on our way. It's 11–0 after one over. Let's get this done. Everyone is focused amid growing delirium. Let's get this done.

Herschelle is given out LBW off the first ball of the second over, and I walk out to join Graeme. Stay calm, I tell myself. Don't do anything stupid. This is your chance to play a proper innings. I punch my first delivery into the covers for a single. That feels OK. Graeme is facing. He drives, edges and is well caught at slip. Justin Kemp comes in at No. 4, and we are rocking at 12 for two after two overs. Stay calm. Stay calm.

Sreesanth is running in. I am facing. The first ball is quick, swinging in and striking me on the pad. The Indians appeal. I fear it is close. The umpire is unmoved. It's OK. I have survived. The next ball is full. I drive it hard, straight to cover, and there is no run. Move your feet, I tell myself again. Move your feet.

Here comes Sreesanth again. He bowls fast and straight. I'm beaten for pace. I play too late and am again struck on the front pad. The Indians appeal yet again, only much louder this time. Umpire Simon Taufel raises his finger. In a moment of chaos, it's all over. I am out for one, and we are now 12 for three.

When Justin Kemp and Shaun Pollock get out in the sixth over, we have collapsed to 31 for five. Within 33 mad minutes, we have slumped from being in complete control – on course for a fifth straight win, on track to bury our jinx and win the trophy – to the brink of the most dismal elimination.

Back on our bench, I look to my left and to my right. All my teammates are stunned. Is this really happening to us again? The crowd is suddenly quiet. Surely it can't happen again.

Mark Boucher and Albie Morkel are still out there. We need 126 to avoid disaster and qualify with a better run rate, and they fight, ball by ball, run by run, reaching 101 for five in the 16th over. We are still battling and, when Mark is unfortunate to be bowled for 36, we need 25 runs from 21 balls with four wickets in hand.

It doesn't happen. We finish on 116, 10 runs short of salvation. We lose. We're out. Nobody says the C-word in our crushed changing room. Nobody needs to say the C-word, but it's the first question for Graeme at the post-match press conference: 'Why did the Proteas choke again?'

There is no easy answer.

The team has lost. I haven't scored any runs. It's a tough night in Durban. Over a couple of beers, quietly, I am starting to despair. I feel average. Mediocre. I need to be so much better than this. Am I going to be dropped? One of the cricket writers says it is time to rest me and give someone else a chance. No one is safe. Even Jacques Kallis was left out of the Twenty20 side. My position has become perilous.

I feel as though I'm hanging on by my fingertips when I am named in the squad that, just a week after the catastrophe at Kingsmead, flies to Pakistan to play two Test matches, in Karachi and then in Lahore, followed by five one-day internationals. Keep your head down, I tell myself. Keep working hard, keep putting the team first. If I can make the changes that are necessary, I will get through this tricky patch.

The tour to Pakistan goes well – both for the team and for me. We win the first Test by 160 runs, and I score 77 in our first innings. The second Test is drawn, and I make 45 and eight not out.

Life gets even better when, in the first one-day international, Herschelle and I make centuries and we win by 45 runs. Confidence is starting to return and, although the home side wins the second and third ODIs, we recover to win the fourth and fifth, following our Test series win with a

3–2 win in the ODI series.

The team is performing well and I am doing just about enough to stay in it. We fly home and secure two emphatic Test victories over the touring New Zealanders, winning by 358 runs in Johannesburg and then by an innings and 59 runs at Centurion. We then win both a T20 international and the ODI series 2–1.

A spirited West Indies team provided our opposition in the second half of the home summer and they surprised us in the first Test in Port Elizabeth before we recovered to win Tests in Cape Town and Durban and nail down a 2–1 series win. We won a single T20 international and then completed a 5–0 sweep in the ODI series.

For my part, I scored half-centuries in each innings of the first Test, then made an unbeaten 103 in our dominant first innings of the third Test in Durban. I had decided to try a new trigger movement, which involved stepping back and across my stumps as the ball is bowled; it felt awkward at first, but I settled into it and managed to pull Jerome Taylor for four to bring up my century just before Graeme declared. There followed decent innings of 45 and 77 during the ODI series, and I was starting to feel reasonably comfortable again.

As one series led to another, I remained figuratively at the crossroads, still building a proper defensive technique and still needing to create an organised and professional support system. Days became weeks, weeks became months and, somehow, despite the best intentions, nothing got done. Two well-known agents had said they would like to represent and manage me, and I needed to choose between them.

Then, out of the blue, my career began to move in a new, unexpected and unusual direction.

Early one Saturday morning I boarded a flight from OR Tambo airport in Johannesburg to Cape Town, where I was required for a commercial appearance with the Proteas. I had been out with some friends most of the previous night and, to be honest, I wasn't in great condition. Looking somewhat dishevelled after only a few hours' rest, I sunk into my seat on the aisle and immediately fell fast asleep.

This much-needed snooze was abruptly interrupted by someone gently poking me in the ribs.

'Excuse me, AB,' said a man in his mid-forties.

'Yes,' I said, still somewhat blurred in thought and speech.

'I think we're going to land in Cape Town in around 15 minutes and I would like to speak to you,' he said. 'Please feel free to stop me at any time, and I'll obviously leave you alone.'

'OK,' I said, wondering where this conversation would lead.

I recognised him. We had met once before, three months earlier at a dinner with a mutual friend, Louis Vorster, the outstanding former batsman for Transvaal and Northerns, and, as the plane began its descent into Cape Town International, this virtual stranger proceeded to tear me apart. He said he knew a few players in the squad and, from what he'd heard, he believed I had huge potential, but that I was wasting my talent. He said I appeared more interested in the next party than in my next innings.

'Let me know if and when you want to get serious and start getting organised,' he concluded.

I was taken aback. Some of what he had said was exaggerated and unfair, but some not. By now, our plane had come to a halt and other passengers were collecting their hand luggage and disembarking.

As he made his way to the exit of the plane, my mind was racing. I didn't know much about this individual, but he had worked at the top level of South African sport for more than 20 years, first as a journalist and sports editor, then as a CEO in rugby and then as a general manager in broadcasting. He seemed to know what he was talking about and, although I wasn't going to admit as much to him, I did need to be better organised off the field. So I made my way off the plane and started to search for him in the baggage-claim area.

'Excuse me,' I said, tapping him on the shoulder. 'I understand what you're saying. As it happens, there are two agents who want to get involved right now. If you would really like to help, would you mind speaking to them both and then letting me know what you think? I would value your opinion.'

He agreed, and did indeed call me three days later. He didn't think there was anything wrong with either of the agents, but said he thought I needed to find someone who was going to do more than arrange a few commercial deals and take 10% of my earnings. He said I needed someone I could trust, who would assemble a professional support team, who would be able to help me through a very busy period of my life.

'Someone like who?' I asked.

'I don't know,' he replied.

'Will you do it?' I asked.

He seemed ready for the question. 'I'll be happy to help you,' he said, 'but this is the only way it will work. I will create and lead the professional support team and we'll manage everything so you can focus on your cricket. In return, I don't want a commission on anything. In fact, I'll never take a cent from you. What I do want is your commitment to apply yourself completely to being the best cricketer you can possibly be.

'And don't think this is a great deal because you can save some money and carry on as usual on the quiet. There are rarely any secrets in professional sport, and this is not going to be three strikes and you're out. This is going to be one strike and you're out. People talk, and if I hear of you being anything less than fully committed, in any way, or if you are ever less than completely honest, then we'll simply stop everything.'

'OK, that's fine,' I agreed.

This arrangement duly started in December 2007 and it remains in place almost nine years later. I have kept my side of the deal, and he has been incredibly helpful and supportive to me. He says he does not want payment: first, because he earns a living elsewhere and, second, because he wants me to be 100% sure that his advice is motivated not by financial gain, but by what he genuinely believes is best for me.

He has always remained low profile; in fact, he does not want his name or his role to be included in this book, but his role – at least – is included on my insistence because he is part of my story.

As chairman, he assembled a professional support team, which met for the first time in February 2008, and which now meets every quarter, usually at the Investec offices on Atterbury Road in Pretoria.

Brendan Ross, a calm, knowledgeable and experienced Wealth Manager at Investec in Pretoria, agreed to deal with all the banking and investment issues. Johan Heunis, the respected former Northern Transvaal and Springbok fullback and partner at Heunis & Straeuli Attorneys, agreed to deal with legal issues, reviewing contracts; and Eben Gerryts, from PricewaterhouseCoopers, was asked to bring his broad experience in working with the likes of Ernie Els to assist me in dealing with tax and accounting issues.

Brendan, Johan and Eben were effectively installed as the three wise men, providing me with trusted, expert professional advice on every business proposal and investment. This structure meant I could stay detached from these decisions, and focus all my attention and energy on the game.

Millie de Villiers, my mother, who had been managing most of these tasks on her own up until this point, remained a key member of the team. Lindie Claassens, another outstanding professional from PricewaterhouseCoopers, was asked to manage my accounts, and Jacques Hugo, from Investec, expertly assisted with my investments. Lastly, it was agreed that I should appoint a personal assistant, who would deal with all correspondence and contracts, and generally make sure I was in the right place at the right time.

A search was launched and, following a series of interviews at the Daan Swiegers clubhouse on the University of Pretoria campus, Letitia

Greyling emerged as the outstanding candidate. Introduced to us by Martin van Jaarsveld, my old friend from Bela-Bela, she is a wonderful person whose kindness is only matched by her efficiency. In so many ways – big and small – over all these years, she has been fantastic.

The support team changed my life because they took responsibility for everything beyond the cricket, providing a stable, organised and professional source of common sense and proper advice. Where there had been pressure and uncertainty, they brought discipline and confidence, and I will always be extremely grateful.

As time passed, the chairman of the group became a source of regular support for me, even from his home in England or wherever he may have been in the world. We would communicate almost every day, usually by WhatsApp, but also by phone and email, discussing anything and everything that might be on my mind, and always agreeing on the best way forward.

His experience in elite sport meant he understood the pressures associated with being an international cricketer and equipped him to help me cope with, first, the stress created by the unrealistic expectation that I would score runs every time I bat and, second, the extraordinary amount of time I would have to spend away from home – international cricketers accept a travel schedule that even the best-paid and most energetic business people in the world would consider entirely unacceptable.

'REPS,' he told me one day. 'That's the key – REPS.'

He had created an acronym to help me recognise and overcome the challenges of my profession, an acronym to help me survive and thrive in a relentless environment of unrelenting pressure.

The *R* in REPS stands for '*Recognise* the thin line between success and failure'. As a batter, the line between being out for nought and scoring a century is very often as thin as a strand of hair. Some days you play and miss, survive and go on to make runs; other days you feather an edge and get out cheaply. That's the nature of the game, but problems arise when

ABOVE: Family portrait – brothers Jan, left, and Wessels, father AB, mother Millie and me, looking clean and neat for the occasion.

ABOVE AND LEFT: *Oerbuds* – my three oldest friends, in the same winning Warmbaths Primary School cricket team and playing golf many years later: Johan Scheepers (second from left in the pink golf shirt, and flexing his muscles in the cricket team); Chris Swanepoel (in the turquoise golf shirt and with the hat in the cricket team); and Stoffel de Beer (in the purple golf shirt and fourth from the right in the cricket team). I am holding the bat.

OPPOSITE: Rugby – playing for the Affies 1st XV, the Wit Bulle, against Nelspruit High School, and, LEFT, with future Springbok Pierre Spies at the KES festival in Johannesburg.

ABOVE: Fans – with brothers Jan, left, and Wessels, dressed up, hyped up and ready to watch the 1995 Rugby World Cup final on television.

BOTTOM LEFT: Old Affies playing for the Proteas – Jacques Rudolph, left, and Faf du Plessis, right.

RIGHT: Smiles – receiving an award from Gerald Majola, CEO of Cricket South Africa.

OPPOSITE: Maiden Test century – raising my bat after reaching three figures for the first time in a Test, against England at SuperSport Park, Centurion, in January 2005.

BELOW: Debut – Dale Steyn and I played our first Test in the same match, against England in Port Elizabeth in 2004.

ODI action – RIGHT, keeping wicket during a successful tour to Bangladesh; OPPOSITE, batting in Pakistan; and, BELOW, keeping my eye on the ball during a limited-overs match in Durban.

Celebrating – RIGHT, passing 200 for the first time in a Test, against India in Ahmedabad, 2008; and BELOW and OPPOSITE, with Graeme Smith, who took the time to teach me so much about professionalism and leadership.

Role models – OPPOSITE, Makhaya Ntini, a great bowler, always humble, always kind, always generous, always friendly; ABOVE, Jacques Kallis, the greatest Test cricketer of all time, who so often helped me with my technique; BELOW, Mark Boucher, the 'big brother' who showed me what it means to be competitive, to be a fighter who never gives up.

Winning in England – ABOVE, diving at silly point to catch Steve Harmison and, BELOW, celebrating a notable series victory in 2008.

success prompts wild celebrations and failure leads to dark despair.

The point of working hard to recognise and remember the thin line between the great days and the bad days, between getting praised by all and sundry and getting criticised is to even out the roller-coaster ride of being a professional sportsman, to reduce the motion sickness caused by being up, up, up one day and down, down, down the next, to temper extreme reactions, somehow lowering the highs and raising the lows. It is simply a plan to survive the psychological pressures of living and working under a constant spotlight.

The *E* in REPS stands for '*Enhance* key relationships'. There is so little spare time in a professional sporting life and so many people – sponsors, officials and media – all demanding your attention that it becomes very easy to lose sight of the very few people who really matter in your life.

In my world, enhancing key relationships means always making time for my wife and son, for my parents and my brothers, and for my oldest friends, always ensuring they remain the top priority and never allowing myself to become so dazzled by fickle flatterers that I fail to give time and attention to those who need it most.

The *P* stands for '*Prepare* for life after cricket'. Every sportsperson knows that the day will come when either the advancing years or injury will force them to step out of the limelight, to pursue a second career and probably earn considerably less money. This scenario is not a possibility; it's guaranteed. Proactively preparing for life after cricket, through further education or relevant work experience, brings the twin benefits of, first, removing any sense of fear of the future and, second, encouraging self-confidence.

As you start to realise that you can actually be successful at something else other than scoring runs or taking wickets and that you can one day earn a decent living beyond the game, so you start to feel less defined by the numbers that appear after your name on the electronic scoreboard, and so the intense life of playing cricket at the highest level becomes more tolerable, and so you survive a little longer.

The *S* stands for '*Stay* close to the cross'. Religion is, naturally, a personal issue but, for me, feeling close to and mindful of God enables me to function as a human being. I started to subscribe to a monthly booklet called *Every Day with Jesus*, and got into the habit of reading the entry every single morning.

REPS has remained with me all these years, at the forefront of my mind as much when things are going well as when they're not. It's neither a secret code nor a magic formula, but it helps.

On another occasion, early in 2008, the chairman of my support team asked me to meet him at the Wanderers Stadium. It was a normal weekday in Johannesburg and, with people going about their business on Corlett Drive, he suggested we meet each other at the main gate, walk straight in to the stand and then sit quietly in the back row.

The famous Bullring was completely empty and completely silent.

'Imagine this place is full of South Africans,' he said. 'Imagine they're standing and cheering, imagine they are waving national flags and hugging each other, imagine they are smiling and laughing, imagine that – for just a moment – amid all the uncertainty and excitement of change, amid the anxiety caused by rising crime and a falling rand, they are actually feeling great about their country and optimistic about the future.

'And imagine that it is you standing out there in the middle, in the middle of all this joy and celebration, humbly raising your bat in recognition of the applause, batting with all the talent you have been given, completely maximising your ability to play this game, entertaining and thrilling the crowd, helping the Proteas to another victory.

'That is the high road, AB. That's the opportunity before you, and you can take it by being prepared to make all the sacrifices, by being totally committed. It's not an easy road. In fact, it's a very difficult road.

'You are 24 years old but, unfortunately, you can't behave like any other 24-year-old. Most people your age are starting out in their professional careers and they will probably reach their peak in around 20 years or so. For you, this is prime time right now. This is when you need to be exclusively and relentlessly dedicated to being the best you can be.

'Sometimes it will seem like a burden and a responsibility, though it will – hopefully – more often feel like an honour and a privilege, but you have the capacity to be a force for good in the country. You have been given a great talent. Use it. That is the opportunity.'

I was listening.

He was clearly in full flow and, while it all seemed a little dramatic and overstated, I understood the point he was making. I realised I had reached a crossroads in my career. I knew I needed to take the high road.

Time would tell.

So what happened?

I am always wary of quoting the statistics because they genuinely don't mean that much to me but, for what it's worth ...

At the beginning of 2008, I was averaging 36.36 in 33 Test matches and had scored three Test hundreds. Between 1 January 2008, and now, at the time of writing in May 2016, I have averaged 58.26 in a further 73 Test matches and scored an additional 18 Test centuries.

At the beginning of 2008, I was averaging 36.46 in 59 one-day internationals, having scored three ODI hundreds. Between 1 January 2008, and now, in May 2016, I have averaged 63.44 in a further 141 one-day internationals and scored 21 more hundreds.

These numbers are fine, but the stats never tell the whole story.

CHAPTER 8

2008

The Proteas enjoyed almost unimagined success during 2008, drawing a Test series against India in India, defeating England in England and then overcoming Australia in Australia.

Some observers may have been slow to praise a young squad, continuing to portray us as hard-working grafters lacking flair and dare, but the fact is we produced plenty of great cricket in a great year. Within the space of 12 months, this talented and happy group played 14 Test matches, winning 11, drawing two and losing one, and played 19 limited-overs internationals, winning 14, drawing one and losing four.

The team that started the Test against the West Indies at Newlands on 2 January 2008 was Smith, McKenzie, Amla, Kallis, Prince, De Villiers, Boucher, Harris, Nel, Steyn and Ntini.

The team that started the Test against Australia at the Melbourne Cricket Ground on 26 December 2008 was Smith, McKenzie, Amla, Kallis, De Villiers, Duminy, Boucher, Morkel, Harris, Steyn and Ntini.

Success led to confidence, which led to stability, which led to more success, which led to more confidence, which led to more stability, which led to more success; and so the upward spiral continued.

It was a memorable year packed with memorable days.

Saturday, 23 February 2008

We are playing in Bangladesh and we're in trouble. After the high of coming from behind to secure a 2–1 win in the home Test series against the West Indies and then sweeping the ODI series by five matches to nil, we are being put under pressure by the emerging Test nation in front of their own supporters.

It's early on the second day of the first Test at the Shere Bangla Stadium in Mirpur and, in reply to the home team's first innings of 192, we are resuming under pressure at 76 for four ... and that soon becomes 77 for five when Ashwell Prince is run out. As the next man in, I join Johan Botha at the crease.

The pitch is slow and the occasional ball keeps low, so I am careful but decide to counter-attack, and proceed to pull, cut and drive, at one point heaving Shakib Al Hasan over mid-wicket for six.

Johan and I are slowly turning the tide of the Test. Our total has reached 145 for five, and, on 46, I am facing the right-arm off-breaks of Mohammad Ashraful. The ball pitches short – so short that it actually bounces twice. I aim to swipe the ball away to leg, but it loops up off a leading edge and is caught by the bowler. There is a loud appeal and umpire Steve Bucknor, one of the best on the circuit, gives me out.

No way, that must be a no ball. I stand my ground. It's got to be called a no ball if the ball bounces twice, doesn't it? I'm sure that's the rule. As far as I know, that's the rule. That was certainly the rule when we played garden cricket at 20 Mentz Avenue. I wait around and ask the other umpire, Aleem Dar. You're out, he says.

Seriously? I'm not happy as I head back to the pavilion. In fact, the umpires are right and I am wrong. Law 24 clearly states that a no ball must be called if the ball bounces *more than twice*; it bounced only twice, so I am out.

'Well, if that's the law, it's a bad law,' I mutter.

We eventually reach 170 and then dismiss Bangladesh for 182, with

Jacques Kallis and Dale Steyn taking five and four wickets respectively. Set 205 to win in the fourth innings, Graeme, Hashim and Ashwell all make contributions and it is left to Mark Boucher and me to keep our heads and guide us to a notable victory by five wickets. I finish on 19 not out from 80 balls in just under two hours and am pleased with my defence.

We dominate the second Test at the Chittagong Divisional Stadium, with Graeme Smith and Neil McKenzie both scoring double centuries in an epic opening partnership of 415. Dale Steyn takes three of their top five in each innings as we bowl them out twice and power to victory by an innings and 205 runs.

Dale is becoming such a match-winner for us.

The game has produced many outstanding fast bowlers but very few, if any, have matched Dale's capacity to win a Test match with one devastating burst of accurate speed. I remember so many occasions, ever since we played our first-class debuts in the same match and then made our Test debuts in the same match, when I have stood in the field and watched in awe as this remarkable athlete tears through a batting order.

He excels in every kind of weather and on every kind of wicket. He has won Tests all around South Africa, in England and the Caribbean, in India and in Australia. On cloudless days and cloudy days, on green mambas and brown dustbowls, he has raced in over and over again, and been unplayable.

What makes Dale special?

First, he's a true fighter, a genuine competitor who never seeks excuses; it's a fact that he rarely bothers to look at the wicket because he'll back himself to take five wickets in any conditions at any time.

Second, he consistently combines extraordinary pace with extraordinary accuracy; you can be very quick and be a respectable Test bowler and you can be very accurate and be a respectable bowler, but you must be both quick and accurate if, like Dale, you are going to be admired as an exceptional Test bowler.

Third, he is physically blessed with both an incredible sense of rhythm, which makes his bowling action appear so smooth and natural, and an incredibly powerful right wrist snap.

In so many ways, he's a classic predator with an instinctive ability to sense a weakness in the opposition and, in an instant, to find something deep within, to strike and to make the kill. He certainly proves too much for Bangladesh as we follow the 2–0 victory in the Test series with a 3–0 win in the ODIs that follow. Encouraged, we move on to play three Test matches against India in India.

Friday, 28 March 2008

It's the third day of the first Test against India at the MA Chidambaram Stadium in Chennai, and people are saying the temperature has reached 46 degrees Celsius, but that simple statement does not begin to describe the amazing experience of fielding in these conditions. This is cricket in a sauna. We are covered in sunscreen and, as I look around, we're all consistently drenched in sweat.

Adding to our general discomfort, Virender Sehwag is playing perhaps the best Test innings I have ever seen. We had thought we were in decent shape when Hashim's outstanding 159 helped us reach 520 in our first innings, but the outrageously gifted Indian opener is essentially playing T20 cricket in a Test, striking the ball so cleanly and batting on, and on and on … and, in the searing heat, we chase, and chase and chase.

'Veeru' eventually finishes with 319 runs from 304 balls. It is batting from another planet, but we stick to our task and Neil McKenzie's second-innings century ensures we salvage the draw.

Friday, 4 April 2008

I think it is happening. It is finally happening at the Sardar Patel Stadium in Ahmedabad. I am 24 and have been playing international cricket for more than four years and I think, finally, I have learned how to defend properly. Facing Harbhajan Singh's off-spin and Sreesanth's reverse swing, I am feeling secure and solid. Jacques Kallis is batting at the other end, watching and supporting me. His advice has made the difference. Ball by ball, we are working together and guiding our team into a position from where we can win this second Test.

It has been a crazy week. On the evening before the first day, relaxing and chatting with Paul Harris and Mickey Arthur, our coach, in his hotel room, 'Harro' had suddenly piped up and said he thought this will be the match where I score my first double century. It seemed an odd statement to make in front of the coach.

'Why do you say that?' I asked.

'It's just a feeling,' he said.

After the pounding in Chennai, our fast bowlers turn up on the first morning of the Test and sensationally dismiss India for 76 in 20 overs. Dale takes five for 23, Makhaya has three for 18, and Morné claims two for 20. Jubilant team celebrations in the middle follow one after another as India stumble to their second-lowest-ever total at home. We lose early wickets in reply, but Jacques and I take our score to 223 for four at the close.

Now it is the second morning, and Jacques and I are getting ready to resume on 60 and 59 respectively. I happen to see Mickey Arthur in the changing room. The Proteas coach is such a knowledgeable man and such a good man, and, without really thinking, I walk straight up to him and say what's on my mind.

'I feel like I can defend,' I tell him. 'For the first time, I feel like I can defend.'

'Good for you,' he replies.

Jacques and I are back in the middle, aiming to consolidate our position and to build the lead. My batting average in Tests against India is a mediocre 17, but I feel organised and secure.

Harbhajan bowls the second over of the day. I am facing. The first ball is floated and landing on off and middle. I reach forward and defend, head still, soft hands. There is no run. The next ball is also flighted. I watch it carefully and, turning the blade of the bat, prod the ball just wide of the crouching short leg.

This feels different. I have learned to play the ball so much later. I'm not forcing anything. I'm not trying to hit everything for four. I am letting the ball come to me. Is this happening? Each careful block feels so good. In fact, each careful block feels better than a boundary. At last, I feel in control.

Jacques and I continue to make progress, at the end of each over meeting in the middle of the pitch and chatting, keeping each other focused, keeping each other going. Jacques gets a break when a ball from Harbhajan rolls against a stump but doesn't dislodge the bail, and we take the total to 302 for four.

This is different. Sourav Ganguly is brought on to bowl the last over before the lunch interval. I am on 98. He's a part-time medium pacer. Keep concentrating, I tell myself. Don't give anything away. Don't take any risks. I walk across my stumps and shoulder arms to his first ball, and I leave the second ball as well.

The ball is not doing much. OK, get ready. This is it. I'm not going to enjoy my lunch if I'm stuck on 98. Let's get this over and done with right here, right now. I decide to paddle sweep the next delivery. I am pre-meditating, making up my mind on precisely what stroke I'm going to play before the ball has been bowled.

Ganguly bowls fractionally outside off stump. I shuffle across the crease, crouch down on one knee and manage to paddle the ball down to the fine leg boundary. The four runs bring up my fifth Test century, and I am overwhelmed by a sense of relief and satisfaction. OK, I tell myself, now carry on.

We bat on into the afternoon until Jacques plays on and is bowled by

Sreesanth for a fine 132. I am then joined by Mark Boucher and we continue to score at four or five runs an over. I pass 150, glancing Harbhajan for four to fine leg, and the runs flow into the evening. Maybe Paul Harris did know something after all.

Bouch eventually falls LBW to Kumble for 21 and, when Morné Morkel is out for one, Paul Harris walks out to the middle. I have reached 184 and am now only 16 runs short of fulfilling his prediction. Five overthrows help me on my way as RP Singh shies at the stumps and misses and the ball races away to the boundary. I work a few more singles and a two, and take my score to 194, as Harbhajan continues his marathon spell.

Don't give it away, I repeat to myself. Don't give it away. Keep concentrating. I take two steps down the wicket to his first delivery of the over, and drive the ball straight, but the fielder at long-off does well and we settle for two. I tuck a single away to square leg off the second ball and Harro nudges an easy one off the third. Hardly pausing for breath, Harbhajan turns, rolls in again and bowls … and, with soft hands, I prod the ball away.

Here he comes again. This time, it's a low full toss. I drive past extra cover and the ball speeds away to the boundary. That's my first double century. I punch the air and hug Paul Harris in the middle and, so many miles away, watching on television back in Bela-Bela, my parents and brothers celebrate as well. These are the important moments when all the sacrifices – all the sacrifices everybody has made over all the years, the infinite number of lifts to practice and the endless games in the back garden – all seem so worthwhile.

I take my score to 217 not out by the time bad light and showers bring an early close to the second day. Graeme declares overnight and our bowlers return to dismiss India for a second time, winning the match by an innings and 90 runs inside three days, taking a 1–0 lead in the series. This Test feels like a turning point in my career. For me, the

city of Ahmedabad, on the banks of the Sabarmati River, will always
be special.

India very rarely lose a Test series at home, possibly because they have
such exceptionally constructive working relationships with the grounds-
men at their home venues. We arrive in Kanpur to play the third and last
Test and are not hugely surprised to find an underprepared wicket at the
Green Park Stadium.

Graeme wins the toss again, which usually helps on the subcontinent,
but we are bowled out on the first day, fading from 152 for one to be all
out for 265. Still we fight hard and reduce the home side to 279 for nine
towards the end of the second day. Parity on first innings will give us a
chance but, on the second evening and into the third morning, Sreesanth
and Sharma proceed to add 46 runs for the tenth wicket.

There is almost nothing in cricket, or maybe in life, as frustrating as a
tenth-wicket partnership that, over by over, edged single by edged single,
stolen run by stolen run, takes a match away from you.

So it proves in Kanpur as India somehow reaches 325. With the pitch
quickly deteriorating, we subside to 121 all out in our second innings.
India win, and the series ends in a 1–1 draw.

Five days later, the world of cricket is forever changed by the launch
of the first Indian Premier League (IPL), a 20-over competition contested
by eight franchises. Most of the world's leading cricketers are put up
for auction and the team owners bid against each other, paying players
extraordinary sums of money for seven weeks' work. I am signed by the
Delhi Daredevils for US$300 000, an average salary in the IPL, an astro-
nomical sum for me.

Saturday, 12 July 2008

Our team briefing at the close of play has started, and Graeme Smith is
not happy. We have been outplayed in the first two days of the first Test

against England at Lord's and our pre-tour hopes of becoming the first South African team since readmission to win a Test series in England appear to be forlorn.

We all know the history. Kepler Wessels' touring squad drew the series 1–1 in 1994, Hansie Cronjé's side lost 2–1 in 1998, and Graeme's team drew 2–2 in 2003. We all believe we have the ability to set the record straight, but we have not started well and the captain is clearly agitated as he addresses his players.

'We can't give our wickets away so cheaply,' he says. 'AB, that wasn't good enough.'

What?

Did he say my name? Is he blaming me?

Doesn't he understand how I play? If somebody like Monty Panesar is going to bowl at me with a slip, I'm going to take him on and hit him straight back over his head. That's how I play. If Graeme doesn't understand that by now, then he really doesn't understand me. I am disappointed. Is he really blaming me?

Maybe Graeme is still annoyed because he won the toss and sent England in to bat, and they proceeded to score 593 for eight, with Ian Bell and Kevin Pietersen both scoring big hundreds. To be fair, it seemed a reasonable decision at the time, with something in the wicket but, for once, our bowlers misfired.

We know we need to bat well on the third day – the celebrated Saturday of the Lord's Test, one of the highlights of the English summer – but we are poor, losing wickets regularly and giving the capacity home crowd so much more to enjoy than just their chilled champagne and their salmon sandwiches.

When Neil McKenzie is bowled by Panesar in the second over after lunch, we are struggling at 83 for four and Ashwell Prince and I come together and set about the task of rebuilding the innings. Panesar and Stuart Broad are on a roll and I am simply trying to survive, scoring four runs from my first 21 balls. We gradually start to settle and, taking very few risks, we manage to take our score to 156 for four at tea.

Into the evening, Panesar switches to bowl around the wicket and I am keen to seize the initiative.

In my mind, in cricket, above everything else, you want your opponents to be playing under pressure. Batsmen put pressure on the bowlers by scoring freely; fielders transfer pressure to the batsmen by chasing with such intensity that twos become ones; and bowlers impose pressure by limiting the run rate and taking wickets.

Transferring pressure is always the key in this game and, as we try to secure a foothold in the Test, still trailing by more than 400 runs, I want to put the pressure back on Panesar and the other England bowlers by scoring runs, and so spreading the field. We have to get on the front foot. This is a battle we need to win ...

Panesar bowls wide outside off. I'm not tempted and leave it. The next ball is straight, and I play it back to the bowler. Seize the initiative, I tell myself. Transfer pressure. I take two steps down the wicket to the third delivery but Monty sees me coming and bowls quicker and flatter. I prod the ball to mid-on.

This is the game. This is the struggle. I love it. Come on, Monty, what have you got now?

He moves in again and this time he gives the ball a little more air. It's there to be hit and, in an instant, I take a step down the wicket and aim to flick the ball over the head of Jimmy Anderson who is fielding at mid-on. Go on, go on, fly, ball, fly. It doesn't. Anderson stretches and grasps a fine catch two-handed above his head. I am out for 42, having batted for more than two hours and facing 119 balls. It is hardly a slog.

Is that giving my wicket away cheaply? I don't know. Perhaps it was.

Ashwell continues to thrive after I am out and completes an outstanding century, but he receives little support and we are dismissed for 247 and asked to follow on. Batting again, we reach 13 without loss at the close, but we appear to be heading for a heavy defeat, and nobody is smiling at the team briefing.

'Come on, guys,' Graeme says. 'We can do so much better than this.'

The captain is right, of course, but I still don't understand why he has chosen to single me out for criticism in front of the entire squad, especially when I actually did stick it out and batted for a full session; many others didn't. Maybe he knows how I will react. Maybe he knows I will be angry and will want to prove him wrong. In the end, I know he has always backed me and I know he has my best interests at heart.

As soon as the briefing ends, I leave our changing room and walk down the stairs of the famous pavilion at Lord's, passing the stewards in white blazers at the door, turning left, keeping my head down as I stride past happy hordes of England supporters in the Harris Garden, and eventually reach the Grace Gates.

A friend is waiting for me in his car parked on St John's Wood Road and, as I get into the passenger seat, I catch sight of a familiar figure crossing the road immediately in front of us.

'Is that Jeffrey Archer?' I ask.

'I think so, why?'

'I've read all his books. My entire family are all massive fans.'

'Well, go and say hello to him,' says my friend. 'He loves his cricket.'

So I jump out of the car and introduce myself to Lord Archer, who could not have been friendlier. He says he will arrange for a copy of his new book – *A Prisoner of Birth* published a few months earlier – to be delivered to our changing room the next morning. He has regularly sent me his books ever since.

I read most of the 412-page novel during the course of the next two days while sitting on our balcony, in between keeping an eye on the cricket, as we demonstrate fantastic application and courage in adversity. Graeme, Neil and Hash all score centuries as we bat and bat and bat, and ultimately secure a creditable draw.

Friday, 18 July 2008

'How can you claim that catch? You should be ashamed of yourself.'

Another Test, another day and another established cricketer is furious with me, and he's lambasting me over lunch.

Graeme speaks up on my behalf. 'Leave him alone and go away,' he says, as tempers begin to fray.

It's the first day of the second Test at Headingley in Leeds, and the usually calm England player is clearly livid with me because he thinks I claimed to have held a catch at second slip when, as far as he was concerned, I must have known the ball had touched the grass.

In truth, I simply didn't know whether or not the ball had carried. Everything happened in an instant and my first reaction was to ask Graeme, who was fielding at first slip, what he thought. He said it didn't matter because the umpire had referred the decision to his colleague watching on a screen in the stands.

So I stood there in the middle of the field, alongside everyone else – my teammates, batsmen, umpires and the crowd – watching the slow-motion replay on the giant screens; and the pictures showed the ball had bounced off my right hand and hit the ground before my left hand scooped it up.

Even before the 'NOT OUT' verdict appeared on the screen, an angry chorus of boos had started to rumble around the entire ground, each and every one of them directed at me. It was a difficult moment but, in all honesty, I had not known whether or not the ball had carried. I had only asked the question.

Over the salads at lunch, the England players are not letting the matter rest.

'That wasn't clever, young man,' says one senior England player as he passes our table.

A couple of my teammates bluntly tell him to move on.

After the high-scoring draw at Lord's, the series is catching fire in the dining room at Headingley. I don't mind. I don't enjoy being the centre of controversy, but I wasn't sure and that's the fact.

Kevin Pietersen cracks a quick 45 during the afternoon, but our fast bowlers soon regain control and England are dismissed for 203 in only 52 overs and three balls. Dale and Morné each take four, Makhaya and Jacques take one. Make no mistake, when this quartet of fast bowlers is firing, we look an exceptionally strong team.

Saturday, 19 July 2008

The spectators are booing me – and it's not just one or two people expressing mild displeasure as I walk out to bat in our first innings at Headingley. It feels like each and every one of the 8 000 supporters sitting on the Western Terrace are booing me, all of them reacting to the grounded-catch furore of the previous day.

No problem, I tell myself. I'll show them what I can do.

I take guard and prepare to face my first ball. Darren Pattinson, on his debut, is running in and bowls a perfect out-swinger. I play defensively and miss. The crowd roars. The breadth of a hair is all that stands between me surviving to continue my innings and me getting a tiny edge, being caught behind, being out for a golden duck and being mocked all the way back to the pavilion by a boisterous capacity crowd eager to see me punished.

Mercifully, I survive. Our total is 143 for four. Ashwell Prince is batting beautifully again and, together, we start to build the partnership that we need to consolidate our position. It's very hard work. Jimmy Anderson is showing why he is widely rated as one of the outstanding bowlers in the world, beating me several times. I am struggling and scratching around and, inevitably, I receive abuse from the fielders every time I play and miss.

Bring it on, I think. I keep battling, determined not to give anything away.

Ashwell and I manage to stick around and stick together into the afternoon and then into the evening, and, with the boos starting to subside, we take our score to 322 for four when bad light stops play. The following day, the third morning of the Test, we continue to make progress until, with our fifth-wicket partnership worth 212 runs in 74 overs, Ashwell is out for an excellent 149, his second century in as many Tests.

I am still not timing the ball as I would like and still not batting fluently, but at Headingley – as in Ahmedabad three and a half months earlier – I am digging in and building a score, accumulating runs. I reach 99, requiring just a single to reach a significant century eked out in adversity. The next over is a maiden. I face three balls in the following over, and block each delivery. Ten minutes pass. Twenty minutes pass. Twenty-five minutes pass.

To the growing amusement of my 'fans' on the Western Terrace, I seem to have got stuck on 99. The run remains frustratingly elusive and every dot ball that passes is being greeted by an ironic cheer. Another over goes by. Stay calm, I tell myself. Don't panic. I play and miss. It's now 34 minutes; it feels like 34 days.

Salvation arrives in the form of a single nudged to mid-off off Freddie Flintoff. I breathe deeply and, almost immediately, start to relax, start to time the ball and start to play some attacking strokes.

The runs are flowing now, and I take my score from 100 to 150 in just 54 balls. I move on to 178 before I finally edge a ball from Stuart Broad and am caught one-handed at slip by a flying Freddie Flintoff. It has been a significant innings for me, an ultimately rewarding eight and a half hours in the trenches.

We are eventually bowled out for 522, which means England start their second innings 319 runs behind. They wilt under the scoreboard pressure and are blasted out for 327. Our fast bowlers are charging in with real intent and I am pleased to support their efforts, managing to hold one of the best catches of my career, diving full length in the slips to dismiss Ian Bell.

Graeme and Neil knock off the nine runs required to win in seven balls, and we win the Test by 10 wickets with a day to spare.

Saturday, 2 August 2008

This may be the most enjoyable fines meeting in the history of South African cricket. It is nearing midnight, more than five hours after victory in the third Test in Birmingham gave us a winning 2–0 lead in the four-Test series, and the Proteas are still in the visitors' changing room at Edgbaston, still celebrating together.

I look around and feel so pleased, pleased for Mickey Arthur and his coaches who have worked so hard for this historic series win, pleased for Graeme, Jacques and Bouch, pleased for the other players and management, pleased for the whole group because we have made history together, becoming the first South African squad to win a Test series in England in the modern era. Right here, amid the laughter and the sweat-stained kit, the shared joy and weariness, the warm glow of collective satisfaction, lies the essence of team sport.

These moments are so precious because it is the hope and belief that such moments lie ahead that drives us, as individuals and as a squad, through the tough times, through all the travel and training, and because it is the memory of these moments that will remain with each of us for the rest of our lives.

I look around the changing room, and feel so blessed and so privileged.

Neil McKenzie is in full flow, running the fines meeting with Mark Boucher.

'Jacques Kallis, come forward please,' he says. 'We all know you have given so much to this team. You have even given most of your hair. Graeme usually makes you bowl into the wind and you always do as he asks, even though you know very well it will make your hairline recede even faster.'

With that, Neil produces an electric fan and says that, in recognition of his huge sacrifice, Jacques will have to down a few beers with the wind blowing in his face, just the way he likes it.

So the fines and the humour continue long into the night.

It had been a remarkable Test match, decided by one of the very finest innings I had ever seen.

England had batted first and, even though we secured a useful first innings lead of 83 runs, the home team seemed to have put themselves in a winning position when they scored 363 in their second innings. We were set 281 to win; in all the history of Test cricket at Edgbaston, no team had ever successfully chased such a total.

Graeme and Neil provided a solid foundation with an opening partnership of 65, but we lost four quick wickets and were battling at 93 for four. Graeme and I steadied the chase, adding 78 runs in an hour and 40 minutes, but a further 100 runs were still required when I was out for 27, edging a catch to first slip.

Our captain was simply not going to be denied. Batting under constant pressure for almost six hours, he proved magnificently resolute. He was joined by Mark Boucher and led us to victory by five wickets, finishing unbeaten on 154 out of our total of 283 for five. With courage and concentration, with great skill, he had single-handedly transformed a match we would have lost nine times out of 10 into a sensational triumph.

Edgbaston security staff eventually persuade us to leave the ground just before midnight but our celebrations are only just beginning. A substantial group of players, including Paul Harris and me, head for Broad Street in the centre of Birmingham where we crawl from pub to pub, and then from club to club.

We arrive back at our hotel just after five o'clock in the morning and decide it is still not quite time for bed, so we order more beers to our team room. Then, an hour or so later, with our party still in full swing, the fire alarm goes off and an emergency announcement says it is necessary to evacuate the building immediately.

The lifts are out of action, so we gingerly make our way down 12 flights of stairs and join the rest of the hotel guests who have assembled in the street. While they are dressed in pyjamas and dressing gowns, as you would expect at that hour, we are still wearing our T-shirts and jeans … and smiling inanely.

Nobody cared.

We had won a Test series in England for the first time since 1965, and neither defeat in the fourth Test at The Oval nor a 4–0 defeat in the ODI series that followed would remotely tarnish the memory.

Thursday, 27 November 2008

We are efficiently taking control of the second Test match against Bangladesh at Centurion, having won the first by an innings and 129 runs in Bloemfontein. Ashwell is batting brilliantly again, on his way to another big hundred, and I am making my way to the wicket with our score on 134 for four.

Shakib Al Hasan is bowling. I defend my first delivery and, next ball, advance down the wicket, but fail to make contact as the ball turns dramatically … and I'm stumped, out for nought. I am surprised. The ball hardly ever turns that much on the second day at SuperSport Park. Perhaps it hit a crack in the pitch.

As I make my way back towards the changing room, another thought strikes.

'Isn't that the first time I have been out for a duck in a Test match?' I wonder to myself.

It is. The records show I played 78 innings in Test matches before I failed to trouble the scorers on that quiet Thursday at Centurion Park. Aravinda de Silva, with 74, stands second on the all-time list of cricketers who have played the most Test innings before a duck, followed by Clive

Lloyd and Ross Taylor, both on 58.

More importantly, *we* make progress and defeat Bangladesh by an innings and 48 runs.

Sunday, 21 December 2008

Please forgive me
If I act a little strange
For I know not what I do

I am arriving at the Western Australian Cricket Association (WACA) for the fifth day of the first Test between Australia and South Africa, and the lyrics of David Gray, the English indie rock singer-songwriter, are flooding my senses via my headphones. I love his music. My whole family loves his music. It is pure and clean and beautiful, and it always gets me in the zone to perform because, against all the odds, against all the precedents in cricket history, we glimpse an extraordinary triumph.

Feels like lightning running through my veins
Every time I look at you

The numbers are simple. We are preparing to resume our innings at 227 for three, chasing an all-but-impossible target of 414 runs to win. We need only 187 more runs. It doesn't seem much, until you count them down one by one. Then it seems a lot. Then, when you factor in the deteriorating pitch, the widening cracks and the uneven bounce, and an Australian team genuinely expecting they will close down another routine win, then 187 more runs begins to feel like a chasm, a divide between what seems possible but never happens.

Jacques Kallis and I are batting. He is 33 not out. I am 11 not out. We have work to do.

What a Test match it has been.

We had arrived in Australia encouraged by the series win in England and thinking we could be competitive. As a squad, we were settled. As individuals, we were in form. We thought we could do well. We *thought* we would do well. I am not so sure we really *believed* we could or would do well ... at least not until the first morning of the first Test when the mighty Australians batted first and, after six blurred overs, were reeling at 15 for three.

It was exciting and exhilarating. The crowd was stunned into silence. We had landed the first punch.

They recovered of course and, at one stage, it looked as if the dangerous Andrew Symonds would take the Test away from us, but he was dismissed by Paul Harris and they were eventually 375 all out.

We stuttered in response. Graeme and Hash both batted well but each fell in the 40s and it was left to Jacques and me to take our score from a precarious 110 for three to a reasonably secure 234 for three. We were settled, planning to maintain our dominance and secure the first innings lead we felt would be necessary.

Then, in an instant, typhoon Mitchell Johnson ripped through our middle order. There are very few bowlers in the world who can literally turn a Test match on its head within the space of a few overs. Johnson is one of them. He took five wickets in quick succession ... boom, whack, boom, whack, boom. We collapsed from 234 for three to 241 for eight, looking every inch the latest South African side to subside with a whimper in Australia.

Typically, Mark Boucher dug in for a while, and hung around with the tail, scoring a priceless 26 as we staggered to 281 all out, still 94 runs behind. We were fighting hard. That's what we always did. And yet, somehow, we seemed to be always chasing the game, always a decisive step behind the home side.

We kept competing when Australia batted for a second time. In fact, we appeared to be right back in the game when they stumbled to 162 for seven but, as ever, just as we threatened, just as they wobbled, they seemed to find another gear. Brad Haddin and their lower order scored runs. The tail wagged. We simply could not close and, when they were finally all out for 319, our target had grown and grown and grown, reaching 414.

That seemed to be just about that, ran the consensus.

'Stuff that,' Graeme Smith figuratively told the consensus. Our captain settled and began to score freely. Hashim also settled and began to score freely. The runs flowed and our total passed 100, and then 150 and, watching on TV in our changing room, some of us began to wonder. No, it was surely too many.

We reached 172 for one and were just starting to dare to dream ... when, like two meaty slaps to the face, Graeme and Hash fell within three overs. Jacques and I came together at 179 for three, and played a few strokes, still swimming against the tide and reaching stumps on the fourth day at 227 for three.

> *Please forgive me*
> *If I act a little strange*
> *For I know not what I do*

Jacques and I are walking to the crease on the fifth morning. Just over 5 000 people have turned up to watch the last rites at the WACA and, as far as I can tell, the Australian players appear unconcerned. Following the retirement of the Waugh brothers, of McGrath and Warne, they are not the team they once were, but they are still strong and they know it. They believe and they strut. I envy their self-assurance.

While batting in our first innings, I had decided to try to transfer some pressure to their spinner, Jason Krejza. I charged down the wicket. He saw me coming and dropped the ball short. I tried to adapt and, looking rather ungainly, ended up going down on one knee and slog-sweeping the ball to deep mid-wicket.

'What kind of cricket is that?' Matthew Hayden scoffed, fielding at slip. 'What is this guy doing?'

'I'll show you one day, bud,' I said to myself.

So I stored away the irritation.

Only 187 runs required, I ponder. Only 187 runs required to silence the doubters. Jacques and I finally reach the crease and execute the standard cricketer's fist-pump before heading to our respective ends. He looks so calm and confident. I look at him and feel confident as well.

We enjoy batting together. In fact, our last four partnerships in Test matches have been worth 112, 5, 256 and 124. Come on, I mutter quietly, let's get this done.

The Australians are running in hard, hunting early wickets, but we continue to prosper until, with our partnership worth 124 runs, exactly as many as our partnership in the first innings, Jacques is caught by Mike Hussey off Mitchell Johnson for 57. We are 303 for four, with 111 runs still required to win.

JP Duminy, playing his Test debut, joins me in the middle. He scored one in our first innings and looks understandably nervous, but I very clearly remember our partnership while playing for South Africa Under-19 against England at Worcester six years earlier. We'd done it before and we can do it again.

The Australians are working hard, running in with real conviction, chatting, unnerving. We are playing carefully, taking few risks, gutsing it out and seizing anything loose. We reach lunch at 322 for four, and start to sense that the home side is getting nervous. We cajole our score to 362 for four by drinks in the afternoon. The sledging is almost non-stop now, between every ball, between every over, but JP and I hear nothing.

Ponting turns to Johnson. We survive. Less than 50 are required now, less than 40, less than 30. We set small targets for ourselves, another 10 runs, then another 10 runs. We reach them, and we set another. Only when the runs required dips into the teens do I allow myself to feel confident.

I reach my century, JP reaches his 50. This is happening. Johnson bowls. JP pushes the ball past cover. Symonds is chasing but we are running ... one, two, we turn again and go for three – and we make it. We've done it. We've scored 414 to win. It is the second-highest fourth-innings run chase in all the history of Test cricket. JP and I hug each other in the middle, and our teammates pour out of the pavilion to celebrate.

Matthew Hayden, a true competitor, walks over to shake my hand.

Wednesday, 31 December 2008

'Wake up, Abbas, wake up. Everyone's already in the team bus. We're all waiting for you.'

It is Paul Harris speaking, and it is the morning after the night before – the morning after we had beaten Australia in the second Test at the Melbourne Cricket Ground, and become the first South African team ever to win a Test series in Australia ... the first ... ever, making more history on the penultimate day of a great year.

'Wake up,' Paul repeated. 'Wake up.'

I hate being late, and pride myself on almost always being on time. This was an exception. After jumping out of bed, frantically throwing my clothes into my suitcase and rushing down the stairs and out of the hotel, I was correctly welcomed onto the bus by a chorus of catcalls and we caught our flight to Sydney ... just.

Please forgive me

If I act a little strange
For I know not what I do

It had been another extraordinary Test match.

Australia had won the toss again and batted again, and scored an imposing 394 all out. Shortly after tea on the second day, we were floundering at 141 for six, almost out for the count, with nearly 50 000 spectators roaring their Australian team back into the series. JP stood firm and remained, and remained and, picking his team off the canvas, scored an unforgettable 166 as we rallied to reach 459 all out.

Morné Morkel had made 26, Paul Harris 39 and Dale Steyn had struck a glorious 76 from 191 balls in just under four hours at the crease. It was truly the fightback of all fightbacks, and the Australians, suddenly batting under pressure, could manage no more than 247 in their second innings. Ricky Ponting followed his first innings century with a typically defiant 99, but the match had turned decisively in our favour.

We were left with 183 runs to win the Test match and the series and, amid an almost surreal atmosphere, we reached the target for the loss of only one wicket soon after lunch on the fifth day. It was almost too much to take in. Australia had not lost a home Test series for 16 years of total dominance, but they had lost to us.

The celebrations followed and the champagne flowed long into the night, through another memorable team fines meeting, and more memorable times spent within the Proteas of 2008.

We had won 11 Tests in the calendar year, a feat matched at the time only by the West Indies in 1984 and England in 2004. We had completed an amazing 10 successful fourth-innings run chases of more than 175 runs during the year and Graeme Smith had contributed 913 runs to these undaunted pursuits.

Each player had played his full part in a settled squad and coach Mickey Arthur deserves high praise, but it was our captain who merited the greatest accolades; he had led consistently and brilliantly from the front throughout this golden year, scoring a grand total of 1 656 runs in 15 Tests, at a remarkable average of 72.

Special captain: Graeme Smith. Special team: Proteas.

Special year: 2008.

CHAPTER 9

SOUTH AFRICA, RIGHT OR WRONG

Representing South Africa remains a massive privilege.

It's true the international cricket schedule is demanding, with long periods spent away from home. And it's true that the pressure to perform in match after match is relentless, with so much resting on the simple number appearing after your name on the scoreboard or in the newspaper, there for all to see. If it's a 100, you're a hero. If it's a 0, you are quite literally a zero. There's no point complaining; that's the reality.

However, it is also true that very few individuals are given the honour of essentially going to work over and over again with the name of their country emblazoned on their chest or on their back.

I am a South African, and I am intensely proud to be a South African.

There are currently 196 sovereign states on this planet and, of course, each and every one of them is special to most of the people who live there. Each and every country cherishes its own history, traditions and identity, and it would be foolish to suggest that any one is somehow superior to any other.

That said, South Africa is special to me.

It is special primarily because of the people who live here, the overwhelming majority, the fundamentally good people who want nothing more than for our country to grow and develop, to prosper and realise

its enormous potential, who want to look after their families and neighbours, who are prepared to work hard.

I see these people everywhere, in schools and in offices, in the streets
and in the malls, on farms and in villages, in the grandstands and at
sponsors' functions; and I genuinely don't see white or black, or coloured or Indian; and I genuinely don't see Christian, Muslim or Hindu.
I see only South Africans.

Sometimes we lose sight of the bigger picture.

An amazingly diverse group of people has gathered at the southern
tip of the African continent, assembled from so many different back-
grounds and cultures and, emerging from a past filled with brutal pain
and conflict, these people have somehow managed to unite behind one
Constitution and beneath one flag.

The scale of the South African miracle should never be overlooked.

Huge challenges remain – challenges of poverty and inequality, of crime
and economic uncertainty, of leadership and corruption – but, in my view,
most importantly, there remains in South Africa today a strong sense of
shared responsibility, a general acceptance that we're in this together.

This gives me hope.

In many countries that I have visited, people seem somehow defeated, resigned to accepting the status quo and content to blame ongoing
problems on the government or bankers or anyone else. In South Africa,
maybe naively, tens of millions of us continue to feel personally involved
and invested in building the nation.

We have a precious national spirit, a collective drive, a *gees*.

It is the *gees* of the small boy who chases after a ball, who trips and
falls, who grazes his knee, who picks himself up with not even a glance
at the blood, who runs again and who reaches the ball.

It is the *gees* of the worker who rises at four o'clock every morning and
takes three taxis and three hours to get to work and then makes the same
trip home, just to provide for his family.

It is the *gees* of the policeman who lives to protect his community, the *gees* of the teacher who lives to educate children, the *gees* of the doctors and nurses who live to heal the sick, the *gees* of the businessman who creates wealth and jobs; it is even the *gees* of the occasional honest politician who wants to improve lives.

It is also the *gees* of a national team that gives everything – absolutely everything – on the field, that always works hard and never gives up under any circumstances, that simply strives to make people proud.

It is this *gees* that makes our country special. It is this *gees* that makes me feel so privileged to go to work, both at home and around the world, with the words 'South Africa' on my chest.

Make no mistake, it is impossible for me to exaggerate the surge of pure and unequivocal excitement that I feel every time I arrive back in South Africa after spending a few weeks or months abroad. It is home, of course, but there is something more, something more that touches me in the most profound way.

Many people have crafted words and music to explain the essence of this amazing, mysterious place, and most of them seem to come from other countries!

> *It's gonna take a lot to drag me away from you*
> *There's nothing that a hundred men or more could ever do*
> *I bless the rains down in Africa*
> *Gonna take some time to do the things we never had*

The well-known chorus of 'Africa' is fantastic, but it is sung by Toto, a US rock band, and the lyrics were written by American David Paich, who was so moved by watching an early 1980s documentary about pain and suffering in Africa that he created a song about what he would do *if* he was there.

Johnny Clegg is certainly an authentic African – even if he was born in Lancashire, England – and I have always loved his music. He's a true genius and, together with his band Juluka, he produced such great songs as 'Scatterlings of Africa' and 'Asimbonanga' that have for many years touched the souls of many South Africans.

> *Asimbonanga*
> *Asimbonang' uMandela thina*
> *Laph'ekhona*
> *Laph'ehleli khona*

The Zulu lyrics are translated as *We have not seen him, we have not seen Mandela, in the place where he is, in the place where he is kept,* and refer to the global desire to see Madiba during the 27 years he was kept in prison, a period when the South African media were banned from publishing his image.

I would challenge anybody to google 'Clegg Mandela' and watch the YouTube video of the moment in Frankfurt in 1999 when, completely unannounced, the former president joined Clegg on stage during 'Asimbonanga' and not to feel enthused by the enduring potential of the new South African dream.

'It is music and dancing that makes me at peace with the world, and at peace with myself,' Mandela announces, before asking Clegg to repeat the song and urging the German audience to dance.

I met Nelson Mandela when the Proteas squad was invited to visit him at his home in Houghton, Johannesburg, before leaving to compete in the World Cup in 2007. He was seated in a wheelchair and appeared frail, but the presence of the greatest South African was extraordinary.

Long Walk to Freedom, his autobiography, is a remarkable book that I really enjoyed. He wrote:

I am fundamentally an optimist. Whether that comes from nature or nurture, I cannot say. Part of being optimistic is keeping one's head pointed toward the sun, one's feet moving forward. There were dark moments when my faith in humanity was sorely tested, but I would not and could not give myself up to despair.

Isn't that the key? Isn't that what we must all do? Can we keep our heads pointed towards the sun and keep our feet moving forward, and never give ourselves up to despair?

He also wrote:

I always knew that deep down in every human heart, there is mercy and generosity. No one is born hating another person because of the colour of his skin, or his background, or his religion. People must learn to hate, and if they can learn to hate, they can be taught to love, for love comes more naturally to the human heart than its opposite. Even in the grimmest times in prison, when my comrades and I were pushed to our limits, I would see a glimmer of humanity in one of the guards, perhaps just for a second, but it was enough to reassure me and keep me going. Man's goodness is a flame that can be hidden but never extinguished.

Even in the grimmest of times, as South Africans, we can cling to the truth that, deep down, the overwhelming majority of 53 million citizens are fundamentally good people who desperately want this 'rainbow nation' to prosper and succeed, to settle into stability, and that, eventually, this collective desire will prevail.

If it is the *gees* and the spirit of the people that motivates and inspires me, it is the sight and feel of the land that sustains and nourishes me, the smell of African soil.

Every minute spent in the bush is a blessing.

When I was young, we used to visit the Kruger Park as a family. We would stay in a rondavel in one of the camps, and drive around the park in a Volkswagen camper van, looking for animals. As the youngest brother eager to prove myself, I found it almost impossible to resist the temptation of triumphantly declaring I had spotted, say, a lion or a buffalo, when in fact I hadn't seen anything. I think I was quite irritating.

I am not so crazy about game drives these days. For me, the greatest pleasure lies in just being in the bush, just enjoying the environment, just being there, feeling close to nature and feeling close to God; and, of course, the entire experience improves dramatically when your cellphone can't pick up a signal.

In recent years, I have invested in exotic wildlife with my father-in-law, John Swart. We bought some sables and we keep them at a place called Shakama, north of Bela-Bela. The investment works well but it is emotionally even more rewarding to watch these remarkable animals grow and to see the herd multiply.

'A World in One Country' was the promotional line used by South African Tourism a few years ago, and they weren't wrong if you consider that, beyond the bush and game parks, South Africa offers coastal cities such as Cape Town and Durban, miles of beautiful beaches, the winelands, the Garden Route, the Drakensberg and much more.

I have got to know the country as a cricketer, not as a tourist.

Pretoria may not be the first place on every visitor's itinerary, but it should not be missed. It's relaxed and calm, and when the jacaranda trees blossom in September and October it puts its best foot forward. From a cricketing point of view, SuperSport Park is my favourite ground in the country.

It's where, in 1995, I watched the Proteas for the first time. It's where my father bought me the Jonty Rhodes cap, which became the most prized possession of my childhood. It's where I have always seemed to score runs and play reasonably well, and it's where they would always arrange a braai for the players at lunch on the Sunday of the Test match, serving steaks and chops – by far the best food on the South African cricket circuit.

It's also home to the Titans, the provincial franchise that provided me with an important break in the game soon after leaving school, and to which I remain affiliated all these years later.

The unavoidable reality in South Africa is that playing for the national team means you will have very few, if any, opportunities to play for your franchise, and it's a pity I have been such an absentee in recent years. Jacques Faul, the Titans CEO, is one of the brightest cricket administrators in the country and, in years to come, when I have time, I look forward to giving something back to the organisation that first gave me a chance.

Cape Town is generally acclaimed as one of the most beautiful cities in the world. I agree, which is why we bought an apartment in the Mother City. Table Mountain, Kirstenbosch, Clifton, The Twelve Apostles, Hout Bay, Boulders Beach can all be counted among the jewels of the Cape – alongside Newlands cricket ground, a place where exceptional natural beauty is matched by exceptional enthusiasm in the stands.

A full house at Newlands generates the most exhilarating atmosphere of any ground in South Africa and, for me, the New Year Test in the Cape is always the most enjoyable match of the year. The supporters are invariably impassioned and knowledgeable, which may partly explain why, as a team, the Proteas have tended to perform consistently well at Newlands in recent years.

Port Elizabeth should not be underrated. The Eastern Cape city is quiet and dignified, and St George's Park enjoys the distinction of having hosted not only the first cricket Test match played by South Africa but also the first rugby Test match played by the Springboks. These days, the resident brass band always ensures a fun atmosphere and the famous old ground still provides players with probably the best nets in the country.

Durban is warm in winter and very warm in summer, and Kingsmead is one of the most picturesque grounds in the country. Situated a few hundred metres from the Indian Ocean, the pitch can be a mystery. I have scored several centuries there but, for one reason or another, it has generally felt like hard work.

In the heart of the country, in the middle of the Free State, Bloemfontein is a tidy and well-organised city, and Springbok Park is a tidy, well-organised and excellent cricket ground. I have also enjoyed playing in both Kimberley and Potchefstroom, the kinds of places where the facilities are outstanding, the crowds sympathetic and where no one will be remotely bothered if you prefer to walk around without shoes.

The Wanderers Stadium in Johannesburg ranks among the leading cricket stadiums in the world, and the famous old Bullring is some place when a capacity crowd turns up to watch a day-night international. The grandstands seem to tower over the outfield and there is always a great vibe on the grassed bank in front of the changing rooms. The renovated home changing room is the best changing room in the country – maybe even the world.

These are the stadiums where international cricket is played in South Africa; these are the places where, summer after summer, I go to work and, over the years, I have learned to be well prepared.

Some cricketers are notoriously superstitious, and it's also true that the mothers of cricketers can be notoriously superstitious – I understand that my mother insists that nobody is allowed to move while I am batting. But, for some reason, I have never been superstitious at all. I have a few settled routines, but that's all.

A batsman requires a reasonable amount of equipment, so it's important to be organised.

I usually carry four or five bats in my cricket bag and, before each innings, I will look at them and feel them and make a decision on which one to use on any given day. If a bat feels good, I will generally keep using it until it breaks. If it feels really good, I won't use it in the nets – just to make it last as long as possible. A bat can last for a week or a month or a year, and I will mark the top of the handle with a 'W' for warm-up and then 1, 2, 3 and 4.

There are quite a few bats in the garage at home, and one of my regrets is that I didn't write on the bats after I played a significant innings. It would be quite good to know which one is which.

Kookaburra has been kindly supplying me with bats ever since 2000, when I was a 16-year-old schoolboy. It's an Australian company, but the brand is distributed in South Africa by JRT Crampton Ltd, and I have always been helped by Chris Bryant, the kindest and most generous man you could ever wish to meet.

It was Chris who signed my first contract all those years ago and, ever since – whatever I have needed, wherever I have been in the world – he has always made sure I have received everything on time. Nowadays, his daughter, Nicola Ludlow, helps to manage the business, and the service remains outstanding.

Chris also provides me with batting gloves, pads and a thigh pad. There are usually six pairs of gloves in my bag because, if possible, I like to use a new pair for every major match, but the same pair of pads and the same thigh pad will see me through an entire season. Every batsman obviously needs to wear a protective box and, in recent years, I have preferred to wear not one, but two boxes fitted together.

Some batsmen choose to wear various forms of arm protection as well. I don't wear anything on my arm because I don't want the bowler to think I'm worried about being hit. However, I always wear a helmet when batting, even when I am facing slow bowlers, because the ball can still ricochet up and hit my face. As far as I am concerned, anyone who decides not to wear a helmet when batting is not brave ... they're just stupid.

I have grown accustomed to batting with a towel tucked into my waist at the front. I've always had issues with sweat and sensitive eyes, and I use the towel to wipe away the sweat. In fact, I don't feel right when I don't have a towel tucked into my waist – that's about as close to a superstition as I get.

Puma has been providing me with top-quality footwear for as long as I remember, and I always keep both a pair of batting shoes and a pair of fielding shoes in my bag.

Carefully prepared and properly equipped, I am then ready to go out and play for South Africa. That's what I do. I play *for* South Africa. That is, and will always be, the greatest privilege of my life.

What kind of South Africa? In my mind, it's the South Africa described by Alan Paton in his book *Cry, the Beloved Country*, which was published back in 1948. It is, as he wrote, 'a great and peaceful South Africa in which the world will take pride, a nation in which each of many different groups will be making its own creative contribution'.

We have some work to do, but we'll get there.

CHAPTER 10

THE MAGIC CARPET

After a while professional sport can start to feel like a treadmill on which you go around and around, making repeated circuits of the same flights, the same hotels and the same stadiums, playing over and over again against the same opponents, dealing with the same officials and the same journalists, year after year.

Perhaps some degree of monotony is unavoidable and even understandable, but I have always worked hard to approach every match with precisely the same boyish enthusiasm with which I approached every game I played with my brothers and their friends in the garden at 20 Mentz Avenue.

I have never known any other way.

Every match, every home series and tour needed to feel like a peak in its own right, an emotional and physical challenge to be embraced. Play every match as if it is your last, I used to tell myself, because, you never know, it might prove to be exactly that. Nothing can be taken for granted.

Looking back over the past 12 years, I have played a significant volume of cricket: more than 100 Test matches, more than 200 one-day internationals, more than 70 Twenty20 internationals, three ICC Cricket World Cups, three ICC Champions Trophies and no fewer than six ICC World Twenty20 tournaments, many provincial matches with the Titans and nine seasons in the Indian Premier League, initially in

Delhi and latterly in Bengaluru.

If you look back at all this cricket, it *can* start to seem like a treadmill. However, the important point is that I have never looked back. I have always looked resolutely forward, keeping my focus on the next innings, the next match, the next challenge; in my mind, the next task is the only task that ever matters.

Some sports people may be able to master the so-called professional arts of pacing yourself through a long season, preserving energy, even going through the motions at stages, but I have never even located such gears. For me, it's always been full-steam ahead.

The day I lose that boyish enthusiasm for the game will be the day I stop playing. It has not happened yet, and I hope it doesn't happen for a while, but there will be no escape when that day dawns. If I no longer feel engaged and excited by the challenge, there will be no pragmatic decision to keep going. That day may come suddenly, without warning.

For the past 12 years, living the life of an international cricketer has never felt to me like living on a treadmill. On the contrary, it has felt like a wonderful adventure of great days and tough days, of huge challenges and extraordinary experiences. It has felt like a magic carpet ride.

2009

If we believed the Test match victories in Perth and Melbourne at the end of 2008, securing the series win in Australia, would herald a new era of world dominance, we were quickly disappointed. In all my time with the Proteas, we have always competed well against the Australians and have enjoyed a few notable triumphs, but we have never managed to dominate them for a sustained period of time. As a country, as a team, the Aussies always hang in there and always bounce back.

So they regrouped and won the third Test in Sydney and both T20 internationals. We regained some form to secure a 4–1 victory in the ODI series but, as both teams travelled west for the second leg of the summer, a series in South Africa, the momentum was shifting in their favour.

The results don't lie.

The first Test at the Wanderers in Johannesburg: Australia won by 162 runs. The second Test at Kingsmead in Durban: Australia won by 175 runs. We were not being beaten at home; we were being thumped at home, and we travelled to Cape Town hoping to find some salvation, some crumb of consolation in the third Test at Newlands.

My personal form was decent (I had scored a century in Johannesburg), but I was being drawn into conflict with Ashwell Prince. We both wanted to bat at No. 5 but it had become clear one of us would be asked to open. The selectors decided I would keep the place in the middle order and an increasingly public rivalry boiled over the next weekend when we were playing against each other in a match between our respective provincial sides, the Titans and Western Province. Harsh words were spoken on both sides. I regretted the saga because I admired and respected Ashwell as an outstanding cricketer and as an outstanding man.

He responded in the best possible way. When we had dismissed the Australians for 209 in their first innings, he opened our reply and scored a fine century, turning the tide of the series. His efforts created a platform for me to play one of the most satisfying innings of my career. With Jacques Kallis moving serenely towards three figures, I walked out to bat on the second evening and aimed to drive home our advantage.

Saturday, 21 March 2009, dawns bright and sunny at Newlands. Resuming my innings on 39, I am especially keen to do well because I know my father is watching from his seat in the grandstand. He is working as a full-time GP back home in Bela-Bela, which means he rarely has time to watch cricket. However, on this particular day, the dates have worked out and he is here, and I want to impress him.

We lose two early wickets but I manage to survive, reach my hundred with a push past cover and begin to play some strokes. I am batting with Albie Morkel, my good friend, enjoying myself …

Andrew McDonald is running in to bowl his medium pace. I am facing, on 117 not out, feeling confident. I pull the first ball of the over, and it goes for six. I heave at the second ball, and it goes for six. I launch myself into a drive at the third ball, and it soars for six over long-on.

Albie is beaming when we meet in the middle of the pitch.

'Listen,' he says, 'you've got to go for this now. You've got to try to get six sixes in one over.'

'Hold on, Albs,' I reply, 'we're playing Test cricket here, not Twenty20.'

The fourth ball is a little shorter, and I manage to pull it into the crowd at cow corner. That's four sixes from four balls. The crowd is excited, urging me to hit two more sixes and make some history, but it's not meant to be. I charge at the fifth ball, planning to drive it straight, but Andrew sees me coming and bowls a yorker at my feet. I manage to dig out a single past cover point.

Newlands is buzzing and I reach 150 with a full-blooded drive over mid-on. Another boundary, driven through extra cover, takes our score to 623 for seven, South Africa's highest score against Australia. It's becoming a special day. I'm in the zone and everything is going my way.

I am eventually caught on the mid-wicket boundary, out for 163 from 196 balls in just over five hours, including seven sixes and 12 fours. The Cape Town crowd is generous in their appreciation as I head back to the pavilion, but I hear the applause of only one man, the applause of my father. I have scored the ninth Test hundred of my career but it is the first time I've scored a Test century with him in the stadium.

We are eventually bowled out for 651 and, despite Mitchell Johnson's defiant unbeaten century, Paul Harris takes six wickets and guides us to victory by an innings and 20 runs. Our form is maintained when we win both T20 internationals and the ODI series by three matches to two.

These successes in the shorter format of the game inspired general confidence that this team could be successful at the 2009 ICC World Twenty20 tournaments, played in England, and we started our campaign impressively with a 130-run victory over Scotland. Albie Morkel and I had managed to add 50 runs in 19 balls as we made 211 in 20 overs, and Dale Steyn and Wayne Parnell reduced the Scots first to 50 for six and then 81 all out.

With hosts England losing their opening match to the Netherlands at Lord's, cricket writers started to proclaim the Proteas favourites for the title, showing the home side precisely how to dispatch lesser teams and cope with the pressures of playing in a World Cup. Criticism can be dispiriting, I thought, but praise can be significantly more dangerous.

The format of the competition meant our next match, against New Zealand at Lord's, was a dead rubber, but we worked hard to defend a low total and edged a one-run victory. It wasn't pretty, but it was another win, another step on the path to winning an official ICC trophy, on the way to getting rid of our dreaded reputation. Don't mention the C-word.

Moving into the so-called Super Eights, we overcame England at Trent Bridge, and when we defeated the West Indies at The Oval media flattery reached a new level. 'In an unpredictable format,' wrote one journalist, 'the powerful and resolved South Africans look unbeatable.'

A further victory over India at Nottingham, when I contributed 63 runs from 51 balls in a low-scoring contest on a low pitch, was our sixth T20 victory in a row, and we moved towards a semifinal against Pakistan with a growing belief that this would be the tournament when we would hold our nerve, when the little moments would go our way.

Jeremy Snape, our excellent team psychologist, even dared to mention the C-word. He told us how the 'chokers' had become the 'stranglers', making reference to our bowlers' ability to exert control, restrict the run rate and defend relatively low totals. Coach Mickey Arthur was pushing the same messages, that we were a team that had moved on from the disappointments of the past, a team with no fear of losing.

In team meeting after team meeting, in huddle after huddle, we listened, and we believed the mantras. As a group and as individuals, we craved this title. After all the pain, this was our moment, surely.

Shahid Afridi had long been recognised as one of the most gifted players in the game, capable of producing brilliance on one day and something less than brilliance the next. On the slow turner at Nottingham, we had desperately wanted it to be our day; it turned out to be Afridi's day.

He batted at No. 3, drilled his second ball over mid-on for four, scored 51 runs from 34 balls and helped Pakistan reach 149 for four from 20 overs. Our fielding had been excellent throughout the tournament but, on this big day, it had inexplicably frayed at the edges. Never mind, we told ourselves, we can get these runs. Graeme and Jacques opened and took us to 39 after five overs. We needed only to hold our nerve and we would get there, surely.

Graeme was out in the sixth over. Afridi prepared to bowl the seventh. His slider dismissed Herschelle Gibbs, and I joined Jacques at the crease. Saeed Ajmal was bowling well, and conceded only three runs from the eighth over. Afridi prepared to bowl the ninth. Jacques took a single from the first ball. I pushed at a leg break, gave a chance and was dropped by the wicketkeeper. Stay calm. Maybe this would be our day. Afridi ran in again. I aimed to cut. It was the slider. I was bowled.

Suddenly, at 50 for three, we were in trouble. Jacques and JP Duminy steadied the innings, consolidated and kept us in contention until we needed 45 runs from the last four; then the target was 39 from the last three. I could barely bear to watch from the dug-out.

Albie Morkel went out to bat when Jacques was caught at long-on, and we required 29 from the last two overs. It was tough. One big over would make the difference, taking us to the final where we wanted to be, where we had imagined we would be; but the one big over never came.

The 19th over was going to be crucial and Umar Gul, the Pakistani fast bowler, delivered a series of impeccable yorkers. We only scored six runs.

An unlikely 23 runs were required from the last over and, although JP did his best and fought till the end, we finished seven runs short.

Our dressing room was very quiet afterwards. Nobody said the C-word. Nobody needed to say the C-word. Each player sat alone with his thoughts, coping with the knowledge that his family and friends would be sharing the gut-wrenching disappointment at home, realising that cricket fans around the world would be thinking the Proteas had choked again.

Mickey remained wholly positive. 'OK, it didn't go our way today,' he said, 'but we've played some fantastic cricket here and this team needs to look forward. We're going to host the ICC Champions Trophy tournament in South Africa in September and we'll be ready.'

He was right, of course, and the stage was set, surely. We were ranked the No. 1 ODI team in the world, and were playing at home, with each of our three pool matches scheduled for SuperSport Park in Centurion. At last, the dice were loaded in our favour, surely. This was our time, surely.

Sri Lanka were our first opponents, and we ran into Tillakaratne Dilshan, who crashed 106 off 92 balls and helped his team to reach a total of 319 in 50 overs. Graeme led from the front again, but our pursuit lacked conviction and, almost literally, dissolved in the rain that fell in the evening. In the end, we were well beaten by 55 runs on the Duckworth/ Lewis method. Where we had anticipated excited euphoria, we found damp disappointment.

The weather had scarcely improved when we played New Zealand at the same venue two days later and, under grey skies, the Kiwis batted first and scrambled to 214, something for them to defend.

Ideally, in such situations, in such tournaments, the Proteas would return to their dressing room, chase a reasonable target with the minimum fuss and get the job done. In that perfect world, bowlers would bowl and batters would bat, we would all field with intensity and that would be that.

Unfortunately, when the Proteas compete in an official ICC tournament, it is far from a perfect world. It is far from perfect because, whether we like it or not, whatever any of us say, we do carry the burden of history. It is far from perfect because, at any given moment, as individuals and as a team, we tend to feel strangled by the pressure and the weight of expectation, and what should be easy can suddenly feel almost impossible.

Golfers know all about the 'yips', a movement disorder that makes straightforward short putts suddenly appear terrifyingly difficult. Something seems to scramble the brain and even established professionals have been known to suffer the 'yips' and take five or six shots to get down from two or three feet from the pin. At times over the years, it has felt as though the Proteas, as a team, have experienced a kind of collective 'yips' in ICC tournaments.

Back in Centurion, I told myself to get my mind right. We needed to reach the target of 215 to beat New Zealand and remain in the 2009 ICC Champions Trophy. And for once, we did go out and get the job done. Hashim and Jacques played well, I scored an unbeaten 70 and, in a surge of relief, we eased over the line with almost nine overs to spare.

OK, we said, let's keep going. We're No. 1 in the world, we're playing at home etcetera, etcetera … and, in a highly competitive pool, we knew we needed to beat England to reach the semifinal. They won the toss and batted first and, with Owais Shah and Eoin Morgan finding form, posted 323.

Graeme Smith led our chase heroically. Gallant and brave beyond words, he batted on when wickets kept falling around him; he batted on when he started to suffer severe cramp and was denied a runner; he batted on and on and simply refused to accept the prospect of defeat. He had moved his score to 141 from 134 balls when he fell in the 47th over … and we fell 22 runs short, beaten by England, bundled out of our own tournament.

Our dressing room was silent again. In black and white, South Africa had hosted three major ICC tournaments on our own soil – the ICC Cricket World Cup in 2003, the World Twenty20 in 2007 and the ICC Champions Trophy in 2009 – and we had not reached a single semifinal.

Andrew Strauss led his England team back to South Africa for a full tour at the end of the year, and we remained frustratingly inconsistent. We lost the first T20 international, but won the next. We lost the first ODI, but won the next on a truly glorious day at Newlands when I managed to score 121 in a winning total of 354. We travelled to play the decider in Port Elizabeth and were dismissed for only 114. The series was lost.

Four Tests and more frustration followed. We should have won the first Test in Centurion, but they held out for the draw on the last day, finishing with nine wickets down. We then collapsed on the fourth afternoon of the second Test in Durban, routed by Graeme Swann, and lost ...

2010

We created another winning position in the third Test at Newlands but again failed to deliver a knockout blow; for the second time in the series, England were nine wickets down at the end and escaped with a draw.

Finally, we completed the task in the fourth Test in Johannesburg when Graeme scored yet another outstanding century. The victory meant the series was drawn, but we knew we really should have won.

After the triumphs of 2008, the disappointments of 2009 had left a sense of annoyance and agitation within the squad. There seemed to be more than enough ability and experience in our dressing room for the team to dominate all formats of the game, and yet, now and then, for no apparent reason, we underperformed and let ourselves down.

It was certainly not Mickey Arthur's fault, but he nonetheless stepped down as coach before our tour to India, to be replaced by Corrie van

Zyl, a knowledgeable and likeable man respected by the players. Notwithstanding the change, our form remained strangely inconsistent.

One week, we were brilliant, winning the first Test in Nagpur by an innings and six runs, with Hashim scoring an unbeaten 253, Jacques making 173 and Dale taking a sensational 10 wickets in the match. The following week, we were less than brilliant, losing the second Test in Kolkata by an innings and 57 runs, even though Hashim sustained his brilliant form by scoring centuries in each innings and leading a rearguard action that came within nine balls of saving the Test at the end of the fifth day.

India's win meant the Test series was drawn, and they duly retained the No. 1 position in the official ICC Test rankings.

Our roller-coaster continued into the three-match ODI series. We went down in Jaipur when we were defeated by a single run and were then whipped in Gwalior when Sachin Tendulkar scored an unbeaten 200 in a total of 401, but our fortunes were revived in Ahmedabad when Jacques and I each scored centuries and we claimed the consolation win.

Another year brought another ICC limited-overs tournament, the World Twenty20 in the Caribbean ... and yet another disappointing experience for the Proteas. We lost to India, defeated first Afghanistan and then New Zealand, but then lost to England and needed to beat Pakistan at the Beauséjour Stadium in Gros Islet to qualify for the semifinals.

On another big occasion, we restricted them to 148 in 20 overs and felt well in the game. Then, inexplicably, we struggled to inject any momentum into our run chase and finished 11 runs short. 'We were just not good enough,' Graeme told the media afterwards. 'I guess we have run out of excuses in this situation. It's very, very disappointing.'

We had failed but, true to character, nine days later, we were playing brilliantly. Remaining in the Caribbean, we started a full tour of the West Indies by winning a T20 international series by two matches to nil and then sweeping an extended ODI series, five matches to nil.

This was more fun, and we maintained our momentum in the Test series, comfortably winning the first Test in Trinidad after we dismissed the home team for 102, drawing the second Test on a flat wicket in St Kitts and sealing the 2–0 series win with a clinical victory in Barbados.

I enjoyed every minute of the tour, hitting the ball consistently well and scoring 102, 41, 70, 57 not out and 13 in the ODI series, followed by 68, 19 not out, 135 not out, 31 not out, 73 and 4 not out in the Test matches. It felt great to be in decent nick, although this success was punctuated by a moment of acute embarrassment during the second Test.

My stomach had begun to rumble as I took my score into the 80s. I wanted to play through the distress but there was no avoiding the anatomical reality that I would need to leave the field and take a toilet break, even though such events are unusually rare in international cricket. I was facing Sulieman Benn. Feeling increasingly pressed for time, I drove to the sweeper on the cover boundary for two, swept a boundary and then reached my tenth Test century with a straight drive into the crowd. Two defensive prods later, at the end of the over, I sheepishly told the umpire I was sorry for any inconvenience, but I really did need to spend some time in the pavilion.

The match had to be stopped for five or six minutes while I left the field – much to the amusement of both players and spectators who seemed to realise what was happening. The general situation was certainly not helped by some of my teammates, who chose to throw a toilet roll at me when I emerged from the pavilion to resume my innings.

Our success in the Caribbean was followed by impressive T20 and ODI series wins at home to Zimbabwe, and spirits within the Proteas squad could hardly have been higher. Since being eliminated from the World Twenty20 with a whimper, we had played 18 international matches in the five and a half months between Wednesday 19 May and Friday 29 October and not lost once, winning 17 games and only drawing the Test in Barbados.

By then we had travelled to the Middle East to play a T20 series, an ODI series and two Test matches against Pakistan in the United Arab Emirates (UAE), their home away from home.

Our extraordinary winning streak continued with victories in both T20 internationals and the first one-day international before, on 31 October in Abu Dhabi, we appeared to be cruising to another decisive win when Abdul Razzaq rescued his side with an innings of 109 from 72 balls.

Undeterred, we travelled an hour down the road to Dubai, won the third ODI, narrowly lost the fourth and then won the fifth to secure victory by three matches to two. The team was settled and successful – Amla, Smith, Kallis, De Villiers, Duminy, Ingram, Botha, Peterson, Morkel, Steyn and Tsotsobe – and our minds started to turn towards the challenge, and the opportunity, of the 2011 Cricket World Cup just three months away.

First, we prepared to play two Tests against Pakistan in the UAE. We would certainly have won the first Test in Dubai if we had held our catches, but we were ultimately denied by Younus Khan's resolute century on the fifth day, and the match ended in a draw.

The second Test was played at the Sheikh Zayed Stadium in Abu Dhabi and, having been sent in to bat, we found ourselves in serious trouble at 33 for three on the first morning. Jacques and I remained at the crease, weathered the storm and gradually dragged our team back into the match. Jacques reached his century in the evening, but fell just before stumps.

There was work to be done on the second day, Sunday, 21 November. I woke early and called home to wish my mother a happy birthday, and said I wanted to make it a special day for her.

So we continued to advance our total. Umar Gul was not happy and spent most of the morning chuntering about a decision that had gone against him the previous evening. The Pakistanis were bowling well and it was proving a difficult wicket, but I continued to make progress, and reached 150 by working the ball off my hip through mid-wicket.

Wickets kept falling at the other end, but nobody gave anything away. Dale Steyn batted for more than an hour, at one point driving the spinner for a straight six, and Paul Harris also fought hard, creating time for me to continue my innings ... and I reached my second double century in Tests by striking two boundaries in one over from the agitated Gul.

Even when Paul fell with the total on 477 for nine and my score on 206, Morné Morkel strode out to the crease, put his head down, worked hard and so enabled me to keep moving towards a milestone.

Graeme Pollock had for many years held the record for the highest score by a South African batsman in Test cricket, and it seemed to many that his epic innings of 274 against Australia at Kingsmead in 1970 would duly stand the test of time. Then Daryll Cullinan scored an unbeaten 275 against New Zealand in Auckland in 1999, a score that was matched by Gary Kirsten, batting against England in Durban later that same year. The record stood for four seasons until, in July 2003, Graeme Smith produced his amazing innings of 277 against England at Edgbaston in Birmingham.

Now, in Abu Dhabi in 2010, as our tenth wicket partnership continued to frustrate the bowlers, I edged nearer and nearer to the record. At one point, I started to wonder whether we were going to declare but Graeme let me keep batting, keep moving towards his record. I passed 250 with a straight drive for six, looked across to where my teammates were sitting, and saw our captain standing and leading the applause.

Morné and I added 91 runs in the 11 overs before tea, and as I walked off the field my thoughts drifted back to our home in Bela-Bela, where I knew my mother was spending her birthday, watching the cricket on television, as usual insisting that nobody move while I was batting.

We resumed after the interval and, eager to reach the landmark and get on with the Test, I drove the third ball of the first over after tea for six, bunted the fourth delivery past the bowler for four and then took a single off the fifth. With Gul bowling the next over, I scrambled two past point and then flicked a single to mid-wicket, and so took my score to 278.

Graeme instantly made the declaration with our total at 584 for nine, but I will always be grateful for his generosity, his willingness to give me my moment in the sun. The feat of setting a new highest score by a South African in Test cricket was an important moment for me and my family, a moment that had seemed unthinkable during all the years when I was simply trying to smack as many boundaries as possible.

Records are made to be broken, of course, and I was also genuinely pleased for Hashim Amla when he duly raised the bar even further by scoring an unbeaten 311 against England at The Oval in 2012.

Both the Test in Abu Dhabi and the series against Pakistan in the UAE were eventually drawn, and our squad returned home to complete the year with an appetising three-Test home series against India.

It was perhaps one of the strangest anomalies in international cricket. Jacques Kallis, one of the greatest batsmen of any era, had not scored a double century in a Test match; at least, he hadn't until the first Test match against India at SuperSport Park just before Christmas 2010, and I was thrilled to be batting with him when he set the record straight.

We had dismissed the Indians for 136, with Morné Morkel taking five for 20, and were aiming to bat ourselves into an unassailable position. Graeme and Alviro Petersen delivered an opening stand of 111, and both Hashim and Jacques moved serenely towards their centuries.

Once I joined Jacques at the crease early on the third morning, we set about the task of taking charge of the Test, utterly dominating the attack and enjoying every moment of another wonderful day. I was fortunate to reach my century just before lunch from only 75 balls, the fastest century ever scored by a South African in a Test match but, more importantly, Jacques continued to advance towards his maiden double hundred.

Finally, just after half-past one in the afternoon, he glanced a ball to the fine leg boundary and moved his score to 201. I was thrilled for him, and the Centurion crowd bellowed their approval. Among our many partnerships while representing our country, this ranked among the best.

Graeme declared our innings at 620 for four soon afterwards, and we proceeded to bowl out India for a second time, eventually winning the Test by an innings and 25 runs, despite Sachin's brave century.

The Indians were desperate to retain their ranking as the No. 1 Test team in the world, and they predictably fought back to win the second Test in Durban, coming out on top in a low-scoring contest in which only VVS Laxman managed to score more than 50 runs. The teams headed to play the third Test in Cape Town with the series poised at 1–1.

2011

The giants of the game came out to play at Newlands. Jacques made a big hundred in our first innings, then Sachin made a big hundred in their first innings before Jacques made another hundred in our second innings. Batting under pressure, the Indians held their nerve and held on, ensuring that both the third Test and the Test series were drawn.

There was little between the sides, and the limited-overs internationals proved just as competitive, with India winning the T20 match and the Proteas winning the first ODI, then narrowly losing the second and third, but recovering to win both the fourth and fifth to secure a 3–2 victory.

We were winning and, as the squad prepared to fly to participate in the 2011 ICC Cricket World Cup to be played in India, Pakistan and

Bangladesh, South Africans dared to hope again. Around the country, in the big cities and small towns, in the schools and the offices, quietly, people began to wonder aloud whether this time, this time more than any other time, we might just find a way to compete, and realise our potential, and win.

For me, personally, winning an official ICC Cricket World Cup with the South African team had become my burning ambition.

CHAPTER 11

LOOKING EAST

There is an African proverb that says each of us has a decision to make each and every day of our lives. As soon as we wake in the morning, whatever our circumstances, we all have the power to decide whether we look east and see the sunrise or whether we look west and see darkness.

In essence, each of us has the power to decide whether to see the good or the bad in any situation or experience, whether to see the good in people or the bad in people. Apart from extreme circumstances, it seems as if, in everyday life, so much of what we see and feel is ultimately what we choose to see and feel. This applies as much to South African cricket as it does to anything else.

You can review the performance of the Proteas squad over a four-year period between the eve of the 2011 Cricket World Cup and the eve of the 2015 Cricket World Cup, and you can essentially decide whether to see a talented squad that consistently worked hard, that lost only one of 13 series and that very often brought pleasure and pride to millions of their compatriots ... or you can decide to see 'chokers' that failed to triumph at the 2011 World Cup or the 2012 World Twenty20 or the 2013 Champions Trophy or the 2014 World Twenty20.

Everyone makes their own choice.

I choose to look east. I choose to recall winning series in both England and Australia in 2012, defeating Pakistan at home and away in 2013 and winning a series in Sri Lanka in 2014. I choose to remember the good days, the great occasions and experiences in many parts of the world. Beyond the results, beyond the matches won and lost, I reflect upon so many golden seasons spent playing cricket alongside so many wonderful people ... wonderful people who became wonderful teammates and eventually wonderful friends.

When Albie and Morné Morkel were named among SA Cricket's five players of the year in 2008, they became the first brothers to receive the award in the same season since Athol and Eric Rowan in 1952. South African cricket has a distinguished history of celebrated brothers: Peter and Graeme Pollock excelled in the 1960s and 70s, Peter and Gary Kirsten thrived in the 1980s and 90s, and the Morkels have illuminated our era.

As far as I can recall, their names were first mentioned in sporting circles in 1996. The Morkels had long been recognised as one of the most prominent families in South African sport, ever since they supplied half of the Springbok rugby team in the 1920s. One branch of the family settled in Vereeniging, where Vat Morkel was an outstanding teacher at a local high school and his sons Albert and Gerard were, respectively, a professional cricketer in the Transvaal Country Districts team and the national discus champion.

The talent was unquestionably in the genes. Albert duly married Mariana, and they produced three sons: Malan, who dismissed Brian Lara while playing for a Gauteng XI in 1998, Albie and Morné.

I met Morné, the youngest brother, first, in an Under-13 match between Transvaal and Northerns at St John's College in Johannesburg. Transvaal batted first and didn't score many. We reached their total reasonably quickly and won the game, but our coach asked if we could continue batting for the rest of our overs.

Since I was scoring freely at the time, I was very eager to carry on, but I saw the tall Transvaal fast bowler was not as happy. He had had enough, seemed close to tears and wanted to go home.

My first meeting with Albie occurred when I was a 15-year-old school-boy and he was playing for the South African Under-19 team; he was a dominant all-rounder who could bowl fast and hit the ball further than anyone else.

As the years passed, the three of us began playing in the same matches and tournaments, generally as teammates, sometimes as opponents, and we got along well. Soon after we started playing for the Titans, we decided to rent a place in Equestria, a suburb east of Pretoria, and to stay together.

Those were great days, and we enjoyed many afternoons and evenings, and late nights and early mornings, when we would braai and have a few beers, and chat. We were almost inseparable, driving together to practices and matches, and to the airport to catch flights ... and so our cricketing and social lives continued until one day Albie announced that he and his long-time girlfriend, Marthmari, were getting married.

'That's not a problem,' Morné and I chorused. 'We don't have an issue if she moves in with us.'

I'm not exactly sure what we were thinking, other than that we didn't want our living arrangements to change, and the four of us did live together for a while until Albie put his foot down and said we should move out of the flat and give him and his new wife some space. Somewhat reluctantly, Morné and I found a place to rent 600 metres down the road but, as the weeks passed, even living this distance from our former flat-mate proved intolerable. Within six months, we moved again and rented the apartment next door to Albie and Marthmari.

Albie produced many fantastic performances for South Africa, with both bat and ball, playing in 108 limited-overs internationals between 2004 and 2015, but the position of all-rounder is notoriously difficult to retain in any international ODI or T20 team simply because the expectations are so unrealistic. People reckon you should win the match almost every time you bat and almost every time you bowl.

You typically bat at No. 7, arriving at the crease when there are runs required off very few overs, so you must swing for glory and be a hero ... or people will say you failed.

And you typically bowl at a stage of the innings when the other team is trying to accelerate, so you either take wickets and exert control and be a hero ... or people will say you failed.

There's rarely any middle ground, which explains why every limited-overs side desperately craves an all-rounder and why there are so few all-rounders who have achieved longevity in the game. Albie is one of them, and it is to his great credit that he fulfilled this role for the Proteas for as long as he did.

Morné has been one of the outstanding fast bowlers in the world for as long as I can remember. Standing four centimetres short of two metres, he has run in and run in over and over again, year after year, consistently troubling the world's best batsmen, finding pace and bounce in almost any pitch. He's also a nuisance to face in the nets, but a physical challenge every now and then never did anybody any harm.

He has produced many, many match-winning spells, occasions when he raced in and literally ripped out the top order of the opposing team. I remember one match at the WACA in Perth, in November 2014, when he seemed to be almost unplayable, claiming five Australian wickets for only 21 runs.

Like most fast bowlers, Morné believes he's an underrated batsman and he has contributed vital runs at vital times in all formats of the game, but his most memorable moment as an international batsman probably remains the incident during the Test against England at The Oval in 2008, when he seemed so disappointed at being caught at short leg that, as he left the crease, head bowed, he walked in the wrong direction.

If you google 'Morné Morkel Oval wrong direction' you can see the clip where he gets out and strides towards the groundsman's shed, realises his error, sees the pavilion away to his left and has to clamber past rows of spectators in the stands before he eventually reaches our dressing room. Aside from this lapse, Morné's sense of direction has been almost perfect over all these years. He has been a great teammate and friend.

2011

The ODI series win over India in January ensured that the Proteas travelled to compete in the 2011 ICC Cricket World Cup with the increasingly familiar blend of confidence in a strong squad and hope that we would play to our full potential. The tournament was being played in India, Sri Lanka and Bangladesh, where we had performed well in the past and, led by Graeme Smith, we were again named among the favourites for the title.

As usual, the format of the quadrennial showpiece event was forgiving, with 14 teams divided into two round-robin groups of seven teams each – the top four in each group advancing to the quarterfinals. Some said the format had been designed to fill television schedules rather than fill anyone with excitement but, as a mere player, I could not possibly comment.

From the perspective of one of the main cricket nations, the event amounted to a period of four weeks' travelling around the subcontinent, knowing you probably needed only to defeat the two minor countries in your group and win one of the other four games to reach the knockout phase. Then, just like seven other teams, you would need to win three knockout matches to win the title and become 'world champions'.

Our campaign began with a hiccup when, during the ceremony before our opening match against the West Indies in Delhi, the playing of a recording of the South African national anthem was suddenly cut short, apparently by some technical fault. In a moment when many teams might have looked around, felt uncomfortable and even giggled, this Proteas team didn't miss a beat. We sang our anthem through to the end.

The impromptu 'a cappella' demonstrated our spirit; one glance at our team demonstrated the ability within our squad: Graeme and Hashim as openers, followed by Jacques, me, JP and Faf, with Johan Botha and Robin Peterson as all-rounders, Dale and Morné leading the pace attack and Imran Tahir as the spinner.

We felt confident and we played in a confident manner, decisively defeating the West Indies in Delhi, overcoming the Netherlands in Mohali, losing narrowly to England in Chennai, but recovering our form to defeat India in Nagpur and secure convincing wins over Ireland and Bangladesh. With five wins from our six group matches, we finished in first place in Group B, and progressed purposefully to the quarterfinals.

I was keeping wicket, a job that was not my first preference, but which I was prepared to do for the team and, as a batsman, quietly, I felt in great nick – maybe the best form of my life.

Chasing 223 against the West Indies, I had come in at 20 for two and managed to score 107 from 105 balls, building a partnership with JP and guiding us to victory with seven overs to spare. Batting first against the Dutch, we were wobbling at 58 for two when Hashim and I added 221 for the third wicket. Hash scored 113 and I made 134 from 98 balls, enabling us to post what proved a match-winning total of 351 in our 50 overs.

Our match against India was billed as a highlight of the tepid group phase, and few were disappointed. Tendulkar scored a fine century, Virender Sehwag and Gautam Gambhir also scored runs, and the home team powered to 267 for one with 10 overs remaining. Our bowlers then staged an almost unbelievable fightback, taking nine wickets for 29 runs in the space of nine overs, dismissing India for a still-competitive total of 296.

It was hot. It was noisy. It was intense. We knew we would have to bat well, and we did. Hash and Jacques laid the ideal foundation. I was pleased to contribute 52 in 39 balls, injecting momentum into the run chase at an important stage, and Faf and Robin took us over the line with two balls to spare.

We were collectively exhilarated to have beaten India. In that changing room, in the aftermath of that important win, we truly believed we could win the World Cup. I had strained a quad muscle while running between the wickets, so I sat out our last two group matches, a convincing win over Ireland and a ruthless rout of Bangladesh, in which we dismissed the co-hosts in front of their own spectators for just 78.

In great form and in great spirits, we were looking forward to playing New Zealand in the quarterfinal in Dhaka ... although, to be honest, in the press conference on the day before the game, we probably should not have told the world how much we wanted to play the Kiwis. They might have scrambled to finish fourth in Group A, but our eager over-confidence ensured they would not lack motivation on the field.

New Zealand won the toss and batted, and Jesse Ryder helped them reach 221 for eight in their 50 overs. Our bowlers had performed well and, in the break, we felt the target was well within reach. We simply needed to keep our nerve and bat properly and, barring catastrophe, we would reach the last four.

Hashim was unlucky to be caught at slip after the ball bounced off the wicketkeeper's foot, but Jacques and Graeme steadied the chase and took us to 69 for one in the 15th over. Jacques and I then settled together, moving our score to 108 for two. We were both playing well and, by the end of the 24th over, we were precisely where we wanted to be, needing only 114 more runs from 26 overs.

Then, within the space of 15 minutes, Jacques connected with a sweet pull shot but picked out the tallest fielder in the New Zealand team and was well caught on the boundary by Jacob Oram on the run, JP was bowled and, two balls later, Faf worked his second ball towards mid-wicket and called me for a quick single. I responded, and ran, and dived, but was caught short of the crease, run out for 35 from 40 balls.

Tempers started to fray. Kyle Mills, New Zealand's 12th man, brought out drinks as I was leaving the field and took it upon himself to start

abusing Faf about the run out. Faf shoved him away and was immediately surrounded by a posse of animated, swearing New Zealanders. It
was ugly and unnecessary. It felt as though the world had gone crazy in
every possible way and, amid the chaos, our dreams were fading.

We had been reduced to 121 for five. The New Zealanders were buzzing, bowling and fielding brilliantly, and we were eventually dismissed
for 172, defeated by 49 runs, eliminated from the World Cup we had
believed we could win, left to confirm our early flights home, universally
condemned as 'chokers', again.

'When the team gets off the plane back home,' Graeme said, 'daggers
and stones will be thrown.'

Some, but not all, of the wounds healed in the seven months that
elapsed between the Disaster in Dhaka and the arrival of the Australian
squad to tour South Africa in October 2011.

Gary Kirsten was appointed to succeed Corrie van Zyl as Proteas
coach and I was asked to take over as captain of the national side in limited-overs cricket, with Graeme continuing to lead the Test team. I knew
I had a lot to learn, and I recognised I had been chosen primarily because
of my performances as a player, but I was determined to embrace the
challenge.

The 'new era' suffered an unfortunate false start when I sustained a
broken finger during fielding practice with Royal Challengers Bangalore
at the Champions League T20 tournament, and was ruled out of the T20
series against the Australians, which was shared, and the three-match
ODI series, which we lost 1–2.

Two epic Test matches followed.

In Cape Town, Australia batted first on what seemed a reasonable
wicket at Newlands and scored 284, including an extraordinary innings
of 151 by Michael Clarke, their captain. Graeme and Jacques Rudolph
launched our reply reasonably well, but we proceeded to collapse in the
most spectacular and embarrassing fashion, from 49 for one to 96 all out

in the space of 11 madcap overs; we were chastened and humiliated.

The daggers and stones were probably being reloaded, but in cricket – as in life – whenever tempted to condemn, it is often wise just to pause for a moment and reserve judgement.

Australia started their second innings and were promptly routed by the swing and seam of Vernon Philander, who was making his Test debut, and Morné Morkel. The mighty Aussies, the renowned battlers in baggy green caps whom we had never beaten in a home Test series since readmission, were reduced to four for one, 11 for two, 13 for three, 13 for four, 15 for five, and then 18 for six, 21 for seven, 21 for eight and 21 for nine.

They were still short of the lowest total in the history of Test cricket (26 scored by New Zealand against England in Auckland in 1955), but their last pair of Peter Siddle and Nathan Lyon ensured they passed that total and batted on, until I caught Lyon off Dale's bowling. Australia had been dismissed for 47.

Batting looked almost impossible and a target of 236 to win seemed a long shot, but Graeme and Hash launched our chase and restored normality. Each scored a century and we won by eight wickets.

The second Test in Johannesburg proved no less exciting.

At first we seemed well set at 241 for four but collapsed to 266 all out. In reply, Phil Hughes and Shane Watson shared an opening stand of 174, but they also lost wickets quickly and were dismissed for 296.

The match was beautifully poised when we started our second innings and, although we teetered for a moment at 90 for three, Hash and I built a partnership and, moving on to 237 for three, appeared on the brink of taking the game away from the tourists, ensuring we could not lose and so securing the series win.

It was all there for the taking and, in all honesty, we should have closed the deal. We didn't. For the second time in the Test, to my intense frustration, I got out when well set, and yet again, the Australians kept battling, kept taking wickets and somehow found a way to stay in the contest, eventually dismissing us for 339.

There was a perceptible sense of irritation in our dressing room but, we thought, maybe it wasn't too bad. We should be OK. In the history of Test cricket at the Wanderers Stadium, no team had ever scored 310 in the fourth innings to win the match. The weight of history was on our side. We simply needed to bowl properly and hold our catches, and we did that on the fourth afternoon, with Vernon running in hard and dismissing Watson and Hughes, reducing Australia to 19 for two. Ricky Ponting and Usman Khawaja stuck around for a while but, after the latter fell to Imran's googly just before stumps, the tourists reached the close at 142 for three, with Ponting still fighting, unbeaten on 54, and Clarke on one not out.

Sporadic rain delayed the start of the fifth and final day, but the skies cleared and, after taking an early lunch, the umpires decided that play would start at 1 pm. We were impatient and excited. As a team and as individuals, we yearned for a home series win over Australia. Let's do this, Graeme said. Let's do this.

We could not have been more motivated and yet, when we eventually ran out to field, the stadium was almost deserted. Only a group of schoolboys was sitting on the grass bank in front of the changing room and our voices were echoing around the Bullring. It didn't matter. There was work to be done …

Vernon rumbled in and clean bowled Clarke. Morné had Ponting caught in the slips. Vernon trapped Mike Hussey LBW and the Australians seemed to be subsiding at 215 for six. Four more wickets, that's all we needed. But the Australians did not subside. Haddin and Johnson battled on, and reached tea at 222 for six, with 88 runs required.

All three results were possible. As the tension increased, the last session started with two boundaries off Philander and then two boundaries off Steyn. After almost five days of intense cricket, after so many twists and turns, the Test and the series remained in the balance. Every single run really did count.

We desperately needed a wicket. Mitchell Johnson stroked Imran for two boundaries through the off-side. The score moved to 276 for six, and just 34 were needed when we took the second new ball. This was our chance, and Haddin finally feathered a catch to Boucher. Siddle came in and hit a boundary, but then fell to Dale. Was the momentum shifting again? They were 292 for eight, still 18 runs short, and we required two more wickets.

Pat Cummins, aged 18, arrived at the crease with a grand total of 27 runs in first-class and limited-overs cricket, and we were swarming all over him. A leading edge produced three more runs. Up in the media seats, a journalist typed into his laptop: 'Four seasons of IPL cricket have not produced anything like this.'

The margins were tiny and, after surviving a series of close calls, Johnson and Cummins took their team to 310, securing a victory that Clarke described as 'unbelievable'. The series was drawn 1–1 …

There are plenty of knowledgeable people in the game who seriously doubt whether Test cricket will be played a decade or so from now. It may have been an epic Test at the Wanderers, they would say, but the last day was played in an almost-empty stadium and, ultimately, there will be no Tests if there is no crowd.

Personally, I am not overly concerned about the future of Test cricket. The commercial reality that ODIs and T20s draw large crowds and generate 95% of the revenue is clear, but the popularity of limited-overs cricket does not mean there is no room for Tests, particularly when the entertainment remains as exceptional as it was at Wanderers in 2011, and when the longer format of the game continues to be enjoyed by a core audience.

Go to Newlands for the New Year Test, or watch the Christmas and New Year Tests in Australia, or attend any Test match played in

England, and you will find committed spectators enjoying Test cricket. Many people predicted the end of roast beef when hamburgers came on the market. Those fears were misplaced because, while the mass market loves the convenience of fast food, a significant core audience still cherishes the real thing.

In my view, Test cricket will continue to be played for many decades to come, played in daylight hours, played with a red ball and played in white clothing. It will continue because it remains the preferred format of a strong group of spectators, whose numbers are not declining and whose passion is not diminishing. I count myself as a member of this audience, and I will be watching Test cricket for many years after I stop playing.

The Australians left for home after a two-Test series, and, strangely, the Sri Lankans then arrived to play a three-Test series. The summer schedule seemed lopsided, but players are not encouraged to worry about such matters. We simply focus on the next match.

We were working ourselves into a dominant position in the first Test at SuperSport Park, and I had moved my score on to 99 when, facing Thisara Perera, I cut the ball firmly towards point where it appeared to be caught by the substitute fielder, Dimuth Karunaratne. I didn't know whether the ball had carried and thought the umpires would call for clarification from their colleague watching a replay upstairs.

Instead umpire Rod Tucker, of Australia, asked me if I wanted a review.

'No,' I replied, 'let's ask the fielder.'

I reckoned we should follow the Jacques Kallis method of dealing with such situations, putting the onus on the fielder to make an honesty call, trusting the 'spirit of cricket' above the technology.

'Did you catch it?'

'Yes,' he replied.

'Are you sure?'

'Yes,' he replied.

Fair enough, I thought. He had no doubts, so I turned and headed back to the pavilion, disappointed to have been dismissed one run short of a century.

Under these circumstances, it was frustrating to watch a replay of the incident later in the day and to see that, in fact, beyond any doubt, the ball had bounced before it was grasped by the fielder. So much for the spirit of cricket, I muttered. In future, I resolved, I would leave the decisions to technology.

We won the Test at Centurion, but then lost in Durban and approached the decider in Cape Town.

2012

For all our talent and ability, we had not actually won a home Test series since 2008. That was the fact. We had drawn five, and we could have – and should have – won most of them. However, it was high time we nailed down a series win in front of our own supporters, and we duly did so, batting with conviction against Sri Lanka at Newlands. Alviro Petersen made a fine 109 and Jacques produced an imperious innings of 224 before we declared at 580 for four.

It had been another special day, and I was pleased to have contributed an unbeaten 160, playing carefully until I reached three figures and then unleashing some flamboyant strokes to entertain the capacity crowd: a few cuts, a few lap-shots, a few drives. Everything was going my way, and I enjoyed every minute.

The first match of the ODI series was played in Paarl, and I captained the team for the first time. I worked hard to prepare properly, tried to think through various scenarios and was relieved when everything seemed to go well. Our plans seemed to work, and we won – and we won in East London, and we won in Bloemfontein.

With the series win sealed at 3–0, the tourists won the fourth and fifth matches, with Kumar Sangakkara scoring a brilliant century as his team successfully chased 313 to win at the Wanderers; he is a high-quality cricketer and a high-quality person, a fine ambassador for his country respected throughout the game.

Next stop ... New Zealand.

The game had moved on from the days when a single touring squad would arrive in a country and play a Test series followed by one-day internationals. In 2012, one Proteas side played New Zealand in three T20 internationals, and won the series 2–1. A significantly different Proteas team played the hosts in three one-day internationals, and won 3–0. And then a third Proteas side set about the challenge of playing three Tests.

Of the team that started the first T20 international at the Westpac Stadium in Wellington on Friday, 17 February, only three players – Amla, Morné Morkel and me – were retained and included in the team selected to play in the first Test match at Dunedin's University Oval 19 days later. The rest flew home.

The horses-for-courses selection strategy recognised the twin realities that, first, certain specialist players were better suited to certain formats of the evolving game and that, second, the physical demands of playing in every single international match were stretching some of the more mature players. Even so, something was lost amid the technical and physiological rationale.

The type of international tour that had once seemed such an adventure for a tight-knit group of 16 players, who were bonded by embracing so many different experiences in so many different places, had been transformed into some kind of military operation where, almost every day, someone would pack their bags and take a taxi to the airport and someone else would arrive, bleary eyed, carrying their suitcase into the hotel foyer.

With all the comings and goings, it was increasingly difficult to predict who would be sitting beside you at breakfast the next morning, but the level of performance remained consistent.

The first Test was drawn in arctic temperatures in Dunedin, and we worked hard to win a closely contested second Test on a difficult pitch in Hamilton, where I scored an important 83 in our first innings and Vernon Philander continued his irrepressible form, taking a total of 10 wickets in the match.

In the third Test at the revered Basin Reserve in Wellington, we batted first, secured a 200-run first-innings lead and then scored briskly to leave enough time to dismiss the hosts and win the match. Traditionalist eyebrows were raised when I executed my first-ever reverse sweep off a fast bowler in a Test match, hitting a ball from Doug Bracewell over the head of gully away to the boundary at third man.

'That stroke doesn't belong in Test cricket,' someone wrote afterwards.

I disagreed. JP and I were going well, doing whatever we could to score as swiftly as possible to set up a winning position. In my mind, there are no such things as 'correct' strokes and 'incorrect' strokes; there is an infinite range of available strokes, each carrying different levels of risk and reward. The skill of any batsman lies in selecting the right stroke at the right moment. In this match at the Basin Reserve, the reverse sweep seemed the right stroke at the right moment – and, with respect, it did go for four.

Our plans were falling into place, and we may well have secured the win if we had held our catches, including one relatively straightforward chance that I dropped in the slips. Even though it was unbelievably cold, even though it was difficult to keep any kind of feeling in your fingers, even though many of us in the slip cordon were desperately hoping the ball would not come anywhere near us, we should have held our catches.

Kane Williamson scored a defiant century on the fifth day, providing an early indication of his potential to become one of the outstanding batsmen in world cricket, and helped his team hold out for the draw, eventually reaching the close with six wickets down. Even so, we were pleased to have prevailed against tough opposition in tough conditions, completing a notable trifecta in winning the T20 series, ODI series and Test series.

In cricket – as in rugby – there has always been, and there remains, a strong bond between South Africans and New Zealanders. In temperament, in general outlook, in an inherent determination to guts it out and be courageous, the two sporting communities seem to have much in common. The contest is always fierce, and there are often flashpoints of temper, but there remains an underlying mutual respect on both sides.

The Black Caps are my favourite and most respected opponents in international cricket; you could say they are my No. 2 team. Characterised by such celebrated players as Brendon McCullum and Daniel Vettori, they are never less than highly competitive on the field and they are invariably great people off the field.

Next stop … England, via the Swiss Alps.

Sports administrators often receive criticism, some of it deserved, but credit should be given when credit is due, and credit was due to Cricket South Africa for accepting Gary Kirsten's unusual proposal and finding the budget for us to prepare for the England tour by holding a training camp with explorer Mike Horn in Switzerland.

Mike is a special person, who has accomplished many remarkable achievements, such as taking six months to swim the 6 992 kilometres from the source to the mouth of the Amazon River and walking to the North Pole in the middle of winter in 61 days of total darkness. His extraordinary energy and enthusiasm as a leader and guide combined with the breathtaking scenery of summer in the Alps to create a magical experience.

Each evening he regaled us with tales of his experiences, underlining the value of daring to have big dreams and of taking enough time to prepare meticulously. He never preached to us, preferring to engage us with his anecdotes and leave us to draw our own conclusions.

Our days were filled with challenges such as rock climbing, walking across ice fields and sliding down waterfalls, but it is the second day that stands out in my memory.

With each of us kitted out in Gore-Tex from head to toe and wearing snow boots, we undertook a three-hour hike through deep snow to the summit of a 3 300-metre peak and continued with an undulating, tiring walk back to the base camp, where we found a truck fully loaded with mountain bikes.

'OK,' Mike announced, 'we're going to cycle over that mountain back to the hotel.'

We gazed up at the peak right in front of us and decided he was joking. Right? No, he was serious. Mike jumped on his bike and told us to follow. What ensued was the most physically demanding experience of my life. We cycled up a steep track for more than ten kilometres – on and on, up and up, pushing ourselves and each other further than we would have imagined possible, getting to a point where we thought we could go no further, and yet carrying on.

When we reached the summit, we expected an easy free-wheel descent down the other side, but we were wrong again. The path down to the village was so steep that several of us decided it would be wiser to carry our bikes and continue the journey on foot. Others opted to cycle, and I saw Alviro Petersen tumble forward over his handlebars and fall so hard that I doubted he would be able to continue. He did.

We were being tested together, and we were going to get the job done together. By the time I arrived back at our hotel, I had rarely felt so exhausted, and rarely felt so exhilarated. As a squad of professional cricketers, we had been taken to places we had never been before, and the experience yielded instant results. Properly prepared and motivated, we were ready to overcome.

The tour began with a warm-up match against Somerset in Taunton, and our planning was rocked by the freakish eye injury, described in an earlier chapter, that forced a premature end to Mark Boucher's distinguished career. Gary Kirsten and Graeme asked me to take over as wicketkeeper, and we carried on.

Properly prepared and motivated, we also played some outstanding cricket.

We won the first Test at The Oval by an innings and 12 runs. After starting slowly on the first day, we increased our intensity on the second day, reducing England from 271 for three to 385 all out. We then batted and batted to reach 637 for two declared, with Graeme making 131, Jacques scoring an unbeaten 182 and Hashim making an epic 311 not out. The home side was deflated, dismissed for 240 and defeated.

To have so comprehensively won a Test match against an England team standing at No. 1 in the Test rankings, and to have lost only two wickets in the process, was an amazing achievement.

Headingley in Leeds is one of my favourite grounds, partly because I have always seemed to score runs there and partly because of the atmosphere generated on the Western Terrace but, in the second Test of 2012, Kevin Pietersen's brilliant century put us on the back foot and we were content to settle for a draw.

The third and final Test was played at Lord's, an exceptional sporting arena rightly known as the home of cricket and renowned for its outstanding atmosphere and stands, ranging from the famous Victorian red-brick pavilion to the remarkable giant space ship of a Media Centre perched at the Nursery End.

In my view, Lord's stands apart because, from the moment they arrive at the ground, players are made to feel so important and valued. Everyone is helpful and attentive – and the lunches always used to be the finest in world cricket, with four main meals and prawns on offer, followed by an amazing array of puddings.

For some reason or another, I haven't managed to score many runs there, and my fortunes didn't change as this decisive Test unfolded as a closely contested arm wrestle. We made 309, after recovering from 105 for five. They made 315 in their first innings after getting into trouble at 54 for four. Another century by Hashim, with some support from me and the lower order, enabled us to reach 351, eventually setting England a target of 346 to win the Test and level the series.

Vernon Philander was producing yet another remarkable performance. He had contributed invaluable scores of 61 and 35 with the bat, and took five for 30 in the England second innings. We survived a scare when Matt Prior looked as if he could inspire a successful chase, but we held our nerve and won by 51 runs.

The 2–0 series victory meant we displaced England as the No. 1 team in the Test rankings. As far as many of us were concerned, the seeds of our triumph had been sown far away in the Swiss Alps.

The ODI series was drawn 2–2, and our victory in a T20 international in Durham offered encouragement that we could move on and mount a strong bid to prevail in the next challenge.

Next stop … the ICC World Twenty20 in Sri Lanka.

I was certainly busy, captaining the team, batting at No. 4 and keeping wicket, and we appeared to be gathering momentum when we defeated Zimbabwe and won a rain-reduced seven-over shootout against the hosts, but our form ebbed away. We were on course to beat Pakistan, but found a way to lose the match, and we were then well beaten by Australia, blown away by an extraordinary Shane Watson innings. We lost our last match against India by a single run, a close finish to end a dismal day when both teams were eliminated from the tournament.

'AB, we should go to the press conference,' said Lerato Malekutu, our outstanding media officer.

My heart sank at the prospect. I enjoyed almost every aspect of captaining the national team, even though I was making mistakes and still learning ... almost every aspect, except addressing the media, especially addressing the media after we had once again been eliminated from an ICC limited-overs tournament.

The C-word was coming, so I addressed the issue before the question was even asked.

'In the big moments, the pressure moments when it mattered, we were found wanting,' I told the journalists. 'We should have closed out that Pakistan game. We know that. It is simple to say but we choked that game. That is a fact. We have to go back and become a better team. There are no excuses.'

The public acknowledgement of failure was not much fun for me, just as it had not been much fun for Graeme Smith, and Shaun Pollock before him, and Hansie Cronjé before him. It will never be much fun until a Proteas team finally goes out and wins one of these ICC limited-overs tournaments. That will happen one day.

For us, in 2012, as ever, there was another series and another challenge around the corner.

Next stop ... a three-Test tour of Australia.

Towards the end of what had been a long year on the road, when we had won in New Zealand and in England and risen to No. 1 in the rankings, we approached the first Test in Brisbane with confidence and our excellent form continued as centuries by Hashim and Jacques helped us to a first-innings total of 450.

The team was looking so settled and strong – Smith and Petersen, Amla, Kallis, De Villiers, Duminy and Rudolph, Philander, Steyn, Kleinveldt and Morkel – and, even after the second day was lost to rain, we maintained the pressure and had the Australians reeling at 40 for three. If Ed Cowan had been dismissed cheaply – instead of escaping because Morné was judged to have bowled a no ball – we might have moved into a strong position.

Instead, the home side took heart and fought back. Cowan made 136, Michael Clarke scored a magnificent 259 not out, and Mike Hussey made 100. They finally declared at 565 for five, and, instead of pushing for the win, we found ourselves batting to save the Test on the fifth day, which we duly did.

Some experts said we should have gone hard for the jugular when we had the chance, persisting with the familiar refrain that the Proteas have been unnecessarily negative; they seemed to forget we were playing a Test series against Australia in Australia. Nothing was going to be easy and straightforward.

The momentum had shifted and the home side took control of the second Test at the Adelaide Oval, once again recovering from 55 for three to reach 550 all out. David Warner crashed 119 in 112 balls, Michael Clarke scored another double century – a remarkable 230 in 257 balls – and Mike Hussey made 103.

We were under pressure and we needed to fight, which we did. Graeme scored a resolute century; Faf du Plessis was playing his Test debut in place of the injured JP Duminy and contributed an important 78; and Jacques Kallis, coming in at No. 9 with a serious hamstring injury, made 58.

These were tough times, testing times. Good teams look strong and settled when things are going well, but it is only the really good teams that remain strong and settled when things are not going their way. Graeme set the tone, as ever, and, collectively, we prepared to draw on all our reserves of courage.

Sometimes simple guts are just not enough. The Australians built on their first-innings lead of 162, pushed hard in the second knock, moved 430 runs ahead and left themselves the better part of a day and a half to bowl us out and take a 1–0 lead in the series. We braced ourselves to bat and to battle to save the Test match and, as we slipped to 45 for four on the fourth afternoon, an emphatic defeat appeared inevitable.

Faf and I – two old Affies – came together in a crisis, and batted, and batted, and batted.

Constantly encouraging each other to keep fighting, to keep concentrating, to leave anything wide, to get in line and defend, to keep going, we survived for five overs, then 10 overs, then 15, then 20 and eventually took our total to 77 for four at stumps on the fourth day. We had scored 32 runs in 29 overs.

We were fighting all right but, even so, the home side needed only six more wickets on the last day. Faf and I resumed our vigil under unhelpfully clear skies, with no prospect of assistance from the weather, and we kept going and kept going. We survived a few close calls and relied on some assistance from the third umpire review system a couple of times, but we kept going and safely reached lunch.

It was hard work, but I was relishing every minute. Ten years after Faf and I had been chased away from a school practice in Pretoria, we were batting to save a Test match in Australia. On a personal level, I wanted to prove to my teammates – and to myself – that I could be more than a stroke-playing dasher, that I was also capable of getting my head down, keeping my concentration and sticking around for the team.

My innings ended in the fourth over after the break, when I was bowled by a ball from Peter Siddle that cut back and took out my off stump. I had batted for just over four hours, faced 220 balls and scored 33 runs without scoring a single boundary and without even coming close to hitting a six. It was the second-slowest innings of more than 30 runs in the history of Test cricket, second only to an innings played by Chris Tavaré, of England, in Madras. More importantly, our partnership of 89 runs in 68 overs had kept alive our hopes of saving the match.

Jacques limped out to bat and scored 46 in just under two hours, but Faf kept going and going. Even though we lost a few wickets in the evening, even though we were never safe until the second-last ball of what was a long, tense and thrilling day, we finally reached stumps at 248 for eight and the Test ended in a draw. Faf remained unbeaten at the end, having scored 110 runs in just under eight hours – a heroic debut.

It may seem odd but, in cricket, a Test match saved can feel as satisfying as a Test match won, and as we travelled to play the third and final Test in Perth there was new optimism in our squad.

Quietly, privately, however, I was becoming concerned, starting to doubt myself. I knew I had played my part in Adelaide, but I had only once scored more than 50 since the tour to New Zealand, and one half-century in 19 innings or one half-century in eight months was not good enough. People were starting to suggest that keeping wicket was having a negative effect on my batting. People were wondering whether I would be dropped.

I began to worry. Should I tell coach Gary Kirsten that I didn't want to keep wicket because it was causing spasms in my lower back and because I wanted to concentrate on my batting? Or should I set aside my personal priorities and continue to keep wicket because the coach and captain felt it was in the best interests of the team?

My decision was never in doubt because the team means everything to me and, by nature, I want to keep people happy. So I decided to keep my concerns to myself and to keep wicket in the decider at the WACA. The reality was that, whether or not I kept wicket, I urgently needed to score some runs.

We won the toss and batted, and were soon struggling at 75 for six. I was caught in the slips for four, but Faf continued his outstanding form and his unbeaten 78 helped us reach a respectable total of 225. We needed to bowl well to stay in the Test, and it was Dale who met the challenge, dismissing four of the top six Australian batsmen. In trouble at 45 for six, they partially recovered to reach 163 all out, but the Test hung in the balance.

After so many sessions spent swimming against the tide in this series, so many demanding days spent fighting hard to stay in contention, we finally sensed an opportunity to seize the initiative. Graeme stepped forward and set the tone with a brisk 84 in 100 balls, and Hashim soon settled into his rhythm.

Jacques also played his part, and it was his wicket that brought me to join Hashim at the crease with our total on 287 for three. I dared not fail and started carefully, only settling when I managed to pull a short ball from Mitchell Starc for four past long leg, and then executed a reverse sweep for three off Nathan Lyon. I reached lunch with 18 runs from 51 balls, and was starting to feel more confident and to move more freely.

We accelerated into the afternoon, scoring freely, and we had taken the score to 436 for four at the end of the 88th over when Hashim was out for a brilliant 196 from 221 balls. Dean Elgar, on his debut, fell soon afterwards, but it was crucial for us to keep the initiative and I managed to take my score from 89 to 101 with three boundaries in three balls from Nathan Lyon: a reverse sweep, a reverse paddle, another reverse sweep.

It feels so good when form returns and the ball starts to ping off your bat again. My first 50 had taken 98 balls, my second 50 came from 33 balls and my third 50 took 31 balls, and I was eventually dismissed for 169, including 21 boundaries and three sixes. This was better. I felt massively relieved.

With more than two days left in the Test, Graeme pressed home our advantage, delaying a declaration, taking the match further and further away from the home team. We batted on and were eventually all out for 569, the second-fastest score over 550 in Test history, setting Australia 632 to win.

Ricky Ponting had announced his retirement and we formed a guard of honour for him when he walked out to bat for Australia for the last time. He had played 168 Tests in 17 years of international cricket and given everything, and I admired the way he was able to walk away from the game on his own terms.

He struck a couple of trademark boundaries before being caught at slip for eight. The crowd gave him a standing ovation, which seemed to get louder and louder. The electronic scoreboard read simply 'Thanks Ricky' and each of us, his opponents, made a point of running across to shake his hand. To coin a phrase, he was a great batsman as great batsmen go and, as great batsmen go, he went … with dignity and respect from all sides.

Australia fought hard, as you would expect, and Mitchell Starc thrashed an unbeaten 68 towards the end, but we eventually bowled them out for 322, won the Test by 309 runs, and won the series 1–0.

'It takes a team effort to win away from home,' Graeme said afterwards. 'Everybody is contributing and pulling their weight. That's the outstanding thing about our team. What we've been able to achieve, it will take a long time for people to understand. To have won a Test series in both England and in Australia in 2008 was special, but to repeat the same feat four years later is the proudest achievement of my career.'

Graeme had led. We had followed. The record shows that, in the space of six years from 2006, we had played 10 Test series away from home, winning eight and drawing two … unbeaten. That is the legacy of a great team, but I know it simply would not have happened without the leadership of a great captain.

2013

My workload had become demanding to say the least, batting in all three formats, keeping wicket in all three formats and captaining the Proteas in both ODI and T20 cricket. Coach Gary Kirsten recognised the situation, and I supported his decision to appoint Faf du Plessis as captain of the T20 side.

Continuity may have been lost but the burden was reasonably shared, with Graeme continuing to lead the Test team, me captaining the ODI side and Faf leading the team in T20 internationals.

Our impressive form in 2012 continued into the new year, with two emphatic Test victories over a New Zealand touring squad that included a talented left-arm fast bowler named Neil Wagner – the self-same Neil Wagner who arrived at Affies a couple of years after me and who, as a younger boy, had been told to carry my cricket bag around, just as I had once been told to shoulder Jacques Rudolph's cricket bag.

Neil was one of a few South African cricketers who had sensed a lack of opportunity at home, where racial quotas were constantly mooted, and decided to pursue his career in New Zealand. He had taken a massive decision and made it work but it still felt strange: we'd been friends at high school and then teammates at the Titans and, barely a decade later, we were playing against each other in international cricket.

The opening match of the ODI series that followed was lost when we narrowly failed to defend 208 in Paarl, but that was only the start of our problems. We had taken too long to bowl our overs and, according to the ICC Code of Conduct, the consequence of falling six overs short of our target was that (1) the captain – in this case, me – was banned from the next two one-day internationals, and (2) each player was fined 100% of his match fee.

Rules are rules, as they say, but it had been an exceptionally hot and windy day and we had conceded no fewer than 18 extras, which meant we had had to bowl the equivalent of three additional overs. I felt that such mitigating factors should be taken into account but David Boon, the former Australian batsman turned ICC match referee, was adamant that the guidelines should be upheld and the full punishment should be imposed.

This saga frustrated and embarrassed me, and it provided a few of the experts with an opportunity to cast further doubt on my ability as a captain. Oh well, I told myself, control the controllables. I resolved to learn and move on, but it was hard to sit in the stands and watch as we lost in Kimberley before winning in Potchefstroom.

Next up … Pakistan arrived on tour.

'And,' the critics chorused, 'when will they learn AB should not keep wicket in Tests because his technique is not sound enough and the added responsibility obviously affects his batting?'

My position on the wicketkeeping issue remained the same. It was not something I particularly wanted to do but, as far as I was concerned, my personal preference was secondary. If the coach and captain believed it was something I should do to assist the balance of the squad, then I was perfectly prepared to do the job; and the more the experts said I couldn't handle both roles, the harder I tried to prove them wrong.

In the first Test against Pakistan at the Wanderers, I held six catches as the tourists were bowled out for 49, and then took that to a total of 11 dismissals in the match, equalling the world record for a wicketkeeper set by Jack Russell, of England, at the same venue in 1995. I then scored 103 not out in our second innings, becoming the first player to claim more than 10 dismissals and make a century in the same Test match.

Of greater significance, Dale took 11 wickets and we won the first Test by 211 runs. Our excellent form produced a close-fought win in Cape Town and a convincing victory in Pretoria, and we took the series 3–0. For me, the runs were starting to flow again: 61 and 36 at Newlands were followed by 121 at SuperSport Park.

Keep in mind the 'R' in REPS, I told myself: 'Recognise the thin line between success and failure.' Remember that it's just as important when things are going well as it is when they're not going so well.

These were good times. The Pakistan team included talented players such as Younus Khan, a world-class batsman I always enjoyed watching, and Saeed Ajmal, one of the most skilful right-arm off-break bowlers I ever faced, but I managed to produce innings of 65, 4, 128, 75 and 95 not out in the ODI series and we fought hard as a team, going 1–0 up, losing, going 2–1 up, losing and then winning the deciding match in Benoni.

In excellent spirits, our squad flew north to compete in yet another

IPL days – LEFT, playing for Delhi Daredevils in Durban when the Indian Premier League came to South Africa in 2009; and, BELOW, batting for Royal Challengers Bangalore in the IPL Champions League, with Mark Boucher keeping wicket for the Eastern Province Warriors.

Second home – the Chinnaswamy Stadium in Bengaluru is a great place to play cricket and there have been many memorable times playing for Royal Challengers Bangalore in the Indian Premier League, together with the brilliant Virat Kohli, ABOVE, and, BELOW, playing for South Africa against India in India.

Great days – RIGHT, Danielle,
my fiancée, being serenaded
at Muldersdrift after we got
engaged; BELOW, Danielle,
my wife, on our wedding day,
30 March 2013; and OPPOSITE,
with our newborn son, AB,
22 July 2015.

Down time – ABOVE LEFT, with my brother Wessels and his son Josuah, and ABOVE RIGHT, proud father with AB junior at Herolds Bay; and BELOW, together in the bush.

2015 Cricket World Cup – ABOVE, with Hashim Amla, as we make progress through the tournament; BELOW LEFT, in deep discussion with Dale Steyn as the semifinal against New Zealand goes down to the last over, and, BELOW RIGHT, facing up to the reality of defeat.

100th Test – ABOVE, with my parents, Millie and AB de Villiers, my PA Letitia Greyling, my mother-in-law Alida Swart, and Danielle, who all attended the match in Bengaluru; and, BELOW, batting during the Test.

Fightback – OPPOSITE, batting during the demanding home series against England, when we won the fourth Test at SuperSport Park, Centurion, and restored some national pride.

Test trials – OPPOSITE, batting with Hashim Amla against England in 2015/16, just before being asked to succeed him as Test captain; ABOVE, sharing some refreshment with Joe Root, the England batsman, after the third Test; and, BELOW, airborne while fielding at the Wanderers.

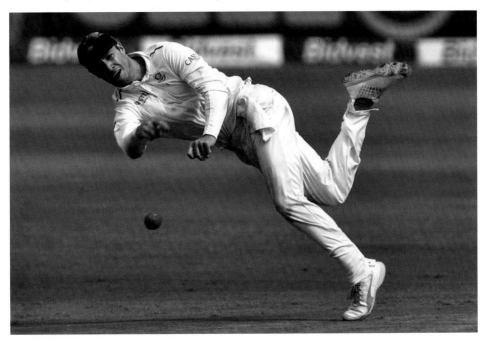

ABOVE: Some days everything comes together ... playing in pink against the West Indies at the Wanderers in January 2015, and, LEFT, some days nothing comes together ... our 2016 Twenty20 World Cup campaign ended in disappointment with defeat against the same opposition.

ICC limited-overs tournament, the 2013 ICC Champions Trophy tournament in England. We were by now standing at No. 1 in the ODI world rankings. We were playing well and, as we completed our preparations in Amsterdam, we dared to hope again.

We worked hard, we spoke about being mentally strong, we thought we were doing everything right ... and we were disappointed again. Nothing clicked. We lost a warm-up match against Pakistan, and then lost our first match in Group B against India in Cardiff before beating Pakistan in Birmingham. Our fate would be determined by the result of our third and last group match, against the West Indies in Cardiff and, at the end of a nervous day spoiled by rain, the match was tied and we qualified for the last four with a greater net run rate. At last, after cursing their names so many times, Duckworth and Lewis finally felt like friends. Maybe our luck was changing.

A semifinal against hosts England at The Oval loomed and, in the pre-match press conference, I spoke about the opportunity to perform in a big match and to banish our reputation.

We were unfortunate to lose the important toss on a humid morning when both teams would have bowled first, but there were no excuses for our batting. Poor shot followed poor shot, and we crumbled to 80 for eight in the 23rd over. The contest was essentially decided well before lunch and, even though David Miller's fighting 56 helped us to post an almost-respectable total of 175, England cruised to an easy win.

As captain, I felt responsible and I felt sad ... sad for players who had desperately wanted to do well, sad for the people at home whose hopes had been raised again and been dashed again, and particularly sad for Gary Kirsten, our coach, who had decided not to accept an offer to extend his contract for two more years.

Gary's reputation as a coach extends across the cricketing world and is based on his special ability to bring out the best in anyone, to motivate and inspire. He is bold and innovative and, having guided us through so many great days, he deserved so much better than to finish on such a dismal day at The Oval.

Russell Domingo had been a member of Gary's team for two years, and he was rightly promoted to take over as head coach. I knew him to be an exceptional person, and I knew I would enjoy working with him.

But sportsmen are nothing if not resilient and, as ever, after suffering a major disappointment, we moved on to the next challenge, and the next tour. There would be no soft landing for us, and no easy start for Russell, as we headed to play five one-day internationals and three T20 matches in Sri Lanka.

Kumar Sangakkara welcomed us to his world with an astonishing innings of 169 off 137 balls in the first match, and then, as ever smart, humble and level-headed, he welcomed us to dinner at his restaurant in Colombo. I did lose five out of five tosses in the series, but Angelo Mathews managed his team with tremendous skill and the home side deserved their 4–1 win. We did salvage some pride, however, winning the T20 series 2–1.

We set out on the road again in October, playing two Tests against Pakistan in the UAE; the first Test was lost in Abu Dhabi, our first defeat in 15 Tests, but we bounced back to win the second Test in Dubai, a match at which Graeme wrote yet another chapter in his book of great innings for South Africa.

He had been under pressure. Some were doubting his form. Others questioned. He made them all look fools by scoring 234 runs in more than 10 hours at the crease, concentrating, straining every sinew for the cause. I was privileged to bat alongside him in a partnership that added 338 runs for the fifth wicket. My innings of 164 paled by comparison, and we won the Test by an innings and 92 runs.

There is a photograph of me hugging Graeme when he had reached his century, with him lifting me clean off the ground. I posted it on Twitter with the words 'never count this guy out'. At risk of repeating myself over and over again, for the umpteenth time in these pages, we were privileged to play for such a captain.

Our form was improving again, and we produced some excellent cricket to win the ODI series 4–1, including a famous win in the opening ODI: Pakistan had needed only 19 runs from 55 balls to win, with six wickets left, but we had fought back, grabbed wicket after wicket and, amazingly, won by two runs.

Such drama enthused and excited everyone, and we advanced to sweep the T20 series 2–0 in the UAE before both teams flew to South Africa and continued what was starting to feel like an endless series of limited-overs matches, with two more T20 matches (1–1) and three more ODIs (1–2).

After 14 matches against Pakistan, we were relieved when India arrived to play three ODIs and two Test matches around Christmas, if only because they would provide fresh opposition. In fact, they didn't provide much opposition at all in the one-day internationals. We won comfortably in Johannesburg when 20-year-old Quinton de Kock helped us to score 358 in 50 overs, and we won in Durban with Quinton scoring another century.

The youngster scored a third century in a row in the third ODI at Centurion, and I also reached three figures as we took our total to 301, but the match was washed out by torrential rain.

MS Dhoni's side seemed to be struggling, but they remained a hugely talented group of cricketers and they raised their level of performance to play a full part in a thrilling first Test ...

India win the toss and bat at the Wanderers, and Virat Kohli shows discipline and skill to score a century against a dangerous attack in difficult conditions, helping his side to 280 in their first innings. In reply, Graeme and Hashim guide us to 130 for one, but we collapse to 146 for six and struggle to 244 all out.

The Test is poised. Batting seems difficult, but the tourists appear to be taking the initiative as Cheteshwar Pujara and Virat Kohli gather momentum and start to score freely.

'AB, do you want to bowl?'

I realise Graeme is speaking, but I am surely mishearing him.

'AB, we need to try something different in the last over before tea. Do you want to bowl?'

'Sure,' I reply, with all the confidence of someone who has sent down a grand total of 38 overs of dibbly-dobbly medium pace and occasional off-spin in my entire professional career.

The Test match pauses while I remove my wicketkeeping gloves and pads, hand them to Hashim, who is going to replace me for this one over, and try to appear calm as I pace out my two-step run-up.

First ball: short and wide, slapped to the cover sweeper for one by Cheteshwar. Second ball: Virat sympathetically and kindly leaves a wide half-volley and Hashim collects. Third ball: Virat pushes a single to the covers. Fourth ball: Cheteshwar drives off the back foot and runs two. Fifth ball: dragged down, it's called a wide outside off stump. Sixth ball: it turns and Cheteshwar defends with respect. Last ball: Cheteshwar plays the ball to mid-off, no run.

Having somehow survived this barrage of top-class bowling, the Indians reach tea at 109 for two and thrive into the evening and the next day. They are eventually bowled out for 421, leaving us an apparently impossible target of 458 runs to win. The travelling journalists are already beginning to prepare triumphant reports of what they are calling 'one of India's greatest Test wins'.

In fairness, our prospects don't look great with more than a day and a half left in the game and, even though Graeme and Alviro open our innings with a steady century partnership, we lose three quick wickets and Jacques gets a poor LBW decision, and we appear to be slip-sliding away at 197 for four.

With a sense of déjà vu, I walk out to join Faf at the crease. It's a simi-lar situation to that which we faced in Adelaide a year before, with the crucial difference being that the target against Australia back then was certainly beyond our reach, but this target set by the Indians is *almost* certainly too much, *not quite* certainly.

Faf and I agree to adopt a positive mindset, to go after anything loose rather than simply to block everything and play for time. History sug-gests we have little chance, but what does history know? Let's go and make history. We reach lunch at 237 for four, focused on surviving but still daring to dream.

Overs come and overs go. Zaheer Khan takes the new ball, searching for what could be the crucial breakthrough. He strays down leg, and I manage to feather-glance a boundary to fine leg. Next ball is a full toss, and I whip it past mid-wicket for four. Maybe, just maybe we can … pos-sibly. Ishant Sharma charges in and over-pitches, and I flick the ball for four. The next ball is too full, and I help the in-swinger to the boundary.

We bat past drinks. The Indian bowlers are starting to appear frustrat-ed. The fielders look anxious. We reach tea at 331 for four. It's happening. It's possible. With six wickets still standing, we need 127 runs in the last session to secure one of our 'greatest Test wins', not one of theirs.

Faf reaches his century. I follow him into three figures soon after. The spectators are applauding every run. Extraordinary events are unfolding before their very eyes.

With 56 runs needed, I aim to steer another single down to third man, but the ball hits the inside edge of my bat and clatters into the stumps. I feel distraught – out, bowled for 103. Faf and I have added 205 runs for the fifth wicket. We are within sight of victory, but I had wanted to take us over the line.

JP Duminy hits a four and is then bowled. Vernon Philander joins Faf, and the runs flow until only 20 are needed from the last five overs. Faf drives towards mid-off and calls for a quick single. Rahane gathers, throws and breaks the stumps with a direct hit. Faf sprints and dives ... and is short, run out for a heroic 134.

Now what? Has there ever been a more thrilling Test? Sixteen runs are needed from the last three overs, but we are seven wickets down. Do we dash for glory or do we play it safe and make sure we don't lose? Dale walks out to join Vernon, carrying an instruction to be careful and maybe set up a dash in the last over.

Mohammed Shami is bowling. Dale is facing and he leaves anything wide. He then plays the ball into the off side but declines the single. Dale plays out a maiden over. A few spectators boo. It's a two-Test series, and defeat would be a disaster. The downside of losing is greater than our need to win. The Indians feel the same way, and MS puts nine fielders on the boundary as Zaheer bowls the penultimate over. Vernon plays out another maiden.

Shami bowls the last over of the day and, only when it is impossible for us to lose, Dale drives him straight back over his head for six. The Test is drawn, as we finish on 450 for seven, eight runs short ...

We all backed the decision. All three results had been distinctly possible with three overs left, but both teams had peered over the edge and pulled back from the brink. In a two-Test series, there was no margin for error, and a crazy over or two in Johannesburg could have put the series win out of reach.

Jacques Kallis had announced his intention to retire from Test cricket after the second Test, starting at Kingsmead in Durban on Boxing Day 2013, and, thankfully, we played well and were able to give Jacques a proper send-off, winning by 10 wickets and securing a 1–0 series win. At the end, escorted by all his teammates, he walked around the field, carrying the national flag and accepting the applause of the crowd.

It had been another tight match. Replying to India's first-innings total of 334, we had reached 113 for three when I walked out to join Jacques, aware we could be batting together in a Test for the last time. I remember feeling mixed emotions as I took guard, sad because an era was ending, yet happy because I had enjoyed so many opportunities to play alongside a cricketer I so admired and a person I liked so much.

The statistics show that we batted together 44 times in Test matches, adding a total of 3 108 runs with an average of 75.80 runs per partnership. We shared in 13 stands of more than a hundred between 2004 and 2013, suggesting there was roughly a one-in-three chance of us sharing a century stand when we batted together.

Among all the pairs of batsmen in Test history who batted together more than 40 times, only three claim a higher average number of runs per partnership: Justin Langer and Ricky Ponting of Australia, Jack Hobbs and Herbert Sutcliffe of England, and Mohammad Yousuf and Younus Khan of Pakistan.

In Durban, I was pleased to be standing at the non-striker's end when Jacques followed the fairytale script and reached his 45th and last Test century playing his 166th and last Test. Our partnership was worth 127 runs when I was out for 74, but Jacques continued and we reached a total of exactly 500 all out.

Dale did the rest: he had taken six wickets in the Indian first innings, and proceeded to claim the crucial wickets of Pujara and Kohli in one devastating spell of world-class fast bowling. The tourists were bowled out for 223, and our openers knocked off the 58 runs required for victory without a problem.

At the end of another successful year, we were on top of the world, statistically speaking, standing at No. 1 in both the ICC Test rankings and the ICC ODI rankings. As a Test team, remarkably, the records show we had only lost one of the previous 25 series, a run of success that stretched back to 2006.

2014

Michael Clarke brought his Australia team on tour for three Tests in February and March and we looked forward to what was another opportunity to end the jinx and win a home series against Australia.

Mitchell Johnson revelled in the conditions at the first Test in Centurion, bowling with rib-pummelling pace and fine control, and, while I was pleased to reach 91 in difficult conditions, we were dismissed for 206 in the first innings and then bowled out for 200 in the second innings. We were well beaten.

Another great fast bowler dominated the second Test at St George's Park in Port Elizabeth. After JP and I scored centuries, helping us reach 423 in our first innings, the Australians were eventually set a target of 448 runs to win, with two days left to play. We seemed in a dominant position, but Chris Rogers and David Warner took their opening stand into three figures and, with rain forecast on the last day, we were running out of time.

In our time of need, Dale produced a remarkable spell of reverse swing, taking three wickets for 11 runs in five overs, dismissing Michael Clarke, Steve Smith and Brad Haddin. The Australians collapsed from 126 without loss to 216 all out, and we duly secured victory by 231 runs, levelling the series at 1–1.

Australia won an important toss in the deciding Test at Newlands, and big centuries from both Warner and Clarke enabled them to declare their first innings at 494 for seven. We were batting under scoreboard pressure. Sensing weakness, Johnson and Harris were storming in. We managed only 287 in reply, and when they reached 22 without loss at stumps on the third day, the tourists appeared to be taking control.

'Guys, can you gather around?' Graeme asked quietly.

Players were packing away their kit in the dressing room, and I remember sensing that this was not going to be the usual captain's pep talk at the end of what had been a demanding day.

'I've decided to retire from all forms of international cricket at the end of this Test.'

The room fell completely silent. Nobody moved.

Graeme continued: 'This has been the most difficult decision of my life, but it's something I have been thinking about since my ankle surgery last year. I have a young family to consider and it seems to me that retiring at Newlands is the best way to end it because I have called this place home since I was 18 years old.'

Of course, after more than a decade as captain, after so many colossal performances, Graeme had many times over earned the right to step aside precisely when he wanted, but I was concerned about the impact on the team. As Oscar Wilde might have put it, to lose one legendary player could be considered unfortunate but to lose two legendary players within the space of barely eight weeks seemed careless. Replacing Jacques was going to be difficult. Replacing Graeme would also be difficult. Replacing both at the same time would be impossible.

In an ideal world, we would have returned to Newlands on the fourth day, dismissed Australia for very few and chased down the target, giving our captain one last victory to enjoy. Unfortunately, the tourists raced to 303, effectively batting us out of the game and setting us an utterly impossible target of 511 to win.

Graeme opened our second innings with Alviro, and was given a guard of honour by the Australians as he walked out to bat for South Africa for the very last time. One last defiant century would have been appropriate but, instead, he scored only three runs before fending Johnson and being caught at short leg. He walked slowly back to the pavilion as the applause of opponents, teammates and spectators alike reverberated around the ground.

We would have liked to have saved the match at least, and we fought hard. Hashim batted for two and a half hours while making 41, and I stuck around for five and a half hours, scoring 43 from 228 balls before being caught behind off the excellent Ryan Harris. Faf, JP and Vernon all made the Australians sweat for their wickets and, with only five overs left and two wickets still standing, we seemed set to secure the draw.

Clarke was concerned and threw the ball to Harris, who immediately obliged with a perfect yorker to end Dale's brave resistance. When he clean bowled Morné two balls later, Australia had won.

We then lost two T20 internationals against the tourists, and both teams travelled to compete in another edition of the now biennial ICC World Twenty20 tournament, being hosted in Bangladesh.

Our strategy was to direct all our energy towards getting the basics right, resisting the temptation to try anything too smart, but in our opening match against Sri Lanka we fielded poorly and then lost our way in what should have been a reasonable run chase, losing wickets regularly and eventually finishing five runs short.

The margins were small, and we won our next match against New Zealand when Dale bowled a magnificent last over. The Black Caps had needed only seven runs to win, but he held his nerve, bowled fast and accurately and ensured we squeaked to a two-run win. As one writer commented, we had produced an 'anti-choke'.

After beating the Netherlands, we faced England in what amounted to a quarterfinal. Faf had been banned from the match following another technical over-rate violation, so I captained the team and managed to score 69 not out in 28 balls as we reached 196 for five in 20 overs, a competitive total. The English chased hard but we bowled and fielded well, and deserved to win and advance to a semifinal against India.

The pre-match stats were not encouraging: it had been 14 years (five Champions Trophies, five World Cups and three World T20s) since we last won a knockout match at an ICC event, and India had never lost a semifinal in any tournament under the calm and collected captaincy of MS Dhoni.

We batted first and made 174 for four, which seemed a par total in

Dhaka, but it was made to look inadequate when Virat Kohli, the leading run-scorer in the tournament, maintained his form, paced both himself and the innings perfectly, scored an unbeaten 72 and took India to victory with an over to spare.

Some observers said I should have batted higher than No. 5 in the order, while others – including Faf as captain – insisted I am more effective when coming in after the 10th over in T20 cricket. My position, as usual, as dull as it may seem, was to do what the coach and captain felt was right for the team. I felt sorry if anyone was disappointed because I declined to stamp my feet, make a fuss and insist on batting at No. 3 – but that was not my way.

It was also not my way to put myself forward to succeed Graeme as Test captain. Some people within the game – such as Mark Boucher, Jacques Kallis and Mike Procter, the former convenor of selectors – said publicly that they felt I was well qualified to lead the Test team, and I would enthusiastically have accepted the job if it was offered to me, but I was not going to start phoning people and organising any kind of campaign.

Eventually, on Tuesday, 3 June, Hashim was appointed as the new Test captain. Andrew Hudson, the convenor of selectors, confirmed I would continue as captain of the ODI side and Faf would remain captain of the T20 team. Three captains in three formats ensured that the burden of responsibility was spread around, but we would have to work hard to ensure the leadership systems did not become fragmented and disjointed.

In all sincerity, I was pleased for Hash. We had known each other since we were 13 years old when we played in school matches. I clearly recall one particular cricket week at Hilton College, when I was playing for Affies and there was a brilliant young batsman wearing spectacles and scoring runs for Durban High School.

I had so much respect for him, both as a human being and as a cricketer, and admired the way he appeared so calm and controlled in the emotional world of professional sport.

The new structures would be tested on tour to Sri Lanka, and all went well. We won the ODI series 2–1, with Hash scoring a century in the first and second matches, and Quinton and me each scoring centuries as we won the decisive third match. Showing considerable skill, Hash led the Test team first to victory in Galle and then to a hard-fought draw in Colombo, and we celebrated a notable Test series win in Sri Lanka.

Our minds were starting to turn to the next World Cup, to be played in Australia and New Zealand at the start of 2015, and Cricket South Africa had planned a thorough and detailed eight-month programme to ensure we would be properly prepared.

We won an ODI series against Zimbabwe 3–0, and then won four out of five matches in a triangular series with the Zimbabweans and Australia, eventually beating the Aussies in the final.

Next we flew west for a virtual dress rehearsal: travelling to play in the host countries of the World Cup, trying to become familiar with hotels, training facilities and venues. We played three ODIs in New Zealand, winning the series 2–0 with one rained off, and then played three T20s and five ODIs in Australia.

We were performing well and victory in the opening T20 international against Australia in Adelaide meant we had won no fewer than 11 of our last 13 limited-overs internationals. Morale was high, and we seemed to be getting into the extremely useful habit of winning. Then, almost overnight, our form suddenly dipped and we lost six of the next seven matches against the increasingly confident and chipper Australians.

Some commentators began to scoff at our unprecedented preparations, but I was not especially concerned. It would have been better if we were winning, but we were making mistakes and learning; we knew we would have to field well and we knew we could not afford to give away too many extras.

Lastly, a very significant silver lining to the dark cloud was that the run of defeats significantly reduced the level of expectation back home and that, we decided, was a positive development.

As an island of five-day cricket amid the unrelenting torrent of ODIs, we enjoyed the Test series against the West Indies. In the first Test at SuperSport Park in Pretoria, Hashim and I took the score from a precarious 57 for three to a position of control at 365 for three. He scored 208 and I made 152. The bowlers rose to the challenge, dismissing the tourists for 201 and then 131, securing victory by an innings and 220 runs.

Poor weather ensured the second Test ended as a draw in Port Elizabeth, but we clinched the series win with a convincing victory at Newlands. I managed to score 148 and helped build a first innings lead, and we dismissed the West Indies for 215 before scoring the 124 needed for victory by eight wickets.

Confidence was returning after the setbacks in Australia and, even though we lost both T20 internationals against the West Indies, we performed well in the ODI series, winning in Durban, winning well in Johannesburg when I scored 149 in 44 balls – as described in the opening chapter – winning in East London, losing by one wicket in Port Elizabeth and then wrapping up a confidence-boosting 4–1 series win in Centurion.

As a captain, I was happy. As a squad desperate to win the World Cup, we were ready.

CHAPTER 12

INSPIRED BY INDIA

Above all, the chanting makes me feel humble and privileged and, of course, obliged to score some runs.

It is difficult for me to understand how someone from a relatively small town in rural South Africa can be so fortunate and so favoured that when he walks out to bat, or simply takes guard, in almost any cricket ground in India, he can be greeted by tens of thousands of happy people chanting his initials.

A-B-D! A-B-D! A-B-D!

I am not arrogant, big-headed or self-important. I am simply grateful to God for giving me the talent to entertain people, for giving me the skill to hit a cricket ball in a way that excites people. I have wondered about these events and arrived at the conclusion that it remains His talent and His skill effectively being manifested through me. I genuinely feel so blessed to be following the path He has chosen for me.

As far as I can recall, the chant started in 2012, during the fifth season of the Indian Premier League (IPL). Royal Challengers Bangalore (RCB) were chasing 182 to beat Deccan Chargers at the Chinnaswamy Stadium and I walked out to bat when we were struggling at 106 for three, with six overs and one ball left. Our form had been inconsistent and we needed a win to stay alive in the competition, but the in-form Chargers appeared in control. With 39 runs needed from 18 balls, we decided our best option was to take risks, to attack and see what happens.

Dale Steyn, my long-standing friend and teammate, was preparing to bowl the 18th over ...

I pull the first ball for a low-trajectory six over mid-wicket. The second ball is a perfect yorker in the blockhole, which I manage to dig into the leg side for two. The crowd is starting to chant. I listen. It is my second season in Bangalore, and our outstanding supporters very often chant R-C-B! R-C-B! R-C-B!

This is different. It sounds like different lyrics set to the same tune.

A-B-D! A-B-D! A-B-D!

I focus on Dale, who is running in again.

The third ball is slower. I swing hard and hit the ball just hard enough to reach the boundary. The grandstands turn into a swirling sea of red flags again and the chanting resumes, louder.

A-B-D! A-B-D! A-B-D!

The fourth delivery is full and straight, pitched on middle-and-leg. I step away to the leg side to make room, to free my hands and drive the ball over extra cover and into the crowd. A slogan flashes on the giant screen. YOU CAN'T PUT FIELDERS THERE, it reads. I look around. The atmosphere is amazing.

Dale races in and bowls the fifth ball outside off-stump. I premeditate, step to the off side, crouch down on one knee and then, swivelling, manage to paddle the ball to the boundary behind square leg.

A single to third man off the sixth ball means we have taken 23 from the over.

A-B-D! A-B-D! A-B-D!

Still on strike at the start of the 19th over, I take two steps down the wicket and drive the first ball to the extra cover boundary. The second ball is driven on the up past the bowler for four and the third ball is pulled into the crowd for six. Everything is going our way, and 37 runs have come from nine balls.

Syed Mohammad, my partner at the crease, whips the next ball for four and, in what seems the blink of an eye, a match we had looked like losing is won with more than an over to spare. Our teammates run on to the field to celebrate and Virat Kohli, our captain, is the first person to reach me and hug me.

THAT ONLY HAPPENS IN THE MOVIES, screams another slogan on the giant screen.

I feel exhilarated, and join the post-match line to greet the opposition. Dale smiles as he shakes my hand. We've come a long way from our first-class debuts on the same day at SuperSport Park to this electric night in Bangalore, and he remains a great fast bowler, a great competitor and a great sportsman …

Not for the first time – and not for the last – I had been inspired by India, this great country that has provided me with so many opportunities and has become so important in my career.

It is the largest democracy in the world and the seventh-largest economy in the world. It is a vast and beautiful nation of more than 1.2 billion people, most of whom love cricket. And it is hard to believe that, not long ago, it was a country that many international cricketers used to dread; they would arrive on tour and complain about the hotels, the food, the training facilities and the transport, and could hardly wait to fly home.

Back in 1991, India was a few months away from defaulting on its international payment obligations; in a moment of profound crisis, the government secured an emergency loan of US$2.2 billion from the International Monetary Fund only by airlifting 67 tonnes of its national gold reserves to Europe as collateral. Things got worse. One of the vans transporting the gold broke down on its way to the airport.

A quarter of a century later, India is transformed. Economic growth is running at around 7%, outstripping China, and the experts who study such matters now confidently predict that the total size of the Indian economy will surpass the total of the German and Japanese economies combined by the end of 2019.

Such observations may seem out of place in the autobiography of a mere cricketer but, for me, this extraordinary progress in the last 25 years could hardly be more relevant.

As India has grown and developed beyond anyone's imagination, so has its favourite sport grown and developed beyond anyone's imagination, with the result that India is now the most influential power in world cricket, the leading Indian players are recognised as the superstars of the game, and international cricketers, far from dreading every visit to the subcontinent, now crave nothing more than an invitation to play in India.

In cricket, the most obvious exhibition of this growth, the gleaming, towering skyscraper on the landscape of our sport, is the Indian Premier League, which launched its ninth season in April 2016.

I am very fortunate to be playing during this era, to have been able to enjoy experiences and accept opportunities that were once inconceivable for a boy from Bela-Bela.

My first visit to India with the Proteas, back in 2006, stands clear in my memory. Albie Morkel and I were two excited youngsters on tour and, wherever we happened to be, we grabbed every opportunity to get out of the hotel and see as much of the country as possible. Filming everything on camcorders, we travelled by tuk-tuk (taxis amounting to a covered seat attached to the back of a motorbike), weaving in and out of the traffic amid the constant chorus of hooters; it was hard to understand how almost everyone seemed to remain so calm.

If someone had stopped us on one of these trips, and told us we would both soon be earning several tens of millions of rupees playing in India for two months each year, we would have said they were mad.

The concept of the IPL was simple: assemble the best Twenty20 players in the largest cricket market, sell them by auction to the owners of private franchises based in large stadiums and major cities, create a league with a double round-robin format followed by knockout stages and a final, add razzamatazz and play.

Sporting organisations tend to be criticised, and the Board of Control for Cricket in India (BCCI) received its share of flak over the years, not least for declining to use technology and the review system, and for their intransigence in arranging tour schedules. However, to be fair, the history books will record that it was the BCCI that got the job done and, in 2008, created the tournament that transformed the game. It was the BCCI that built the platform on which cricketers were suddenly being paid up to US$1.5 million to perform for seven weeks.

Their fellow administrators around the world recoiled in shock.

Some responded by figuratively plunging their collective heads into the nearest bucket of sand, trying to pretend that the IPL did not exist; these governing bodies arranged international fixtures at the same time as the new league and so sought to prevent their leading players from taking the opportunity.

Fortunately for me, and many other South African players, Cricket South Africa immediately adopted a more enlightened and proactive approach, embracing the concept of the new league, ensuring the Proteas would never play in the same time window, and so enabling our players to enter the auction and participate.

'AB, you've been bought for US$300 000 per year.'

'What?'

'Serious! You've been bought for US$300 000 per year, and it's a three-year deal.'

It was true. I had been entered into the inaugural IPL auction, and been bought by a team called the Delhi Daredevils (DD) for US$300 000 per year. Around the world, disbelieving cricketers double-checked the numbers.

'Really? Are you sure there isn't one nought too many?'

Albie Morkel had been sold to the Chennai Super Kings (CSK) for US$675 000 per year. Jacques Kallis was going to a team called Royal Challengers Bangalore for a salary of US$900 000 per year.

My immediate response to being contracted for this amount of money was to think, well, I had better play well and score some runs, but, in that first season, the IPL regulation that franchises could sign up to eight overseas players but were allowed to include only four in any starting XI meant I would get few opportunities.

Shoaib Malik, the gifted Pakistan batsman, was usually preferred to me, and I spent most of my time training and travelling, trying to be useful, desperately wanting to prove my value to the team. I played in only three matches but, even so, enjoyed being around players such as Gautam Gambhir and Virender Sehwag, whose brilliant form carried us to the semifinal, where we lost to Rajasthan Royals, the eventual winners.

The average crowd in that first season of IPL cricket was an incredible 58 000 spectators per match. Amid all the jingles, the imported cheerleaders and the shiny kit, the gentleman's game was being turned upside down.

In 2009, concerns that the Indian government could not guarantee security during the run-up up to the general election persuaded the BCCI to make a dramatic decision; barely three weeks before the opening match, they decided that the entire tournament would be moved to South Africa. The logistical challenge was unprecedented, but it was met by the combined skill, can-do mentality and enthusiasm of South Africa's stadium owners, hotel chains, security officials, transport providers, media organisations and supporters. As a country, we made a plan.

The switch in venue was good news for the South African economy, which benefited from an injection of around US$90 million, and it was also good news for me. The Delhi Daredevils coaches knew I would bring local knowledge, and I played in every match, scoring an unbeaten century against CSK in Durban and averaging 45.

After feeling peripheral, everything was much more fun when I was properly involved, on and off the field. If any of the DD players wanted to book a restaurant for dinner or to play golf, I was their go-to tour guide. And we played some outstanding cricket, winning 10 of our 14 group matches, finishing top of the round-robin league and advancing to a semifinal against Deccan Chargers at SuperSport Park in Pretoria, my home ground.

We batted first and scored 153 for eight in 20 overs. That total appeared defendable, but Adam Gilchrist soon proved otherwise. The brilliant Australian crashed 85 runs in only 35 balls, guiding his team to victory with two overs to spare. Deccan Chargers advanced to overcome RCB in the final and win the title.

The tournament returned to India in 2010, and I returned to the ranks of international players struggling to get a game. The Delhi Daredevils coaches selected Paul Collingwood, the England all-rounder, ahead of me, and I made only three appearances during the entire tournament. DD won seven and lost seven of their group matches, finishing fifth, eliminated with an inferior net run rate.

IPL contracts typically last three years and, although some eager DD officials had said they wanted to renew my contract, I really had no idea where I would be playing the following year.

Aside from taking salaries to a new level, the IPL had started to change the game in another important respect. The leading cricketers in the world, used to being rivals on the international stage, suddenly found themselves cast as teammates in IPL teams and many became friends.

In Delhi, I spent a great deal of time with players such as Zaheer Khan, Glenn McGrath, Virender Sehwag and others, going out for dinner, just sitting around, talking about cricket, chatting about life in general, getting to know them as people rather than as opponents, learning about their families and their passions.

Glenn is universally recognised as one of the great fast bowlers, but

I was just as impressed by him as a great human being, and we spent many hours discussing his interest in South Africa and wildlife. As a comparative youngster talking to an Australian legend, I was so pleased to discover we had so much in common.

Others will have shared similar experiences throughout the league with the result that, in my view, year by year, the IPL has gradually taken the intimidation factor out of international cricket.

It used to be huge. Whether you were playing in Kolkata or Brisbane or Leeds or Bridgetown, the fast bowler who was glowering at you after bowling a bouncer or the slip fielder who was constantly sledging you seemed scary because they were strangers, shadowy figures from a foreign land. But nowadays you are not going to be as easily intimidated by someone who, a few weeks earlier in an Indian hotel, was having a few beers with you and telling you about his children.

Most of the players now know each other so well, both as cricketers in a technical sense and as people, that some of the mystery and some of the edge have disappeared. What was once primarily a psychological contest has become a less complex, less layered test of skill between increasingly familiar foes.

I don't know whether this is a good thing or a bad thing, and it's probably a bit of both, and it may just be that I am getting old, but there do seem to be fewer surprises in the international game.

The IPL player auction was held in January 2011, ahead of the tournament, and I was signed by Royal Challengers Bangalore, then owned by Vijay Mallya, the extrovert entrepreneur and businessman. As players, we called him 'Boss' and, for many of us, he became an enthusiastic supporter and friend, a generous host who genuinely cared about the squad.

A few well-timed performances, notably a century from 59 balls while playing for South Africa in an ODI against India in Ahmedabad, may have increased my value but, whatever the reason, I was surprised and, frankly, a little embarrassed when the list of annual player salaries was published after the auction, and US$1.1 million appeared beside my name.

I made my debut for RCB at the Jawaharlal Nehru Stadium against the newly formed Kochi Tuskers Kerala, one of two new franchises whose introduction had increased the number of teams from eight to 10, and I managed to score an unbeaten 54 from 40 balls, including five sixes, as we reached our target of 162 to win the game. I was pleased to be named Man of the Match.

This was the season when the value of momentum became clear. Having won our first match, we proceeded to lose the next three and the fifth was a no-result. We were struggling but nobody panicked and we managed to win the next seven games in succession, eventually finishing top of the league.

Moving to the knockout stages, we lost to CSK in the first qualifier between the first and second placed teams, but recovered to beat Mumbai Indians in the second qualifier when Chris Gayle, the hard-hitting West Indian batsman who had joined us as an injury replacement for Dirk Nannes, produced a typically brutal knock, scoring 89 from 47 balls. RCB advanced to play CSK again, this time in the IPL final at Chennai.

We were ready to perform on the big day but the CSK openers, Mike Hussey and Murali Vijay, scored 159 in fewer than 15 overs, and we actually did well to restrict them to 205 for five.

It was going to be a tough chase, and we had the worst possible start when Chris was out in the first over. We continued to lose wickets, with Virat Kohli dismissed for 35 and me scoring only 18, and we were essentially out of the running at 70 for six in the 11th over. CSK duly claimed a second title.

Chris Gayle, Virat Kohli and I had been assembled as the core of the RCB batting order, and we would stay together for six IPL tournaments, enjoying many great days, many fine partnerships, entertaining electric capacity crowds of 45 000 flag-waving supporters at the Chinnaswamy Stadium in Bengaluru.

Chris batted with incredible power and simplicity, standing tall at the crease and typically bludgeoning the ball in the 'V' between mid-off and mid-on. For him, the bat was a club. For Virat, the bat was a surgeon's knife, and he so often proved himself uniquely skilled at placing the ball in the gaps.

For me, it was a privilege to spend so much time with two of the finest batsmen ever to play the game, training with them, partying with them and getting to know them as friends. There has never been any kind of rivalry between us because we have grown to understand and respect each other.

'Come on, you little biscuit.'

'OK, let's play, you little beauty.'

Virat and I share a liking for nicknames, and we have become very tight over all these years. He is an incredibly generous person, generous with his advice, generous with his time and generous with his support. He's also a ferocious competitor and, many times, he has driven the team, and me in particular, to new heights.

There have been some fantastic occasions when everything clicked and we seemed almost unbeatable but, to be honest, our performances as a team have been generally disappointing. Some have suggested the balance of the RCB squad has never been quite right, with the depth of our bowling rarely matching the depth of our batting but, whatever the reason, we have too often performed below our potential.

In 2012, we won eight of 16 group matches. Chris Gayle averaged over 60 in 14 innings, and I picked up three Man of the Match awards, but we finished in fifth place and narrowly missed out on the knockout stages with a marginally inferior net run rate to CSK in fourth.

The results were too often frustrating, but I was still really enjoying the IPL experience, which was now starting to feel like a genuine gathering of the global cricketing world. One evening, at a private house party, I was approached by Sir Viv Richards, the legendary West Indies batsman of the 1970s and 1980s. I could hardly believe that he wanted to speak to me.

'You are changing the game,' he said.

I smiled, unsure of what to say.

'I'm serious. You're changing the way this game is played. People used to say the same about me many years ago, but I am saying it to you now. You are taking cricket to a new level. Keep going.'

Feeling overwhelmed, I thanked him and tried to change the subject.

RCB started the 2013 tournament in outstanding form, winning six of our first eight matches, but we then lost four out of six consecutive matches on the road. As ever, there were some great occasions, like the evening at Chinnaswamy when we beat Pune Warriors by 130 runs after Chris scored a staggering 175 from 66 balls. However, yet again, we finished fifth and, yet again, we just failed to qualify for the play-offs.

With another cycle of three-year contracts coming to an end, RCB then exercised its option to contract Virat, Chris and me as three of the five players that every team was entitled to retain and effectively keep out of the player auction, which was held in February 2014.

The opening 20 matches of IPL 7 in 2014 were played in the United Arab Emirates amid renewed concerns over security during the general election in India. We won two and lost two matches in the UAE, resumed the tournament in India and remained inconsistent: brilliant one day, pretty average the next.

We finished seventh in the eight-team league in 2014, winning only five of our 14 matches. I was typically being asked to bat at four or five, held back as a kind of safety net to keep us in the game if we happened to lose early wickets. As a result, more often than not, I would come in around the 15th or 16th over and my opportunity to impact the match would be limited to scoring something like a quick 30 off 15 balls.

In an ideal world, I would have preferred to bat in the top three and to have had the opportunity to play a major innings but, in the interests of the team, in what was fast becoming the pattern of my Twenty20 career, in international cricket as well as in the IPL, I was more often than not held back in the middle order.

Our results improved in 2015, when eight teams participated in a double round-robin format, and we won seven of our 14 group matches, including four notable victories on the road.

We defeated Kolkata Knight Riders at the vast and noisy Eden Gardens, an impressive stadium where the playing experience can be spoiled by a dead wicket and a rock-hard outfield.

Virat's classy, unbeaten 62 guided us to a comfortable win over the Rajasthan Royals at the Sardar Patel Stadium in Ahmedabad, one of my favourite stadiums in the world ... the place where I scored an important double century in a Test, the place where I struck a quick century in an ODI (including probably the biggest six of my entire career, struck off the bowling of Harbhajan Singh and landing on the roof of the stands) and the place where lunch typically includes an exceptional pasta station, where you can choose your own ingredients.

RCB's successful travels continued with a win over the Delhi Daredevils at the storied Feroz Shah Kotla cricket ground, where we bowled out DD for 95 and Chris thumped an unbeaten 62 in a comfortable chase.

Our fourth away win was secured against Mumbai Indians (MI) at the Wankhede Stadium in the great city of Mumbai; it was a venue that had been transformed a few years earlier to the extent that, when we returned, it felt like a totally different place. The improvement in facilities was obvious and welcome, but the famous old stadium had character and quite a few fond memories were, quite literally, buried by the progress.

It was a memorable match against MI. I was given a chance to bat at number three, and Virat and I combined to add 215 runs for the second wicket, the highest partnership ever for any wicket in Twenty20 cricket. We ran efficiently between the wickets, turning ones into twos, and twos into threes, launching ourselves at anything slightly short or wide.

I managed to score 133 from 59 balls, and we set what proved a winning total of 235 for one.

We finished third in what was a congested final league, level with two other teams on 16 points, and progressed to play Rajasthan Royals in the eliminator, a match we won by 71 runs in Pune after I made 66 from 38 balls, helping the team set what proved to be a winning total of 180 for four.

After all the frustration, it felt as if we were finally finding form and consistency at the right time, at the business end of the tournament, but two days later we were beaten by CSK in a low-scoring second qualifier, a semifinal, after we struggled to score 139 and they reached the target with one ball to spare.

Bengaluru, formerly known as Bangalore, is known as the 'Garden City' on account of its green spaces and parks, and I have grown very fond of both the city and its people. There is a particular energy on the streets that is hard to explain and wonderful to experience and, every time I return, it feels as if ongoing development has further enhanced the infrastructure … as far as I can tell from the team bus.

In truth, it's almost impossible for any relatively well-known cricketer to walk around the city because they would very soon be submerged by cricket supporters. Just leaving the team hotel requires significant logistical planning: not long ago, I visited Red Monster, producers of a video game that I have endorsed, at their offices in Bengaluru, and they had to hire four security guards to help me get in and out of the building.

The daily life of an IPL cricketer is almost completely contained within an air-conditioned cycle of five-star hotels, team buses, stadiums, airplanes and airports, and almost the only place we ever meet real supporters tends to be in the controlled and sterilised environment of one or other marbled hotel foyer.

In the early years of my career, supporters wanted nothing more than your autograph, but times have changed and cricketers don't have to write any more. Nowadays, with nearly everyone owning a cellphone and almost every phone incorporating a camera, people ask only for photographs.

You always try to oblige, to agree to every request, but there is never enough time to please everyone, and sometimes situations can get out of control, especially if I happen to be with my family. I have watched leading Indian players responding to constant requests by saying 'not now' and turning the other way, but I find the best strategy is to keep walking while assisting as many people as possible; in that way, hopefully, no one is offended.

The ninth season of IPL cricket was launched in April 2016 with the novel introduction of LED stumps that light up when they are broken by the ball, and the debuts of two new franchises, Gujarat Lions and Rising Pune Supergiants, created to replace two former champion teams, Chennai Super Kings and Rajasthan Royals, both of which were suspended for two seasons by the BCCI following charges of spot-fixing and betting.

I have no knowledge of either of these cases, but there is no question corruption continues to cast a shadow over our game. It's probably a fact of human nature that where there is money to be made, there will always be those prepared to go to any lengths to pocket some for themselves. The International Cricket Council, in tandem with the national bodies, has set up proper systems and structures to investigate any events that appear unusual, but it must be hard to catch players who may be collaborating with syndicates betting on, for example, things as obscure as how many runs are scored between the 17th and 26th overs of any given ODI innings.

I have never seen any indication of match-fixing and, if I did, I would report it immediately. I hate it. I really hate to think that cricketers playing with or against me could be deliberately distorting the course of the game for their own financial gain. I simply can't understand it.

The Indian Premier League will surely continue to grow and develop, leading the evolution of the game in many respects, and I hope to participate for a few more years … not least because, taking into account the size of the crowds, the noise and the atmosphere, the most inspiring place to play cricket is India.

क्रिकेट खेलने के लिए सबसे अच्छी जगह भारत है

CHAPTER 13

THE MATCH THAT MATTERS

Shakama Private Game Lodge is located at the foot of the southern Waterberg Mountains, a little more than an hour's drive north of Pretoria; it's one of those places that make our country feel special.

'Well, if we're not going to play golf, what are we going to do?' asked Jan, my older brother, one day in May 2007.

'We could go have lunch at Shakama,' my mother replied.

'What happens there?' I asked.

'It's a game lodge, and I'm helping to sell the plots,' said my mother, who worked as an estate agent.

We agreed and, just as we were leaving after a great lunch, my mother introduced us to the owner, John Swart. He said he wanted us to meet his wife and children, and went to call them.

'This is my daughter Danielle.'

It was the eyes, the beautiful eyes. The long brown hair was striking, but it was the eyes that instantly caught my attention. I said hello, she said hello and, amid the family greetings, that was that.

Back at our car, I asked my mother whether she could get a mobile number for the daughter with the beautiful eyes. A few days later, I sent Danielle a text, asking whether she and some of her friends might want to come out with me and a few of my friends one evening in Pretoria. There would be safety in a group. She replied, and accepted, and eventually turned up with a friend, and we all had a good time.

And that was still that. She was busy with her studies, I was busy with my cricket and, while we came across one another now and then, the rest of 2007 passed … 2008 passed … 2009 passed … most of 2010 passed.

It was Saturday, 4 December 2010, and the occasion was the wedding of my brother, Wessels, at Chateau Larize, near Bela-Bela. Danielle had been asked to sing at the reception, and she was performing 'This Year's Love', written by David Gray, one of my favourite songs. I sat and listened, in awe, entranced.

> *And won't you kiss me*
> *On that midnight street*
> *Sweep me off my feet*
> *Singing ain't this life so sweet*
> *This year's love had better last*
> *This year's love had better last*

It was an amazing moment and, not long afterwards, our relationship finally started to gather some momentum. Danielle was by now living and working in Cape Town, and I was still charging around the world playing cricket, but we saw each other on a regular basis and started going out. Early in 2012, I reached a clear decision that Danielle was the woman I wanted to marry. This was going to be the match that really mattered.

I wanted to do everything properly and so, on Tuesday, 7 February 2012, just three days before I was due to leave for New Zealand with the Proteas, I arranged to meet her parents, John and Alida, in Pretoria, and ask whether they would give me permission to ask their daughter to marry me. I was unbelievably nervous, but I need not have worried. They not only said yes, but also agreed to help me find the right diamond and have the engagement ring made while I was away on tour.

My typically frenetic schedule gave me only three days at home between returning from New Zealand and flying to Bangalore for the start of the Indian Premier League, but I made arrangements to have lunch with the Swart family. It was becoming a military operation and, in a brief window of opportunity when Danielle and Alida stepped away from the table, John discreetly passed me a package containing the engagement ring.

Everything was going according to plan.

I had invited Danielle to spend some time with me in India and, knowing she had always wanted to visit the Taj Mahal, suggested we organise a trip during a break between RCB matches.

'Jim Rydell and Kalveer B Biradar are going to travel with us,' I said.

'Why?'

'There will be crowds, and they will be our security guards.'

That was a tiny white lie. In truth, Jim was a professional photographer and Kalveer was a videographer. Both are closely associated with RCB, and have become good friends, and I wanted them to be present to record the events that would, all going well, unfold during our visit. So the four of us flew to Delhi, hired a car and made the 212-kilometre drive to Agra in Uttar Pradesh. We eventually checked in at the Oberoi Amarvilas hotel and, while Danielle went to change, Jim fixed a hidden microphone inside my shirt.

The Taj Mahal, this staggeringly perfect marble mausoleum commissioned by the Mughal Emperor Shah Jahan in memory of his wife Mumtaz Mahal, was described by Nobel laureate Rabindranath Tagore as 'a teardrop on the cheek of time' and it seems to evoke strong emotions in almost every visitor. As far as I was concerned, it was the ideal place to pop the question, the ideal place to get engaged.

We walked around the main building, and then made our way to a nearby lawn. The sun was just starting to set. Danielle looked fantastic in a simple white dress and, out of the corner of my eye, I noticed Jim and Kalveer standing among some trees approximately 50 metres away, their cameras pointing towards us.

My heart was pounding. I went down on one knee.

'What on earth are you doing?' Danielle asked.

I smiled and started to recite a carefully prepared speech telling her what she meant to me and concluding with the words: 'You're the one I want to live with forever. Danielle, will you marry me?'

At that moment, I took the engagement ring out of my pocket and presented it to her. She looked at it, promptly burst into tears and fell into my arms. A few seconds passed. I held her tightly. A few more seconds passed. I was starting to feel just slightly concerned.

Danielle is a strong-minded person, not afraid to say what she thinks. As these torturous seconds passed, I considered it was not entirely impossible that she could turn to me and say, 'Sorry, bud, that was a nice presentation but this is not going to happen. Would you mind if we go back to Bangalore?'

I was getting anxious.

'Listen, are you going to give me an answer?'

She finally looked up at me and said: 'Yes.'

We were married on Saturday, 30 March 2013, at Shakama, and exchanged vows on almost exactly the same spot where we had first set eyes upon each other just over six years earlier. So many people put so much effort into creating what turned out to be the most amazing day of our lives.

The actual ceremony took place on a piece of land not far from the main lodge, surrounded by bushveld, under a canopy, with an altar and rows of chairs laid out for the 140 guests. Danielle was led down the track from the lodge by her father and, just before she arrived, a song was played that she had written and recorded especially for me. I stood there and listened, and struggled to maintain any kind of composure.

Ek weet daar is nog altyd 'n engel aan my sy,

Vandag is dit so duidelik want jy staan hier voor my.

Jy't my geleer hoe om myself te eer

En jy't gewys wat die liefde is.

Jy's my sielsmaat en ek kan nie wag om alles met jou te deel
nie.

Jy's die rots waarteen ek lê as my wêreld te veel raak.

Jy's my regterhand en die arms wat my altyd kan beskerm.

Jy's die een wat my laat lag en my lig in elke dag.

Vandag gee ek vir jou my hand

En vandag smee ons met mekaar 'n band.

This is translated as:

I know there is always an angel at my side,

Today it's clear because you are standing here.

You have taught me how to honour myself

And you have shown me the meaning of love.

You are my soulmate and I can't wait to share everything with
you.

You're the rock that I lean against when the world becomes
too much.

You're my right hand and the arms that always protect me.

You're the one who makes me laugh and my light in every day.

Today I give you my hand

And today we join together as one.

I was close to tears as the song ended and then, at the exact moment that my bride appeared in the open, it started to rain. In many places, such a brief downpour would have been viewed as a disaster, but not in Africa. On this continent, where water is so scarce and precious, rain is received as a blessing from God, and so it was received by us.

Pastor Danie Nelson conducted the service, which meant a lot to me because he has been a friend of our family in Bela-Bela for many years and has taught me so much about life and faith.

The wedding dinner was held in the main lodge and included an amazing performance by Elvis Blue, the platinum-selling singer and songwriter. He agreed to play out of the kindness of his heart and, at my request, he sang 'Lighthouse'. It's a special song, and I love the chorus.

> *Miles away, I can look down from space*
> *Know where I've been*
> *Know where I am and where I'm going.*
> *Lost at sea I see you shine for me*
> *You are my lighthouse*
> *You are my lighthouse.*

I then carried that theme into my speech, trying to explain how I wanted to be a lighthouse for my wife. I hope it made sense.

Danielle has brought so much love and stability to my life, and I am acutely aware how she has sacrificed her career in financial services and her singing so that she can spend time with me and look after our son, AB junior, who was safely born in Pretoria on Wednesday, 22 July 2015.

We have become a little family now and, without repeating all the well-worn clichés about fatherhood, I will simply say that changing circumstances do change your perspective. For me, there is nothing more precious, nothing more enjoyable, than spending time alone with my wife and son, even if it is in a hotel room in some far-flung corner of the planet.

It's not easy being married to a professional cricketer whose career takes him all around the world for extended periods, and whose time is consistently being claimed by cricket, by sponsors and by media. I am not complaining. I am very fortunate in many ways. But Dan and I know we always have to plan well and make sacrifices to ensure we see enough of each other.

Gary Kirsten once told me how, facing similar challenges, he and his wife, Debbie, introduced a 21-day rule, whereby they would never go longer than 21 days without seeing each other. It meant that, if he was on tour for more than three weeks, she would fly in to visit him, whatever the cost.

They made a decision that seeing each other regularly had to be the highest priority in their lives, and Danielle and I have reached the same conclusion, although we are trying to apply a 10-day rule.

We were separated for the entire eight weeks of the IPL in 2015, and it was tough. Speaking several times a day on Skype is no substitute. In 2016, whenever possible, she and AB junior travelled with me. Living in a hotel is not ideal, but at least we are all together.

I try not to bring cricket home and work hard to be equally as considerate and helpful whether I have scored a century or been out for a duck, whether everything is going well inside the team or whether there are issues that are bothering me, whether we have won or lost.

Danielle always manages to be incredibly supportive, whatever the situation. She has never been a huge follower of the game, which is probably a good thing, but she says precisely the right things to give me confidence when I leave in the morning and is always sympathetic and understanding when I return at the end of the day.

The pressure does occasionally take its toll and, on several occasions in recent years, I have struggled to sleep properly. Some people can get by with just a few hours of rest. I am not one of them. I need a minimum of eight hours of sleep each night, or life can start to become challenging.

I remember getting absolutely no sleep at all on the night before the first day of the second Test against India in Durban in December 2013. I went to bed around 10 pm, as usual, but could not sleep. My wife was with me, and she was dozing off, but I just lay there, wide awake … mid-night … 2 am … For a moment, I thought I heard raised voices in the hotel reception. Were they keeping me up? It was 4 am … 6 am … And then, all of a sudden, it was time to gather my things and join the rest of the squad on the bus to Kingsmead.

This is bizarre, I thought. I am going to play a Test and I have literally not slept for one minute. I was hoping we would bat, so I could maybe get a quick nap in the dressing room, but MS Dhoni won the toss and decided India would bat first, so we were fielding and I was keeping wick-et, which meant I needed to concentrate for every single ball of what, in all probability, was going to be a long and demanding day.

I felt totally exhausted. How would I survive? I was beginning to pan-ic. Calm down, I told myself; take it ball by ball, over by over. I got by. India reached 76 for one at lunch, and I walked straight off the field, into the changing room and slept for 25 minutes of the 40-minute interval. I managed to get through the afternoon as well and, with the Indians 163 for one at tea, lay down and slept for 10 minutes of the 20-minute break.

Mercifully, bad light forced an early close after just eight overs of the evening session, and I was hugely relieved to get back to the hotel, get something to eat and get a proper night's sleep. It had been a troubling experience, but I recovered the next day and took five catches as India were bowled out for 334.

'Just take a sleeping pill.'

That was Mike Hussey's advice several months later when we were chatting during the IPL. The Australian is one of the kindest, wisest and most sensible cricketers I have met, and he explained how he would take a pill before major matches just to make sure he slept well and was prop-erly prepared.

I discussed the matter with my father, a GP, and he assured me it should be fine to take half a sleeping pill every now and then. So that's what I do, and the drama of Durban has not been repeated.

Sleep is precious, and time is precious as well. My schedule tends to be so busy that there is just no time to do everything I would like to do, and I worry that people can feel either let down or brushed off because I don't get around to seeing them or contacting them. There are just not enough hours in the day.

This is a typical scenario: I will meet somebody and we will discuss a project. I will be genuinely enthusiastic and, as ever, eager to please; we will start making plans. Weeks go by. Nothing happens because I have no time to make anything happen, and people may start to think I've lost interest or I no longer care and, on a few occasions, I have probably been guilty of creating unrealistic expectations.

It bothers me a lot. I remember Graeme Smith once telling me that the key to surviving the life of a busy professional sports person is simply to say no. You can't keep everyone happy, he would say, so sometimes you have to say no, you can't attend that event, you can't get involved in that venture. Rather like the character played by Jim Carrey in *Yes Man*, the 2008 film, I too often find it much easier to say yes.

To be honest, whenever the relentless schedule does allow me some free time to myself, I far prefer to spend that time with my family, ideally lying on a bed beside my young son, watching him sleep, quietly wondering what the future holds for him, casually pondering what kind of man he will grow up to be.

He will be exactly what he will be, of course, and I will be completely content to see him develop as he wants but, from what I have learned over the years, most youngsters benefit from being active, from having a fighting spirit, from being able to have fun and from enjoying music.

Being active means getting out and about, participating in organised sport or any kind of exercise, being the kind of person who would sign up to run a half-marathon just for fun. I competed in the Knysna half-marathon a couple of times, first in 2011 with Mark Boucher, Jacques Kallis and Rob Walter, a good friend who was then a conditioning coach for the Proteas and has since become a successful head coach at the Titans.

Having a fighting spirit could mean subscribing to the belief that, when you are involved in any kind of game, you play as if it is the most important thing in the world, sure in the knowledge that as soon as the final whistle sounds and it's all over that very same game becomes the least important thing in the world.

It's only sport, people might say, and they're right, but it is sport and, during the game, there is no alternative but to strain every muscle and fight for every single inch. You need to fight like hell, you need to fight like Rafa Nadal so often fights on the tennis court, you need to fight like Tiger Woods fought through the intense pain in his left knee when he somehow managed to complete the 2008 US Open, and actually won the title.

Being able to have fun means being able to do all of the above while still retaining the capacity to sit back every once in a while, to share a beer with your mates and just enjoy yourself. In my experience, the world-class sportsman who has most effectively and most consistently got this part right is Ernie Els.

Ernie is recognised around the world as a great golfer, with two US Open wins, two British Open wins and 64 other professional titles to his name in a career that started way back in 1989; and he has made enormous contributions in the fields of autism and golf for underprivileged youngsters in South Africa. Above all, however, he remains the same big easy guy with the big easy swing, the big easy smile and the soft heart.

By a happy coincidence, Ernie and John Swart, my father-in-law, both own holiday homes in Herolds Bay, not far from George on the southern coast of South Africa, and, in recent years, we have been able to spend a couple of days in that part of the world between the Christmas and New Year Test matches.

One day in 2012, Danielle and I had been out to lunch and were returning home when I saw a tall, blond man driving his car, and seemingly arriving at his house, and thought he looked familiar.

'Dan, please stop,' I said. 'That's Ernie Els, and I want to meet this guy. He's been my ultimate hero for as long as I can remember. You carry on. I'll be home in five minutes, or so.'

I walked towards where he had parked. His wife and children were already heading into the house, and he must have looked up and seen me approaching from around 20 metres.

'AB, you *bliksem*!' he shouted, with a grin.

'Hi,' I said. 'I just wanted to say hello.'

'Yes, it's great to see you,' he replied. 'We're going to have a beer. Come in.'

He had some American friends, Kevin and Ira, staying with him and Ernie introduced me to them as 'South Africa's Babe Ruth', adding that they could stuff baseball because cricket was a much better game. The Americans seemed to get the idea, and, over a few beers, we all chatted cheerfully for a while, about golf and cricket, baseball and sport in general.

'Let's play golf tomorrow,' Ernie announced. 'I'll arrange a tee-off time at Oubaai.'

'That would be great,' I said, trying to appear only moderately interested in the idea, when, in truth, I was unbelievably excited. Soon, I was also very scared of embarrassing myself because my golf game has declined a little in recent years, ever since my peak when I was 23. I hadn't really had time to play and, when I had managed to get on the course, I had struggled to keep the ball on the fairway. Oh well, I thought, I can't let this opportunity pass. I will try my best.

Oubaai golf club is a beautiful links course, located between the Indian Ocean and the Outeniqua Mountains, designed by Ernie, and, at very short notice, I asked a friend, Jan Potgieter, to be my partner in what would be a special four-ball.

Ernie was six under par after the first nine holes, and we were well down but, to my great relief, I was striking the ball well off the tee … and our host seemed both impressed and surprised by my distance, exactly as my father and brother Wessels had been surprised many years earlier when we were all playing golf, as a family, in Warmbaths.

I was using a three-wood off the tee because my driver was usually just too erratic, and I was quite pleased to walk down the fairways at the par-four 1st, the par-five 4th, the par-four 5th and the par-five 7th ... to find my ball no more than 20 or 30 metres behind Ernie's ball. Jan and I recovered some pride on the back nine, and enjoyed what was an incredible experience, playing golf with a man who knows how to win, and still knows how to have fun.

Lastly, if AB junior turns out to be so inclined, I would very much like my son to enjoy and appreciate music. If he is fortunate enough to inherit his mother's music genes, that will undoubtedly be the case.

When I was growing up, our family home was always filled with music, usually with the golden oldies my parents so enjoyed. I took guitar lessons for two years at Warmbaths Primary School, where I was taught by Jo Fourie, the wife of Louis Fourie, a teacher who later became principal. My interest lapsed for a while at Affies, but a friend of mine, called Johan Booysen, and I enjoyed playing the guitar in our matric year.

Some years later, I took my guitar on tour with the Proteas, thinking it could be useful at social evenings, but the strings snapped and it was awkward to carry around, so I dropped that idea.

It made more sense for me to channel my music energies into writing songs, something I had been doing fairly regularly since leaving school. The process would start with writing a poem; then I would create some kind of melody, try out a few chords on my guitar and develop a tune.

Ampie du Preez is a hugely talented professional musician and we have been friends since we were boys. In 2010 we decided to collaborate and have a real go at producing a proper album. Our commitment was such that we entered into an arrangement with Sony Music and went away for four weeks; we literally cut ourselves off from the world and did not return until we had laid down 20 new songs.

An excellent producer named Murray Lubbe then helped us choose the best 14 songs, which were included in the album, and *Maak Jou Drome Waar* (*Make Your Dreams Come True*) was released as our debut single. I enjoyed the entire exercise, and the song was included in playlists of major music radio stations for a few weeks, but we were not exactly One Direction.

I am pleased to say Ampie has gone on to enjoy a successful solo singing and songwriting career, while I have restricted my musical activities to a few one-off appearances at special events.

In January 2011, Shah Rukh Khan headlined a concert after the Proteas played a Twenty20 international against India in front of 45 000 spectators at the Moses Mabhida Stadium in Durban. SRK, as he is known, is just about as big as it gets in the world of Indian entertainment and, incidentally, he is also the co-owner of Kolkata Knight Riders.

He had approached me a few days before and asked if I would sing a duet with him. He wanted us to perform '*Yeh Dosti*', a popular and well-known Hindi song about friends together. I said that was fine, but I did ask him if, in return, he would let me teach him an Afrikaans song that we could also sing on stage. He agreed and so, for the one and only performance, the two of us sang '*Ryperd*', the song made famous by Dozi.

Shah Rukh is a wonderfully humble and kind person, and we had a great time during the concert, singing the duets and then dancing together with JP Duminy, Wayne Parnell and Makhaya Ntini.

So I wonder what the future holds for my son.

Will AB junior grow up to be active, to have a fighting spirit, be able to have fun and enjoy his music? Who knows? We will see. As I lie on the bed and watch him sleeping, so small and perfect, my only goal is to help, support and encourage him as he grows in his own image, not mine.

CHAPTER 14

THE DREAM

Ever since I was a boy, I have had a recurring dream – the same dream over and over again, to a point where the exact sequence of events could not be more vivid or more clear in my mind.

It is the ICC Cricket World Cup final and I am fielding at cover. The batsman is left-handed and he drives, making a solid connection. I dive to my right, gather the ball at full stretch, spring to my feet, run towards the stumps and take off the bails. We all appeal. The umpire's finger is raised, and South Africa wins the World Cup.

Then, agitated and excited, I wake up ...

The frustration and pain of successive World Cup disappointments linger for me, as they linger for millions of South Africans: in 1992, we were denied by the rain against England in Sydney, which left the scoreboard famously reading 'South Africa to win need 22 runs off 1 ball'; in 1996, we were one of the favourites, but were eliminated by Brian Lara's century in the quarterfinal in Karachi after Allan Donald had been left out.

In 1999, our family was watching together on television when South Africa played Australia in the semifinal in Birmingham, and we needed nine from the last over with one wicket standing. Lance Klusener drove the first two balls for boundaries, and we needed one to win from four balls. Allan Donald was almost run out backing up off the third ball. Next, Lance called for a quick single but Allan didn't hear him and was run out. The match was tied but Australia went through to the final because they had finished higher on the Super Six table. I remember my father being so angry. He could not believe how we had lost. I just ran to my bedroom and cried.

We were all watching on television again in 2003, when South Africa were hosts and we had to beat Sri Lanka in Durban, and we were on course to win with rain coming. There was confusion over the reduced target, and we thought we were on track when the downpour arrived, but we weren't. We were level, which meant the match was tied, again, and so we were eliminated from our own World Cup by the slimmest of margins.

In 2007, we collapsed to 27 for five in the semifinal against Australia in St Lucia and were well beaten by the eventual winners and, four years later in 2011, we seemed on track to win the quarterfinal against New Zealand in Dhaka but then floundered and fell well short of a modest target of 222.

Six Cricket World Cups had inspired so much hope, and delivered six national disappointments.

Still, I kept having the same dream ...

It is the ICC Cricket World Cup final and I am fielding at cover. The batsman is left-handed and he drives, making a solid connection. I dive to my right, gather the ball at full stretch, jump to my feet, run towards the stumps and take off the bails. We appeal. The umpire's finger is raised, and South Africa wins the World Cup.

And still I kept waking up ...

Maybe 2015 was going to be our year. The Cricket World Cup was being hosted by Australia and New Zealand, presenting us with what started to feel like the perfect opportunity to move beyond the history of frustration and pain. As the tournament approached, I started to feel more and more confident that our time had come. As captain, I sensed a real belief within the squad, a collective resolve to banish the 'chokers' tag forever.

Our preparation was ideal, impeccably planned by Cricket South Africa, and we played no fewer than 21 one-day internationals in the five months leading up to the World Cup, trialling various combinations and plans. We won 14 of these games, with two no-results, and began to feel we could beat anyone on our day.

The squad looked strong: Hashim Amla, Quinton de Kock, Faf du Plessis, JP Duminy, Rilee Rossouw, Farhaan Behardien, David Miller and I were the batsmen; Dale Steyn, Morné Morkel, Vernon Philander, Kyle Abbott and Wayne Parnell were the pace bowlers; Imran Tahir and Aaron Phangiso were the spinners.

I was becoming nervous and excited as, in January 2015, we completed our preparations by winning four of five ODIs against the West Indies. It was Russell Domingo who kept us calm.

'It's just another tournament, AB,' our coach said, over and over again. 'We must focus on the basics and not try anything special. We'll give everything, of course, but let's not get too intense or stressed. It's a World Cup and it's not going to change our lives. Whatever happens, I will go fishing afterwards.'

Russell was choosing his words carefully and intelligently, deliberately aiming to lift the burden of pressure and expectation from the players, helping us relax. I like, respect and admire him as a good man. He is not the type of coach who will scream and shout for the sake of looking tough, but his approach should never be misinterpreted as soft. Instead, in his own way, he is able to draw the best out of the people around him.

I felt we combined well as coach and captain. We would address the squad before almost every training session and before every match, and Russell would generally speak first, addressing technical issues such as plans for opposing batsmen, calmly running through the basic mechanics of what we needed to do, and then my task would be to engage the other side of the brain, motivating the players by stirring their emotions.

My theme remained consistent before and during the Cricket World

Cup in 2015, and invariably revolved around the concept of 'Protea fire', which had become so important to all of us.

It had started as Graeme Smith's idea. He had some years before identified the need for the national cricket team to develop its own clear culture and identity, and he wanted to create something around the fighting spirit that, like me, he valued above anything else. In his mind, he wanted the Proteas to be first and foremost a team that is prepared to bleed for each other, one that never gives up, that always fights back from adversity.

The eureka moment came when he discovered that the protea, the national flower after which we were named, embodies all of these precious qualities. When the South African veld has been destroyed by fire, it is the protea that is resilient and grows among the ashes, that fights back and blooms again.

I remember him calling me when I was in Bangalore, and explaining the idea.

'Can you write a song about it?' he asked.

'How do you mean?'

'We need to create a song about Protea fire, which the team can sing.'

I sat on the balcony of my hotel room in India, and wrote a song with a chorus in isiXhosa, translated as 'Forever we'll keep the fire burning'.

Umlilo uhlala uyatshisa
Umlilo uhlala uyatshisa ye
Umlilo uhlala uyatshisa.

Within the Proteas squad, we attach great importance to building on the achievements of the past, honouring and respecting every single person who has played for South Africa, and I included some words in the second verse to reflect this concept of picking up a torch from the great names of the past, and carrying it forward and then handing it on:

To those before us, to those to come,
Today, tomorrow, we'll play as one.

The full lyrics are private, the words shared only among those who are privileged to represent South Africa on the cricket field, but the song has become an important element of the Proteas team culture, and it is sung in the dressing room after every win in a Test match, or an ODI or a Twenty20 international.

It is also sung when we have secured victory in a Test series. On these special occasions, we will traditionally wait in the pavilion until almost everyone else has gone home and then we walk back out onto the field into what is then a completely deserted stadium, and we form a tight huddle and we sing our song.

The concept of Protea fire grew organically among and within the squad over several years and, in October 2014, it was extended into a fully fledged public campaign designed to excite and enthuse all South Africans. Two advertising agencies, Ogilvy and Thackwell & Whittaker, produced some brilliant content, including one two-minute clip that can be seen on YouTube and, even now, sends shivers down my middle-aged spine.

Overlaid on stirring images, the voiceover runs as follows:

> *AB: Men, what does playing in this shirt mean? Each and every one of us is where a million kids dream to be. We get to pull on this shirt and wear the badge on our hearts. We get to sing our anthem and play for 60 million fans, like the heroes who came before us. But what does a protea have to do with all of that? It has everything to do with it. No matter how hot the fire burns, the protea will always survive. It's got the will to grow back stronger, to do what needs to be done. We are Proteas. We are South Africa.*

HASHIM: *We find a way, boys, we do what it takes.*

FAF: *This team never ever gives up.*

HASHIM: *We are the guys that bat with a broken hand, who take five wickets on the flattest deck in the world. Who does that? Proteas do that, boys. We are the guys that bat for eight hours in the hottest weather to save a Test match. For me, boys, that's the Proteas. We bleed, we hurt and we fight together right to the end. That's what makes us what we are, boys.*

AB: *We know who we are, and we know who we play for. We are South Africa.*

ALL: *To the team! Proteas! To the team! Proteas! To the team! Proteas!*

Protea fire meant a lot to me, and I think it meant a lot to the players and coaches. In one sentence, it meant we would always fight, always fight back from adversity and always fight for each other.

As the squad travelled to the 2015 Cricket World Cup, I bought a small green book and stuck the Proteas logo on the front cover. Sitting there on the plane, I wrote the first two pages:

Wed 04 Feb, 2015

ABBAS

I'm sitting next to Vern and Morras on the flight to Sydney, and the two of them are so curious about what I am doing. I just told them now that this book will eventually make its way to them. Let's hope it does.

This is a pass-on book. The idea is for you to write in it and pass it on to anyone listed on the previous page. Please scratch out your name as soon as you receive this book, so that the next person knows who has not written in it yet.

Book rules:
1. *Write your name at the top right of the page.*
2. *Write about anything you want, long or short, good or bad, World Cup dreams, anything.*
3. *You lose this book, you fly home! Just kidding, but please look after it.*
4. *Let's not skip a day.*
5. *You've got this page and the next at your disposal; please don't write more.*
6. *No smut or swearing.*
7. *Break any of these rules, and it will be discussed at the Fines Meeting.*

OK, so here I go. After our send-off @ Melrose Arch, I can't help but think of the World Cup. I'm so excited. My adrenalin is already giving me sweaty palms. I know we're winning this Cup. I've been dreaming about it my whole life. I know you guys believe it too. The obstacles we will be confronted with might seem impossible to overcome at times, but fire in our hearts, the resilience we have and the trust for each other will overpower these challenges.

Personally, I can't wait for the pressure moments, cause I know I'll have a group of incredible human beings and cricket players right behind me.

'To those before us, to those to come, today, tomorrow, we'll play as one. Umlilo uhlala uyatshisa.'

I'm right behind each and every one of you.

Abbas

The little green book was going to travel with us, passed from hand to hand, throughout the tournament, and Hashim made his contribution after our first warm-up match against Sri Lanka in Christchurch. 'It went pretty well,' he wrote. 'Suffice to say, we chased down a decent total after bowling well. The days preceding the World Cup are a good time for the team to get the bonding in order, before the real responsibility begins.'

He passed the book on to Russell, who wrote about missing his sons, Kyle and Liam, and added: 'You guys have no idea how influential and important you are to so many kids back home.' The coach concluded by writing: 'The last thought I have before I go to bed is that everyone is fighting a battle in life … whether it's from within, something at home, financial, emotional, esteem, anything. Everyone wants love. Let's try and make a difference in each other's life. That's quite deep for a fisherman, but we all just need some connection.'

Wayne Parnell was the next recipient of the book, and his contribution reflected on a defeat against New Zealand in our second warm-up match in Christchurch, when they scored 331 and reduced us to 62 for six before Vernon and JP made runs and helped us to 197. We were not fazed by the outcome and Wayne wrote: 'Bags have been packed and shipped to Hamilton and soon we will follow. Everyone is very excited about 15/2/15 because that is when we take the first steps to reaching the MCG and turning our dream into reality #proteafire.'

The format was unchanged from 2011, with 14 participating countries divided into two groups of seven and the top four from each round-robin group advancing to the quarterfinals, followed by the semifinals and the 2015 ICC Cricket World Cup final at the Melbourne Cricket Ground on Sunday, 29 March.

Our opening match, against Zimbabwe in Hamilton, was always going to be tricky and it became significantly more dangerous when we lost the toss and, sent in to bat on a difficult pitch at Seddon Park, found ourselves in trouble at 83 for four. The first pressure moment had arrived sooner than anyone had expected, but we responded well as a team, and David Miller and JP proceeded to rescue the innings.

Dave scored 138 not out and JP made 115 not out as we reached 339 for four in our 50 overs. Zimbabwe fought hard and, in reply, reached 191 for two after 32 overs before we finally managed to apply some pressure, bowled them out for 277 and nailed down a tough victory by 62 runs.

We travelled to Melbourne for our next game, against India, and everyone seemed in good spirits. I was starting to enjoy the responsibility of captaincy and relishing the challenge of leading this group of young men through a World Cup, which, I desperately hoped, would unfold as the highlight in all our careers.

The squad gathered, as usual, at six o'clock on the evening before the match and, after Russell had spoken, I made a couple of points, firstly suggesting everyone should keep their eyes on the ball at all times because that was a good way to stay focused when playing in front of a big crowd in a big stadium; and, secondly, urging everyone to adapt to the flow of the game, recognising when we had the momentum and needed to push on, and also seeing when the game was running against us and being able to pull back a touch and control the damage.

I finished by reading a quotation from a film I had watched with David Miller. *Lone Survivor* was a dramatisation of an actual raid to capture a Taliban leader in Afghanistan by four United States Navy SEALS, in which Marcus Luttrell, played by Mark Wahlberg, was the only one to survive.

The quote was: 'Brave men fought and died building a proud tradition and fear of reputation that I am bound to uphold. I died up on that mountain. There is no question that a part of me will forever be up on that mountain, dead, as my brothers died. There is a part of me that lived because of my brothers. Because of them I am still alive, and I can never forget that no matter how much it hurts, how dark it gets or how far you fall, you are never out of the fight.'

That was my message: it was going to be tough and there would be times when we would need to fight, but the important thing was that we would be fighting together. That was the plan.

'Rely on each other when we feel the pressure,' I concluded. 'Enjoy.'

India won the toss and batted and, though we started well when I managed to run out Rohit Sharma with a direct hit from extra cover in the third over of the game, Shikhar Dhawan and Virat Kohli built a partnership that laid the perfect foundation for India to reach 307 for seven in 50 overs.

MS Dhoni's team backed this up with some really disciplined bowling, giving us nothing loose to hit, and some outstanding fielding, executing run-out opportunities and taking catches. We struggled under pressure from the first ball, and were dismissed for 177, outplayed and decisively beaten. I was disappointed, and told the media the defeat was 'almost embarrassing' but we were not going to panic.

I knew we needed a much-improved performance against the West Indies in Sydney. A camera team travelled with us during the tournament, and their video recording of my talk to the squad on the eve of this match makes it possible to provide a word-for-word transcript:

> *I feel it is that time of the tournament when we really need to focus on freeing up a bit. Relax, breathe deeply and have full faith that we are prepared, because that's what I really believe. Yes, we had a bit of fun today. We didn't hit a lot of balls in the last two days. But we are ready and we must trust each other.*
>
> *We have spoken about obstacles in our way. We had a bad loss against India. Guys are writing bad things about us. We've got injuries going on. There will always be obstacles that come your way. That's part of tournaments like this. We are going to have controversial stuff around us all the time. But we can deal with that because we created this culture and we have to look after it, boys.*

We're going to take it on the field tomorrow, and we're going to show them what it's all about, but I really need us to free up, and relax, and enjoy ourselves, and remember that we have some of the best players in the world and remember that we are going to win this World Cup because we have the best talent.

In my last chat, I spoke about us never being out of the fight. Fight and enjoyment go together really well because you can't fight without enjoying it. We are going to take both on the field tomorrow. We are going to fight, but we are going to enjoy what we do. You can't just do one. You can't just enjoy it because then you will get knocked over. You have to take your fight with you.

No matter how dark it gets, no matter how many people speak badly about us, we cannot stop fighting for one second. We are men and we enjoy competition, and I want to see some of that tomorrow.

OK, manne, lastly, I want to say I will never lose hope as a captain. This is hope right here. I will not stop that, I promise you. I believe in every single oke in this team.

Yes, Parny had a tough game in the last game. I don't care because I know what he is capable of as a player. Yes, Immy will go for a boundary every now and then. Hash didn't score in the last game. The Rock wasn't there. I wasn't there in that last game, but we will not lose hope as a team, boys, not for one second. We know what we can do. We've seen Rilee bat in the nets. We've seen Quinton score three hundreds in a row.

I can go through every single name. Morras has been part of IPL-winning teams. He can land a yorker when he wants to. I've seen that happen. I will not lose hope in any of you, and I'm expecting the same of you. There will be obstacles. We will be down and out in games coming up in the World Cup, but we

are not going to stop the fight, gents. We're going to take it on,
and we're going to run into the wall, together.

That's when we enjoy it and that's how we create memories.
It's when we fight together.

I didn't sleep much in the night that followed, not because I was particularly nervous, but because I was ill, suffering from some kind of
stomach bug, so ill that I called the doctor to give me an anti-nausea
injection at three o'clock in the morning. We won the toss and decided
to bat, and I actually fell fast asleep in the changing room while Hash
and Faf were building an ideal foundation, moving to 145 for one in
the 30th over.

They were then both out in the same over, which brought Rilee
Rossouw and me to the crease with plenty of work still to do. I was feeling quite flat and generally lacking in energy, but I was soon encouraged
by the sight of 'Rolos', as we know him, striking the ball around the
Sydney Cricket Ground. He has a very special talent. As we picked up the
momentum of the innings, I began to feed on his intensity.

Reaching 19 from 18 balls, I was feeling stronger. I moved to 50 in
31 balls, after striking Sulieman Benn for six, four, four, in consecutive
deliveries. Rilee was out for a brilliant 61 from 39 balls, and I carried on
where he left off, attacking everything and reaching my 100 in 52 balls. It
was the second-fastest century in World Cup history, and I celebrated by
beating my chest vigorously. I was feeling quite emotional. This World
Cup meant so much to every single one of us.

Everything was going my way. Jason Holder bowled the 48th over of
the innings, and I managed to score four, six off a no-ball, two off a free
hit, four off a no-ball, four off a free hit, four, two and six; and the pattern continued when the young West Indian captain stuck to his guns and
bowled the 50th and last over, and I managed to strike a two to long on, a
six over square leg, a six over mid-wicket, a four to the long-off boundary

(meaning I had moved from 100 to 150 in 12 balls), a six over long on and one last six over square leg.

I finished with 162 not out from 66 balls, including 17 boundaries and eight sixes. More importantly, as a team, we had posted an impressive total of 408 for five from our 50 overs. I was exhilarated. We had bounced back from the defeat against India and made a clear statement.

Kyle Abbott then dismissed Chris Gayle in the second over of the West Indian reply, and, with Imran Tahir taking five wickets, we were able to bowl them out for 151. True to plan, the players had fought hard and enjoyed themselves, exactly as I had asked the previous evening.

The little green book had been passed to Rilee, who that night wrote: 'I could write ten pages on today's match, but I only have a little space. We had a fantastic base set up when I got my opportunity and Abbas followed soon after. We both played some great cricket shots, but what I remember most was the enjoyment we were having and playing with the flow of the game. Abbas #spiderman decided to leave nothing to chance and played a SICK innings – "cough, cough" – excuse the pun, leading from the front! It was a memorable day for me and I'm glad my parents were there to see it. Jimmy bowling Gayle, QDK's serious stumping of Sammy and Immy's five-wicket haul. It was an amazing day at the office. I am honoured to be part of this special team. Love you guys. #proteafire.'

That's all we were: a group of young South Africans working hard, giving everything to win this World Cup and to make our compatriots, all our compatriots, burst with pride. There was no dark agenda, no secret plan to deny any kind of opportunity to anybody. We simply wanted to play cricket, and to win.

As usual, the players and coach were the most visible elements of the squad, but there were many dedicated and professional people working tirelessly in the engine room, unseen and largely unappreciated by everyone except us, keeping us fit, motivated and impeccably prepared to perform on the field.

An entirely separate book would be required to do proper justice to their contributions, but Adrian Birrell was our assistant coach, providing exceptional support to Russell Domingo; Allan Donald proved an outstanding bowling coach, respected by everybody; and Claude Henderson excelled as our spin-bowling coach. Gary Kirsten and Mike Hussey, two highly skilled and highly experienced cricket men, had been recruited as invaluable consultants, saying all the right things at all the right times.

Dr Mohammed Moosajee was always an efficient, highly organised and sympathetic team manager, while Lerato Malekutu continued to manage the media with a smile, which was no mean achievement. Greg King performed regular miracles as our strength and conditioning coach, and Brandon Jackson was a talented and brilliant physiotherapist.

Riaan Muller managed our logistics, proving himself to be a conscientious and committed individual who ensured our complex travel plans were executed without a hitch, while Zunaid Wadee was the ultimate professional as our chief protection officer. Prasanna Agoram proved a top-class analyst, and Michelle Schmidt took on the crucial role of looking after our wives and families when they joined us on tour.

Tony Irish, Chief Executive of the South African Cricketers' Association (SACA), was another important contributor; he has for many years played a highly significant role in the smooth running of the Proteas and South African cricket in general, always supporting the players and always finding solutions. He has become a good friend to many of us.

Our World Cup campaign seemed to be gathering momentum and the little green book was passed to Dr Moosajee, who finished his notes by writing: 'Prior to our departure for the Cricket World Cup, someone I know well remarked that South Africa have never won a World Cup because, as a country and as a cricket community, we were not as yet ready for it. He further stated the team environment and culture, epitomised in the Protea Fire campaign, is set up in a way that, irrespective of the outcome, we will leave it all out there on the field and we will always be there to support, protect, nurture and care for each other. It's amazing that someone from outside can sense what we all do.'

Playing against Ireland in Canberra, Hashim and Faf both scored outstanding centuries as we passed 400 for the second match in a row, and then closed out a clinical and efficient victory.

However, just as the experts were starting to talk up our chances, we flew back to New Zealand and produced a really poor performance against Pakistan in Auckland. I sensed something was missing in the warm-up, and we simply did not present on the day. Our bowling was decent in dismissing a motivated Pakistan side for 222 but, inexplicably, our batting lacked any sense of urgency and fight, and we fell 29 runs short.

I managed to score 77 from 58 balls before being the ninth man out, and then attended the post-match media conference and completely failed to conceal my feelings of complete dismay.

'I hate losing,' I told the journalists. 'I really do, so I have nothing good to say about the team at the moment. I'm very disappointed. Even though I scored some runs, I'm still disappointed in my own performance. I should have finished it off. I have done it before so many times and I just couldn't cross the line tonight. We have an opportunity to fix things against the UAE, to play a really good game of cricket and to go into the quarterfinals with a fresh mindset, that mindset of believing we are the best team here. I still believe that, but I just have nothing good to say about our performance today.'

Maybe I was too honest and maybe I was too negative, but I was annoyed by the defeat and, when dealing with the media, I have always found it difficult to be clever and artful, to conceal anything or pretend anything. When they ask a question, they get a straightforward answer.

I was even more blunt in the private team meeting that followed.

'Come on, guys, we can't talk about Protea fire and play like that,' I said. 'It's totally unacceptable, and it's not what we are about as a team. Too many of us were basically fooling around.'

We did rediscover our intensity against the United Arab Emirates in Wellington, and I managed to score 99 not out in our total of 341 for six in 50 overs, before we bowled them out for 195. Two of the UAE batsman, Saqlain Haider and Amjad Javed, suffered the indignity of being dismissed by a part-time dibbly-dobbly bowler of medium pace, who finished with figures of two for 15 from three overs. His name was De Villiers.

Five weeks after the first game, the tournament finally reached the last eight stage and, after finishing second in Group B behind India, we prepared to play a quarterfinal against Sri Lanka in Sydney.

None of us needed reminding of the bleak reality that, in all the history of World Cup cricket, no South African team had ever won a knockout match, not one. It was a wretched record and, when the squad gathered at 6 pm on the eve of what would be a huge match, I tried to find the right words:

> I want to read part of this letter I have received from John Smit [captain of the Springbok team that won the Rugby World Cup in 2007]. There's one piece that stands out for me. 'You chaps have created something special over the last few seasons and, for me, that is the difference between my three World Cups. The one we brought home was the one where our team had the strongest family bond. For me, in life, family is a massive deal and being a father made me truly understand the meaning of being in a team: being responsible for one another, supporting each other, defending each other blindly and having a deep-rooted desire for each of your family members.'
>
> I think that's exactly what it's about.
>
> There are a few things I want to say.
>
> First, it won't be easy. It's never going to be easy, boys, especially in the quarterfinal of the World Cup. I know we're going

to go to the final, but there will be plenty of obstacles in our way, but we have come a long way because of our culture and our team values. The respect we have for each other, the joy we have in each other's successes: those are the things that have brought us to here. No hassles. Nobody has boxed each other. No one has got arrogant. We all value our team culture, and these things become so much more important in knockout games.

Guys, we're not eleven in the quarterfinal tomorrow. We're about 30 people in this match, and each and every one plays a role. Each and every one must arrive tomorrow or else we will come up short. It's not about eleven guys. It's not about me or Morras. It's about every single person turning up.

As I've said before, no matter how bad it gets out there, we are never out of the fight. The fight will never end, and it's not going to end, even if we lose it's not going to end because we are going to have to go fight back home. It doesn't end, because we can always turn it around. If they come out with a punch, we have to go back with a punch twice as hard. If they come with 1% extra, we go back with 2% extra.

We must relax because we are good enough. I promise you, there is no need to stress. I promise you, boys, we are good enough to beat any team in the world, and we have shown that over the past few years.

Lastly, we must be obsessed with our vision of winning this Cup. We have to eliminate all negativity by being excited and obsessed by what we want, and that is to win the Cup. We have to see that. If we don't see that, we're not going to make it. Tomorrow, each of us must be completely obsessed by our goal.

Mark Nicholas, the cricket commentator and former Hampshire captain, was interviewing the captains at the toss before the quarterfinal at the SCG and, off camera, he said he thought I looked nervous. I smiled. He was mistaken. In fact, given the well-documented history, I felt amazingly calm and confident. The warm-up had gone exceptionally well, and I sensed we were going to deliver a high-quality performance at the right time.

As it turned out, we played an almost perfect game.

The Sri Lankans won the toss and batted, but were four for two in the fifth over. Kumar Sangakkara and Lahiru Thirimanne threatened to stage a recovery but both fell in their 40s, and what looked a skilful and dangerous batting team were dismissed for only 133 before the end of the 38th over. Our seamers created the pressure at the top of the order, and spinners Imran and JP took four and three wickets respectively.

We reached the target for the loss of only one wicket, with Quinton de Kock scoring a brisk and unbeaten 78 in 57 balls, guiding us to victory with an almost unbelievable 32 overs to spare.

Once again with perfect timing, the little green book landed in the hands of our young, massively talented wicketkeeper and opening batsman, and Quinton wrote that evening: 'We just smashed the Sri Lankans at the SCG. What a great win it was. Weirdly, it was our spin twins (Immy and JP) who just went right through them, with JP taking his first ever hat-trick. After the game, we enjoyed our night to end a memorable day.'

So we made the three-hour flight across the Tasman Sea for the fifth time in the tournament. Having started our campaign in New Zealand, flown to Australia, back to New Zealand, then to Australia for the quarterfinal, we headed back to Auckland to play New Zealand in the semifinal at Eden Park.

The Proteas team for the quarterfinal had been Amla, De Kock, Du Plessis, Rossouw, De Villiers, Miller, Duminy, Steyn, Abbott, Morkel and Tahir, which meant it had included three so-called players of colour as they were designated in the race-conscious corridors of South African sport. None of us within the squad was counting. I sincerely believe we were genuine new South Africans, blind to race and colour. As far as I was concerned, it was just the strongest possible team representing our country.

It was generally assumed the same team would be named to play in the semifinal. That was my expectation as captain, until I was called to a meeting at 5.30 pm on the evening before the match, half an hour before our usual team meeting was due to start, and was told Vernon Philander, who had passed his fitness test a few days earlier, would play instead of Kyle Abbott.

I knew about the Proteas convention that an incumbent player who is injured will automatically go back into the team when he returns to fitness, and Vern was an incumbent. Vernon and Dale had been our regular opening bowlers and were earmarked to lead our first-choice attack and I sensed the selectors thought Vernon would thrive in New Zealand conditions. Even so, it seemed to me, there could have been other considerations.

We had been assured that Cricket South Africa was the only national sporting governing body in the country that had declined to set a target for the number of players of colour to be included in the national team, but there was a delicate balance to be struck and it was generally understood that, as they chose the side, the national selectors would be conscious of working towards providing opportunities for at least four players of colour.

So what had happened? Had Vernon, who was officially classified as coloured, been selected ahead of Kyle, who was classified as white, to ensure there were four players of colour in our team for the semifinal? Or had the decision been made for purely cricketing reasons?

It depressed me even to think of my teammates in these outdated racial terms, as white or coloured, but three players of colour had played in the quarterfinal, so could three players of colour play in the semifinal, or was that not the case?

I was certainly not blind to the wider issues and I regarded the process of transformation in South African cricket not as something imposed upon the game but as something that was morally the right thing to do. As far as I was aware, everybody in the game supported Cricket South Africa in their missionary zeal to ensure all South Africans enjoyed an equal opportunity to play cricket and to reach the highest levels. Cricket's development programme had been launched by Dr Ali Bacher when he was MD of the United Cricket Board, had continued under Gerald Majola and Haroon Lorgat, and was widely and consistently praised.

However, since we all shared an overriding goal to grow cricket among all South Africans, surely the best way of achieving that ambition was to do whatever we could to win the World Cup and to promote the game on the tidal wave of celebration that would then sweep through the entire country? Would anyone really mind if there were three or four players of colour in our side? Would anybody have decided to start playing or start following cricket just because there were four players of colour in the side, rather than three?

My mind was churning but, as the players gathered for the meeting, I had to keep everything together.

'Obviously, it's a huge game tomorrow,' I said, gesturing towards the 11 names on a white noticeboard. 'It will be a massive privilege for these okes to walk on the field tomorrow. Let's stick together no matter what happens out there. No matter what gets thrown in our direction, we're prepared to take it on.'

It was never my plan to say too much and I finished by referring to a specific line in one of my favourite songs; it is called 'I Lived' and was released by the US rock band OneRepublic in 2014.

I said: 'The line is "With every broken bone I swear I lived", and that sentiment goes hand in hand with some of the talks I have done before.

I am saying to you that, when the moment comes, dare greatly. Don't be scared to dare and to risk it all. We have spent a long time together here at the World Cup, and we owe it to each other to promise each other that "with every broken bone" we're going to leave it out there tomorrow.'

My voice had almost faltered over the words 'risk it all', almost cracked with the emotion of everything going on inside my head, but I kept going and introduced the motivational film edited and produced by Andy Croly and Jared Hinde, the talented producer and videographer from the agency, T&W, who generally travelled with the squad and invariably found the images and music to move and inspire us.

I returned to my room and ordered room service with my wife, Danielle, but could not stop thinking about the selection issue. Russell sent me a text message, asking me to stay focused on the task, telling me how much the team needed my leadership; and Gary Kirsten also made contact, urging me to be calm and positive ahead of the big match. I needed to get my head around everything but I was emotional and, so far as I could see, the entire situation seemed so unnecessary and unfair on everybody.

I didn't sleep well that night and remember my first thought when I opened my eyes the following morning was 'I hope Vern will be OK'. I had met him when we were 13, got along well when we played together in the South African Under-19 side and had become good friends.

What's done is done, I told myself, let's go and play. I didn't want to overreact to what, at the end of the day, was just a perception. I didn't know for certain what had happened. Even today, I still don't know for certain what happened. I didn't want to blame anyone. I wanted to treat the issue as just another obstacle to be overcome. We had to deal with it.

Across the field, as we worked through our warm-up routines, the New Zealanders were planning to write their own story, playing in front of their own supporters, desperate to reach the Cricket World Cup final for the first time after they had lost all of their six previous semifinals.

We won the toss and decided to bat first at Eden Park in Auckland, a world-famous venue designed for rugby and being used for one of the biggest matches in cricket. The straight boundaries were unusually short but we had played here many times before, had prepared carefully and were happy with our plans ...

Hashim and Quinton open our innings. Quinton is dropped in the second over, and then Hash is dropped in the third over. Maybe this is going to be our day, after all, but both fall soon afterwards and, from 31 for two, Faf du Plessis and Rilee Rossouw settle into a rhythm and start to make progress. The intensity of the contest is remarkable. Brendon McCullum, the brilliant Kiwi captain, is trying everything. We are fighting hard.

Rilee falls for 39, and I walk out to join Faf at the crease at 114 for three in the 27th over. Here we are again, my old friend from Affies and me, together again, in the heat of the battle. Corey Anderson bowls, short and rising, and my first ball deflects down off my gloves and narrowly misses my off stump. Breathe hard.

We settle and start to ease on the accelerator, taking 11 runs from the 31st over, 11 from the 32nd, another 11 from the 33rd, 13 from the 34th. We seem to be taking control, applying the pressure. I push into the covers and call Faf for a quick single. It's going to be tight, and I sprint as fast as I can and I dive at full length, getting an eyeful of dirt in the process. The throw misses the stumps, although I think I would have been safe anyway ... and then I guide the last ball of the over past third man for four.

In the 35th over, I cut firmly square of the wicket but too high and the ball is flying straight at Kane Williamson, fielding at point, and my heart skips a beat as the ball bursts through his hands and falls to the grass. I survive ... and pull the next ball for six, drive the next for four and drive the next for another four. We are racing along, daring to believe that this may turn out to be our day after all, and we reach 216 for three at the end of the 38th over, appearing poised to launch a real assault in the last dozen overs, to post a score in excess of 350 and effectively, we hope, take the game away from New Zealand.

What's that? Drizzle? I knew light showers had been forecast, but hoped they would come later in the day. The rain starts to fall harder, and the umpires decide we must leave the field. The break in play is frustrating, but we need to stay calm, to accept the weather and focus on controlling the controllables …

We left the field at 4.50 pm, and play eventually resumed at 6.45 pm It was announced that the match would be reduced from 50 overs per side to 43 overs per side, and that the target New Zealand would be set to chase would be marginally greater than our score, supposedly taking into account the reality that we had batted for 38 overs, pacing ourselves as though we were going to bat for the full 50 overs.

It was complex and it was generally unsatisfactory because, in simple terms, we did not believe that the official calculations, following one or other contorted theory, would properly compensate us for the runs we would have scored in the extra seven overs we had expected to bat but were now denied.

However, there was no point moaning. Rules are rules and, just before 6.45 pm on what now was looking like a dry evening, Faf and I returned to the crease, preparing to face the last five overs of our innings. Faf got out off the second ball after the restart, unluckily gloving a leg-side wide to the wicketkeeper, and I was joined by David Miller, possibly the ideal batsman to launch an assault in the closing overs.

David delivered, striking four boundaries in the 40th over and taking a single off the last ball, and then hitting a boundary and two sixes in the 41st over. He continued to find the middle of the bat and was eventually out in the 43rd over, having scored what appeared to be 49 invaluable runs from only 18 balls, and there was still time for JP Duminy to hit a boundary before we finished on 281 for five after 43 overs.

I finished unbeaten on 65 from 45 balls, although any frustration at having faced only seven of the 30 balls bowled since the resumption was soothed by the quality of David Miller's hitting.

After all the calculations, New Zealand's target was increased to 298 in 43 overs. We had batted extremely well under intense pressure, paced the innings intelligently, increased the run rate at the right time and posted a decent score. We could have been out of sight if the rain had not intervened, but I was satisfied with our effort.

The home side had dropped no fewer than four catches, and I realised we would need to bowl and field with real intensity and discipline if we were to finish the job and reach the final ...

Brendon McCullum is one of the cleanest strikers of a cricket ball in the world. If he gets going, no target is too much. He's not the only dangerous batsman in the New Zealand team, but we need his wicket, and we need it as soon as possible. Dale bowls the first over, and 'Baz' hits the fourth ball for six over extra cover.

I have decided Vern will bowl the second over because he is handy with the new ball, but McCullum is clearly set on attacking everything. He charges the first ball and it goes for four byes. The second goes over long leg for six, the third goes for four past square leg, two dots follow, and the sixth ball goes for four behind square on the leg side. We have conceded 18 off the over. This can happen. The Kiwis are off to a flier.

My mind is racing. We need to keep shuffling the bowlers. Dale bowls the third, and concedes six. Morné bowls the fourth and concedes 14 runs. It is nobody's fault. We need to stay calm. McCullum erupts in the fifth over, hitting Dale for six, one wide, four, six, four, four and a dot. That's 25 runs from the over. The Eden Park crowd is cheering as though the All Blacks have scored a try and somehow manage to maintain the level of noise.

I look at the scoreboard. New Zealand are 71 for no wicket after five overs. This is crazy. We need to change something, so I call Imran Tahir into the attack, to bowl only the sixth over of the innings. He's a talented spinner and a fantastic competitor; when we most need him to perform, he does exactly that and bowls a maiden to Martin Guptill.

OK, that's good – now we have a chance. I ask Morné to bowl from the opposite end. McCullum is charging at him, but Morras finds a decent length, cramps the batsman for room, and the New Zealand captain can only club the ball to mid-on where Dale jubilantly takes the catch. McCullum is out for 59 from 26 balls, and is soon followed by Williamson, who plays on. New Zealand are 81 for two at the end of the ninth over and, breathing a significant sigh of relief, I think we may have weathered the storm and can now settle into our rhythm.

Guptill is run out by Hashim's throw and Taylor is brilliantly caught down the leg side by Quinton off JP. The New Zealanders are throwing everything at us, but we are holding our nerve, picking up wickets. Just as the game seems to be swinging our way, Grant Elliott and Corey Anderson start to settle, seemingly hitting a boundary every over, keeping up with the run rate. We have a chance to run out Anderson in the 32nd over, but I am at the non-striker's end and I am simply unable to collect the throw on the half-volley, and the batman scrambles to safety.

The game is getting away from us. We need a wicket now. The Kiwis need 85 from 10 overs, then 79 from nine, then 67 from eight. Tahir goes for eight. We still need a wicket. Running out of options, I bring myself on to bowl, and Anderson's pull passes just wide of square leg. The margins are tiny, but we really need a break.

New Zealand require 47 runs from the last six overs, and I call on Morné again. He concedes a single to Elliott off the first ball, but then bowls a dot ball to Anderson, and another dot, and another dot, and another dot. The pressure is building on the batsman, and the pressure tells when he skies a top edge. Faf gets under the ball and takes the catch at square leg. After a delay while the umpires check the replay to see whether the ball has touched the cable suspending the 'spider cam' high above the pitch, which would have meant it was a dead ball, Anderson is given out.

Has this remarkable game turned again? They now need 45 from five overs, and everything is starting to happen very quickly. Every ball counts. Amid all the noise, if we can stay calm and apply pressure, we will get the opportunities to win the game; we must just take them.

I trust myself to bowl the 39th over but concede four singles and a six, swung over mid-wicket by Grant Elliott. He moves to 62 from 60 balls. It's ironic that the batsman now carrying New Zealand's hopes was actually born and bred in Johannesburg and educated at St Stithians. Grant emigrated in 2001 because he thought his cricket opportunities were limited in South Africa, and he qualified to play for his adopted country in 2008. Good luck to him, I thought, but we really need to get him out.

Immy bowls the 40th over, and concedes only seven runs. We are fighting. Rilee Rossouw sprints to his right and turns what might easily have been a two into just a single. Dale races in again, and Luke Ronchi flicks the ball to deep mid-wicket where Rilee takes the catch.

Dan Vettori walks out to bat, but Elliott has the strike. He slices a two down to third man, and then pushes the ball into the leg side; he runs one and turns for the second, hesitates for a moment and then goes for it. Rilee throws to the correct end, but the ball eludes Quinton's gloves, and the batsmen scurry home. It was a chance to dismiss Elliott.

Now 23 runs are required from 12 balls. Everything is on the line. The tension is incredible. Morné steps up to bowl the second-last over. First ball, Vettori drives and Hashim makes a magnificent diving stop at short cover, but they scramble a single. We can do no more. Second ball, Elliott swings and the ball goes high but lands between two fielders as the batsmen run two. We need a break. Third, Elliott runs a single. Fourth, Vettori drives straight, but now it is Dale who sprints and dives to stop the boundary, restricting them to just a single. Elliott drives the fifth ball past extra cover for four, and then swings at the sixth but miscues … and the ball goes high again and it seems as though either JP Duminy or Farhaan Behardien will take the catch but, amid all the noise, neither hears the other call and neither moves and the ball falls between them, and the batsmen run two.

So it all comes down to this, the 43rd and final over. New Zealand need 12 to win, and Dale marks out his run-up. He is suffering. His hamstring is sore. His calf is sore. But this great fast bowler knows exactly what needs to be done, and he will give everything for the team.

He starts with a slower ball that deceives Vettori, and Elliott charges through for a bye. The second ball is a full toss that Elliott drives straight to cover, and they run a single. Dale is hurting and Brandon Jackson, our physio, runs out to provide some treatment. Ten runs are required from the last four balls, although we realise that nine will be enough for New Zealand because they finished higher in the group stage.

Dale races in again and finds the yorker, but Vettori uses all his vast experience to dig the ball out and somehow squeeze it past the fielder to the boundary at third man. The fourth ball is a bouncer, which Vettori attempts to pull but misses, but Elliott is once again sprinting down the pitch, trying to run a bye to the wicketkeeper; Quinton throws at the stumps and just misses. Grant is riding his luck, but he makes his ground.

Five runs are needed from the last two balls, but a boundary will be enough. I know we still have a chance. I walk up to Dale and ask him what he thinks. He says he's going to try to bowl a yorker. I agree, and walk back to my place in the field, still believing we can win.

Dale bowls … it is good … Elliott swings … and connects … impeccably … and the ball soars high into the Auckland night … into a stand full of delirious New Zealanders … for six. It's all over. It's suddenly all over.

In that precise moment, in that moment of defeat, I think about my dream. I see all the familiar images in my mind's eye, see me diving to my right, gathering the ball, springing to my feet, running towards the stumps and taking off the bails ... and then I look up and see the reality of Dale lying on the pitch, spent and devastated, Faf hiding his face in his palms, and Morné sitting on the grass, so still and so sad.

Maybe 20 seconds pass. Lose properly, I tell myself. So I take off my cap and start to walk around the field, either consoling teammates or congratulating New Zealanders on their victory. I am feeling OK, controlling my emotions well until I come across Dan Vettori, my friend and teammate from Royal Challengers Bangalore; he gives me a massive hug, which brings a lump to my throat and a few tears to my eyes.

'You didn't deserve to lose,' he says.

'It is fine,' I reply. 'Congratulations.'

I want to be strong. I want to show I can accept this disappointment. I compose myself, and continue going through the sporting rituals that follow every international, and finally reach the refuge of the visitors' dressing room at Eden Park. Our wives and families are starting to arrive. Danielle walks in with my parents. I hug her and hug my mother, and then I hug my father and, as he holds me in his arms, he says: 'It's not your fault, AB. It's not your fault.' And that is that. The tears start streaming from my eyes, as all the sadness and disappointment suddenly overflow.

I managed to recover and get through the post-match presentation ceremony, and I was still holding everything together when I embraced the ordeal of the media conference. Some journalists are knowledgeable, understanding and often humorous observers of the game; some can be less kind.

One of the latter breed took the microphone during the 'presser' and asked: 'AB, when you dropped the ball and failed to execute that run out, did you think you had dropped the World Cup?'

I replied: 'If you want to see it that way – that I cost us – then I will gladly take it.'

When the last question had been answered, I returned to our dressing room and Russell and I both addressed the players, thanking them all for their efforts and telling them we could be proud of our performance. We drank a few beers, tried to cheer each other up and went through to the home dressing room to spend some time with the New Zealanders, and to wish them well in the final against the Australians.

There is no doubt that our failure to win the 2015 Cricket World Cup ranks as the greatest disappointment of my cricket career. I genuinely believed we were strong enough. I genuinely believed it was our time. I genuinely believed that, if we had got past New Zealand in the semifinal, we had the ideal combinations of batsmen and spin bowlers to take on Australia at the Melbourne Cricket Ground and potentially win the final. I believed all that, but it didn't happen. It was not, in fact, our destiny.

Let's get some things straight.

We did not lose the semifinal because of the decision to replace Kyle with Vernon. I won't deny the saga was unsettling on the evening before the match but, in the event, Vernon bowled eight overs, bowled well and conceded only 52 runs; his economy rate of 6.50 was only bettered by Imran.

We did not lose the semifinal because of the rain interruption. I won't deny it was frustrating, because we were taking control at the time, but it cannot be cited as a reason for defeat.

We did not lose the semifinal because our strategy was wrong; in almost all respects, in our batting plans, in our bowling changes and in our field placings, we got almost everything right.

So what did go wrong?

In my view, we lost the semifinal because we failed to take five clear opportunities. We put the opposition under pressure, and the pressure created the opportunities, but, through no lack of effort and no lack of desire, as individuals and as a team, we were unable to make the play when it really mattered. Three possible run outs were missed and two catches were dropped. If we had taken one of these chances, we would probably have won. If we had taken two or more of these chances, we would certainly have won. By such tiny margins, dreams either come true … or remain just dreams.

CHAPTER 15

RENEWAL

Birthdays can bring everything into focus. I turned 31 during the 2015 Cricket World Cup, and celebrated the occasion in Melbourne.

I was another year older, another year wiser ... and another year more sore first thing in the morning. At stages, it might be an ache deep within my right shoulder that becomes more acute when I throw the ball, or it could be the pain shooting through my left knee when I set off for a quick single, or it is the general discomfort in my ankle when I need to change direction, either while fielding or batting.

Such niggles and aches are an unavoidable part of every professional sporting life. Very few players ever run onto the field feeling completely fit and pain-free, and 'pain-free' is not a phrase that often applies to international cricketers, like me, who have played all three formats of the game for 12 consecutive seasons.

I didn't say anything to anyone beyond my inner circle of family and friends, didn't want to appear either weak or half-hearted but, moving into 2015, I was feeling the physical strain.

Maybe I haven't managed my body well through all these years. Maybe I should have withdrawn from the team whenever I wasn't feeling even 90% fit, and given various ailments time to heal. Maybe I should have developed the 'professional' knack of putting my own welfare first, pulling back, shifting down a gear or two and easing the strain without ever quite being seen to be going through the motions.

In truth, I know only one way to play the game. It's the way I played every game with my brothers in the back garden at 20 Mentz Avenue, and it's the way I have approached every single one of the 106 Test matches, 200 ODIs and 71 T20 internationals that I have played for South Africa, so far.

Give everything, always. Hold nothing back, always. Put the team first, always. Play through pain, always. Fight and fight again, always. Always, always play the game with the hunger, the enthusiasm and the appetite of the eight-year-old *laaitjie*, the youngest brother, who would run into the garden to play with his older brothers and their friends, relishing the challenge, loving every minute of the contest.

That's the way I play. That's the way I have always played. That's the only way I know how to play. When the day dawns that I can't play this way, when my shoulder or my knee or my ankle is too sore, when I can't generate the same hunger, enthusiasm and appetite, that will be the day I decide to stop playing the game.

This all-or-nothing approach could mean my international career ends sooner than that of others, but I would much rather be the guy who gave everything whenever he played than be the guy who somehow paced himself to play for, say, 16 years. Others will have a different view, and they may be right. I am just explaining my outlook.

To use an analogy, imagine my career as a racing car with a full tank of petrol. Ever since 2004, I have driven that car just about as fast as it can go, foot pressed down on the accelerator, shaving every corner, endlessly going for broke and now, moving into my thirties, there is only so much petrol left in the tank.

When the petrol runs out, that will be that. The racing car will come to a halt. Some may say I should start to drive more conservatively, be prepared to pull back at times and even to freewheel on the clutch, conserve energy, and so make what remains of the petrol last for longer. The point is I can't do that.

In any event, with more than enough petrol still swilling around in the tank, I flew home after the World Cup in March 2015, joined Royal Challengers Bangalore for another IPL tournament and eventually took my place in the Proteas squad, gathered to undertake a two-Test tour of Bangladesh in July 2015.

I opened with Quinton when we won the two T20 internationals in Mirpur and enjoyed the experience; but then – for the one and only time in my international career – I asked permission to leave the tour and miss the two Test matches, because I wanted to attend the birth of my son back home.

The timing was not ideal because the second Test in Bangladesh would have been not only my 100th Test match but also my 100th consecutive Test because I had not missed a single Test played by South Africa since my debut in December 2004. I could have been the first player to achieve this feat, but I've never chased records and, to be honest, there was no chance that I would miss the birth of my son.

Danielle and I decided our son would be named Abraham Benjamin de Villiers, after my father. The first recorded Abraham de Villiers in South Africa was the second of the three brothers who emigrated from La Rochelle, in France, via Holland, in 1689, and it meant a lot to me that, quite apart from continuing this long-standing tradition, my son would have the same names as my dad.

AB junior was born on the second day of the first Test in Chittagong, which was cut short by rain and drawn, and I was preoccupied with changing nappies and being helpful around the house by the time Bangladesh batted on the first day of the second Test, before persistent rain washed out the next four days.

In August, I rejoined the Proteas for a limited-overs series at home to New Zealand, billed as an opportunity for revenge after the World Cup semifinal. The original plan was that I would keep wicket in these matches, but Morné van Wyk took this responsibility, and I was free to take my place in the field.

Fielding has always been pure pleasure for me. Some batsmen do not share the sentiment, but ever since my high school days when Faf and I used to patrol the covers, I have always enjoyed the adrenalin rush of pacing in as each ball is bowled, primed to dive or swoop ... It's not just fielding for me, it's hunting the ball.

During the first T20 international against New Zealand, which we won at Kingsmead, I experienced both sides of the fielding experience, nearly losing a tooth when the ball bounced up and struck me on the chin, and then leaping to my left to take a catch at mid-on.

We lost the second T20 at Centurion, though a significant consolation in defeat was the continuing emergence of Kagiso Rabada, a 20-year-old fast bowler educated at St Stithians, who had made his mark at the Under-19 Cricket World Cup in 2014 and was becoming a regular member of the national team. 'KG' has all the talent and athleticism required to be successful, but it is his strength of character that most impresses me. He works exceptionally hard in practice and in the nets, and he's eager to learn. I spent quite a bit of time with him, offering pieces of advice here and there, and I really enjoy his response when batsmen try to disrupt his rhythm: he simply fights fire with fire.

Moving into the ODI series, Hashim's century won us the game at SuperSport Park, and then Martin Guptill's innings took New Zealand to victory in Potchefstroom. The deciding match was played in Durban and, after a relatively barren run, I was pleased to score 68 in what unfolded as a reasonably decisive victory.

Our next assignment was a full two-month tour of India, which would include two T20 internationals, five one-day internationals and four Test matches, and I looked forward to playing in all three formats. People often ask whether I prefer five-day Tests, ODIs or T20 matches, and my response is dull and predictable: I enjoy all three.

Test cricket remains, figuratively and literally, the ultimate test and it remains most valued by most of the leading players. If anyone wants to be respected within the game, they need to perform consistently well in red-ball cricket, meeting both the physical and psychological challenge, demonstrating both courage and technical skill.

There is usually no hiding place over five days of cricket, and there is certainly no hiding place in a series of four or five Tests with only a few days of respite between each match.

It's the ultimate test for a batsman because the leading bowlers in the opposing team will come at you three or four times during the course of a day's play, whereas you only need to face them for either four or 10 overs in the shorter formats. And it's the ultimate test for a bowler because you usually need to earn your wickets through skill and patience, rather than rely on batsmen to give it away in a run chase.

Simply put, Test cricket remains a pure contest, while limited-overs cricket is manufactured.

ODIs represent the middle ground because, for batsmen, they still give you an opportunity to play yourself in and to build an innings; and, for bowlers, there is still time to get into a groove. T20s are a dash for glory for all concerned, an all-action format where either one innings or one spell of bowling often proves decisive.

However, a player's enjoyment of the game is not determined solely by the nature of the contest and, for me at least, it is easier to get the blood pumping for a T20 match played in front of 45 000 chanting spectators than it is to get going on the fifth morning of a Test when there are 450 people in the ground.

Each of the formats has strengths and weaknesses and, in my view, it is crucial for the future of the game that each format is supported, that each format maintains its place in the calendar.

Leading players may well become increasingly specialised, with most playing only two formats because, with the continuing increase in the volume of top-class cricket, including international series and various

T20 leagues, it could become almost impossible for anybody to find either the time or the energy to play in all three.

Make no mistake, I have enjoyed always feeling involved and jumping between formats over the past 12 years, but there will be an upside to increased specialisation; as future generations of players focus on one or two formats, so skill levels will rise and the quality of play will become better and better.

We started our tour of India with an encouraging T20 win in Dharamsala. Rohit Sharma scored a century and the Indians seemed to be cruising at 158 for one with five overs left, but I loved the way our bowlers held their nerve and their lines and we fought back, restricting the home side to 199 for five. Hashim and I laid the foundation for the chase, and JP and Farhaan took us to a victory in the last over.

The bowlers also performed well in the second T20 international, dismissing India for only 92. The spectators in Cuttack were not happy, and some began to throw bottles onto the field, causing two interruptions in play, but we paid little attention and eased to victory and a 2–0 win in the T20 series.

Any tour is enjoyable when you are winning, and we were in great spirits as we prepared to play the first of five ODIs at Green Park in Kanpur. We batted first and Hashim, Quinton and Faf each made strong contributions, providing the ideal platform for Farhaan and me to build a partnership and set a competitive target. I had moved my score to 80 from 66 balls, with two overs left in the innings ...

Bhuvneshwar Kumar runs in to bowl the penultimate over. Farhaan takes a single for one. I drive one straight six off the second ball, and hit another off the third ball. MS Dhoni saves runs off the fourth, but I take two off the fifth and then manage to slice the sixth ball of the over for a boundary behind point.

My score has moved to 98 and, for some reason, the capacity home crowd of 33 000 seems excited as Umesh Yadav gets ready to bowl the last over of the innings. Farhaan is striking the ball beautifully, and he hits the first three deliveries for four, four and six before pushing the fourth ball into the covers and calling for a single.

The Indian crowd roars. Why are they so excited about a single? Or are they just pleased to concede one run? It soon becomes clear that, in fact, they are making this noise because they want me on strike so I can reach my century.

'A-B-D! A-B-D! A-B-D!'

A shiver runs down my spine. It really does. I can't believe this is happening. To hear people chant my initials when I am playing for Royal Challengers Bangalore is one thing, but to hear so many supporters chanting for me when I am batting for South Africa, the opposition, against India, their heroes, is something else.

'A-B-D! A-B-D! A-B-D!'

Yadav runs in to bowl. I swing … hard, across the line … and miss. The spectators groan. My score stays 98 not out, and there is now just one ball remaining in the innings.

'A-B-D! A-B-D! A-B-D!'

Here comes Yadav again. As usual, I concentrate on keeping my head perfectly still, trying to judge the length in a split second. Yadav bowls … I swing and connect, flat-batted … and the ball soars towards long-on, and over the head of long-on, and into the crowd for six … and the noise in the stadium gets even louder …

We finished on 303 for five in 50 overs, but the match was far from won. Rohit Sharma played another fantastic innings and led what looked like a comfortable chase, until they required only 35 runs from the last four overs. Then Imran Tahir turned the match in the 47th over, beating Rohit with his leg break and clasping a return catch, and using his googly to deceive Suresh Raina and have him caught at long-on.

India eventually needed 11 from the last over, and KG Rabada, aged only 20, prepared to bowl to MS Dhoni, the most celebrated and experienced 'finisher' in limited-overs cricket. As the crowd implored their icon to win the match, our youngster would sink or swim.

He swam, brilliantly ... conceding two, one and one off the first three balls, drawing MS Dhoni to loop a return catch off the fourth ball, and having Stuart Binny caught at mid-wicket off the fifth. India needed six from the last ball, but could manage only two. KG had closed out the game, and we celebrated a special victory.

India levelled the series at 1–1 by winning in Indore, when our batsmen fell short of a moderate target, but Quinton's century and Morné's four wickets took us to victory in Rajkot. The competition was intense and India levelled the series at 2–2 by winning in Chennai, when Virat Kohli scored a hundred in their total of 299 and we succumbed to their spinners, falling short despite my innings of 112.

The deciding match of what had become an outstanding series was played at the Wankhede Stadium in Mumbai, and, happily, we were able to dominate from the first ball of a famous day.

Faf anchored our innings with a magnificent 133, creating the opportunity for Quinton to score 109 from 87 balls and for me to strike a quick 119 from 61 balls, including 11 sixes. We posted an impressive total of 438, and the game was essentially won when KG stepped up to dismiss the dangerous Shikhar Dhawan.

I was thrilled, and told the team afterwards it had been our most complete performance for some time. To have arrived in India and won both the T20 and ODI series was a significant achievement, and the performances of younger players like Quinton and KG suggested that we were witnessing the emergence of a new generation.

We would, however, be brought down to earth in the Test series that followed. India prepared dry, dusty pitches, as they were perfectly entitled to do, and we struggled against their trio of spinners, never really getting a foothold in the contest and giving up our proud record of never having lost a Test series on tour since 2006.

The first Test in Mohali ended within three days. India scored 201, we replied with 184, and India scored 200 in their second innings. Set 218 to win, we were dismissed for 109, with Ravichandran Ashwin and Ravindra Jadeja each taking eight wickets in the match. We had been comprehensively outplayed.

Bengaluru was chosen to host the second Test, which meant my 100th Test match for South Africa would be played in my 'home town' in India. Both my parents and Danielle's parents, and Letitia Greyling, travelled from Pretoria to witness this significant landmark, but they ended up watching more rain than cricket.

Virat Kohli won the toss and sent us in to bat. In all the 246 Tests ever played in India, it was only the twentieth time a captain had chosen to field first. Amid forecasts of bad weather later in the week, his decision gave me a chance to bat on what turned out to be the one and only dry day of the entire Test match.

Ashwin and Jadeja were soon creating problems for us, and I walked out to bat with our score at 45 for three. It was a reasonable cricket wicket and, batting under pressure, it was important for us to be positive and to keep scoring runs. I reached 85 from 105 balls, but was dismissed when wicketkeeper Wriddhiman Saha leapt forward to catch a ball that glanced off my bat and popped up off my pad.

We were all out for 214 and the Indians rushed to 80 for no wicket by stumps on the first day, but that proved to be that. Four days of rain followed, and the Test ended as a damp draw.

I knew we were struggling. We spoke about applying ourselves and about fighting harder, and about finding a way to compete but, for us, the series was, quite literally, spinning out of control.

In the third Test at Nagpur, India batted first and scored 215. In our innings, fast bowler Ishant Sharma opened the attack at one end, Ashwin opened at the other and Jadeja replaced Sharma after only two overs. By the middle of the 13th over, the two spinners had reduced us to a humiliating 12 runs for five wickets. The pitch was almost unplayable, but JP Duminy fought well and made 35. We were finally bowled out for 79 in our first innings and for 185 in our second innings, and defeated within three days for the second time in the series.

The pattern continued in the fourth Test at Delhi. India won the toss for the fourth time in four Tests, opted to bat and made 334 in their first innings, with Ajinkya Rahane becoming the first player on either side to score a century in the series. We were then bowled out for 121 and, once Ajinkya had scored his second century of the match, were set an impossible target of 481 to win. The series was already lost but, as we started our second innings just after lunch on the fourth day, we wanted to show some guts and put up a fight.

Hashim and I came together at 49 for two and batted till stumps and well into the last day, fighting and blocking, making them earn every wicket. Hash scored 25 in almost five hours, and I made 43 in almost six hours. Faf then made 10 runs in two hours as we battled to salvage a draw that would have felt like a consolation victory, but it was not to be and we lost our last five wickets in the final session.

The Indians had played well and played to their strengths, and our bowlers had fought manfully. In the end, we had not scored enough runs to be competitive. Our victories in the T20 and ODI series seemed lost in the dark and distant past by the time we flew home to play a series against a confident England team.

We were starting to look like – to use a dreaded cliché – a team in transition, struggling for confidence, relying too much on too few players and missing the firepower of the injured Dale Steyn.

Maybe a dip in our form was inevitable. No team in the world could afford to lose players and characters as important as Boucher, Kallis and Smith in the space of a few years and not suffer a very significant impact.

Russell Domingo, our coach, was absolutely correct to tell the squad over and over again that no one is irreplaceable, but our challenge was to cope with the absence of three stalwart legends, not just one.

Our margins for error seemed to have disappeared and it felt as though, if we were to prosper, we would need almost all our experienced players to perform well at the same time. If the frontline batsmen failed or if the frontline bowlers lost their line and rhythm, we would quite quickly find ourselves in trouble.

England were encouraged by a recent Ashes win over Australia, and Alastair Cook's squad arrived with what was perhaps then the strongest pace bowling attack in the world: there were fitness doubts over Jimmy Anderson, but he and Stuart Broad, supported by Steven Finn and Chris Woakes, would cause problems for anyone.

The first Test started in Durban on Boxing Day. Dale was back to lead our attack and he gave us the ideal start, removing Cook and Hales. We were taking control at 49 for three, but Nick Compton and James Taylor batted well in difficult conditions and helped the tourists reach a respectable 303 all out.

Dean Elgar demonstrated his huge potential when he scored a fighting century in our reply and I made 49 in reasonable time, but we succumbed to Broad's seam bowling and Moeen Ali's off-breaks, and were eventually all out for 214. A first-innings deficit of 89 runs did not augur well on a tricky wicket.

Dane Piedt, our promising spinner, performed well to take five wickets in the England second innings, but Compton, Root, Taylor and Jonny Bairstow all scored runs as they gradually moved ahead in the game, eventually leaving us a target of 416 to win in the last innings.

We wanted to fight and we tried to fight. Stiaan van Zyl and Dean Elgar both looked in decent form, but neither was able to go on and score the big hundred that we needed, and we were four wickets down at stumps on the fourth day.

Dale and I resumed our innings on the last morning, determined to make England fight for every wicket and still harbouring hope of getting away with a draw. I played back to the third delivery of the day, but the ball skidded on quicker than I expected and struck me on the pad. Moeen Ali appealed and the umpire raised his finger. I called for the decision to be reviewed, more in hope than expectation ... to no avail. I was out.

The next hour or so unfolded as one of the more depressing experiences of my career; our last five wickets fell for 28 runs in the space of 24 overs, and we were defeated by 241 runs. I have never minded losing. I have never minded being beaten by the better team. You accept it and move on. However, on this dismal morning in Durban, with the songs of several thousand England supporters echoing around an otherwise deserted ground, it started to look as though, for the first time in my memory, a Proteas team was losing without a fight.

I know that wasn't the case. I know we were all trying. However, I am simply saying there was a perception that, collectively, we had lacked the appetite for a battle – and that perception hurt.

Frank conversations followed and, on the first day of the second Test in Cape Town, we seemed to be competing more intensely. England won an important toss and batted first on a flat wicket, but KG took three wickets and we were reasonably content to have England at 223 for five at drinks in the evening session.

We were then subjected to one of the most extraordinary batting assaults. Ben Stokes and Jonny Bairstow batted for the last hour of the first day and into the second, adding 399 runs in 59 overs. Stokes struck the ball magnificently and his epic innings of 258 included 30 boundaries and 11 sixes. We were wilting under the onslaught, and Bairstow reached 150 not out before England declared at 629 for six.

'AB, can I have a word with you?' our captain asked.

'Sure, Hash, no problem.'

Hashim proceeded to tell me he had made a decision to resign as captain at the end of the second Test, and wanted me to be prepared because he thought Cricket South Africa would ask me to take over. These were tough days for everyone, and once again I remember feeling so impressed by Hash's honesty and decency.

Nothing was said publicly but, perhaps privately feeling a burden had been lifted from his shoulders, Hash led our fightback at Newlands, scoring another outstanding double hundred. He was supported by me with 88, and then by Faf, who scored 86, as we set about rebuilding our credibility and self-confidence.

Hash was eventually out for 201, and his dismissal brought Temba Bavuma to the crease at 439 for four. Aged 25, raised in Langa near Cape Town and now playing for the Lions in Johannesburg, he batted beautifully, playing with freedom and enthusiasm, cutting and pulling his way to a maiden Test hundred. It was the first Test century scored by a black South African, ever. Even in the midst of what was in many ways a difficult and demanding series, South African cricket was visibly moving in the right direction.

The Test ended as a draw, and it was duly announced that Hash had decided to resign and that I would captain the side for the remaining two Tests of the series. I felt honoured, of course, and pleased to realise a boyhood ambition to become the Test captain, but these feelings were tempered by sympathy for Hashim's situation and the knowledge that we would have to play at the top of our game, consistently, if we were going to fight back and win the series. I believed we could compete with them and beat them, but we could not afford to be fragile.

For most of my career, the Proteas side would approach any Test match at home expecting to win. Those days were gone. Great players had retired, and we had entered a period of renewal.

The third Test at the Wanderers was always going to be a shootout. A result appeared certain, so we were either going to win and level the series at 1–1 or we were going to lose both the Test and the series. There were no half-measures and, as the new captain, I worked exceptionally hard to be as prepared as possible.

To be honest, I really did not enjoy my first few months as captain of the ODI team. I was being pulled in all directions, needing to worry about everyone else, and having no time to prepare myself.

However, as time passed and as I learned to manage the job more effectively and to get more done in less time, I started to enjoy captaining the side, relishing the responsibility and embracing the challenge of sitting down and working out what we were going to do.

Perhaps the main strength of my captaincy has been an ability to read situations as they evolve on the field and to understand the rhythm of the game. There are times when opponents are going well and you need to step back and contain, and there are moments when a weakness appears in the opposition and you need to spot the gap, react quickly, be bold and seize the advantage.

There is no short cut to gaining such skills, and no textbook to teach such skills. You only learn by watching great captains in action – as I watched Graeme Smith for so many years – and you learn, slowly but surely, through years and years of experience against different teams in different conditions, making mistakes and making a mental note to try another option when a similar situation arises in the future.

All of this happens on the field, but you can't overstate the importance of planning and preparation; and so, before each match, I would sit quietly in my hotel room, sometimes for a few hours, developing a specific strategy for each opposing batsman, writing everything by hand, learning everything by heart, for example …

> *Batsman A, an England top-order batsman: bowl straight lines to him; go straight at the start and try to get him LBW; if he gets in, bowl at the fifth or sixth stump; he scores a lot*

of boundaries through point, but he can also get out in that zone; areas of strength can always be areas of weakness, so we could nick him off a wide ball; don't give him too many short balls, because he plays them well and they can help to get his feet going.

Batsman B, a world-class Sri Lankan batsman: in Tests, pepper him with short balls until his feet are nowhere and, as soon as he looks disturbed, nick him outside off; in ODIs, he's a brilliant player of spin, so starve him of spinners and bring mid-on into the circle and invite him to hit over the top; that's his weakness.

Batsman C, a high-quality Australian batsman: bowl straight at all times, giving him no width and no room; put long-off and long-on right back on the boundary because he can score heavily in that area but he can also get out. Give him a few bouncers as well, because he thinks he's good with the short ball, but he isn't.

So preparations continued, until detailed plans for every opposing player had been developed, discussed and debated with coaches and players, and then committed to memory; and, even then, the captain's work is just starting because he needs to be 100% alert and aware whenever his squad is together, travelling or training, eating or meeting, warming up, batting or fielding, constantly asking himself: 'Am I doing the right thing? Do I need to give that guy a boost? Do I need to have a firm word with that player? What will I say at the next meeting? Am I having an impact? Are the selectors thinking the same way? Are the coaches happy with that option? What is the alternative if that doesn't work?'

It never stops.

The only way to keep on top of everything is to address any issue as soon as it arises; nothing can be left until later because a backlog quickly develops and things never get done.

If a bowler shows too much emotion on the field, and gets upset because someone has misfielded or dropped a catch, I will immediately go across and tell him he needs to control himself; if anybody lets their head drop or appears to disagree with a decision, I will very quickly pull them back into line.

Off the field, if anyone is late for a meeting or late for the bus or messing around during practice, I will speak to him straight away and let him know his behaviour is unacceptable. Working with the coach and Dr Moosajee, we try to maintain our standards and culture.

I also make a point of trying to check each member of the squad at least once each and every day; if I can look an individual straight in the eye, and see he is focused and present, then I'm happy.

All this sounds like hard work, but it's also hugely rewarding when a plan goes well and the team plays to its potential, or when a player responds to something you say and performs. The only element of the captain's job that sounds like hard work – and is never anything less than hard work – is speaking to the media. I realise it needs to be done, and I always try to be open and honest, but it is not something I ever enjoy.

Leaders eat last. I read that somewhere and the concept of standing back still appeals to me because, even though I enjoy the captaincy, my preference remains to perform as well as I can and then, without anyone noticing, to slip away while others soak up the limelight. Since I was a boy, I have never wanted to be the face of anything. The team should always be the face.

So, trailing 0–1 in the series with two Tests still to play, we arrived at the Wanderers Stadium. I won my first toss as captain, decided we would bat first and worked hard to keep everyone positive.

Our first-innings total of 313 might have seemed a decent start when considered against the fact that, in the eight previous Tests at the Bullring, the team batting first had only once passed 280. In truth, it was a missed opportunity that would come back to bite us. We wanted to be positive and take the game to England, but too many of us got ourselves in and got ourselves out. I was as guilty as anyone, racing to 36 from 40 balls and then being caught behind wafting on the leg side. All 11 of us reached double figures but no one passed 50.

KG raced in again when England started batting, and we seemed to be getting on top when we had them 22 for two and then 91 for four, but Root scored an excellent century and, with Stokes and Bairstow scoring valuable middle-order runs once again, the touring side reached 323, securing a lead of 10 runs.

We were well in the Test just before lunch on the third day, but, within the space of three crazy hours, it was all over: the match was lost, the series was lost and the English players were celebrating. Our fragility had been exposed yet again, and Stuart Broad had demonstrated his ability to win a Test with one spell. The fast bowler took our top five wickets for one run in a devastating six-over spell, causing a collapse from 25 for no wicket to 35 for five. I was caught behind off the inside edge for 0. Faf resisted for just under two hours and KG hit a couple of boundaries as we scrambled to 83 all out, our second-lowest total in a Test since readmission. England knocked off the 74 runs required for victory within 23 overs, and we were done.

Defeat meant that, according to the ICC rankings, we were formally replaced as the No. 1 Test team in the world by India, and many in the media began to predict the decline of the Proteas.

'How much have you missed Dale Steyn in this series?' one journalist asked at the press conference.

'We miss Dale, we miss Vern, we miss Kallis as well,' I replied, 'but this is the team we have and this is the team I believe in. We created opportunities here, but failed to take them. It is up to the 11 players picked for the fourth Test in Centurion to do something special. That's the way past players like Kallis and Smith did it; they had tough times as well but they fought back and found a way to get back to the top.'

We did respond well in the fourth and last Test, with Stephen Cook, Hashim and Quinton all scoring centuries in our first-innings score of 475. Stephen had been brought into the team as a specialist opening batsman and, while everybody knew he was the son of Jimmy Cook, a great player of the 1980s and 1990s, he quickly made a name for himself by showing a great attitude and great skill in joining the select group of players to score a century on his Test debut. KG took seven wickets as we dismissed England for 342, before Hashim and Temba made runs, putting us in position to declare, setting the tourists an unlikely target of 382 to win.

I was enjoying the captaincy and most of our plans were working, but I was also setting the wrong kind of records with the bat. Following my duck in the second innings at the Wanderers, I had been caught in the slips for 0 in our first innings, and was trapped LBW for 0 by Anderson in our second innings. Three consecutive ducks were unwelcome, but the team was playing well and that's what mattered.

England were dismissed for 101, and we won the Test match by 280 runs. KG had run in again and claimed another six wickets. His match figures of 13 wickets for 144 confirmed his arrival as a top-class fast bowler; it is exciting to imagine what he might achieve in years to come because I know he will work hard and learn fast.

Our revival continued during the limited-over matches that followed. We staged a fine comeback to win the ODI series 3–2 after losing the first and second games, and we then won both T20 internationals. I was pleased to score an unbeaten 101 in our successful chase to win the decisive one-day international and, although the disappointment of losing the Test series lingered, we had regrouped and recovered well from the catastrophic afternoon at the Wanderers. It was good to see the players smiling again.

Spirit was renewed.

Our minds were turning towards the 2016 World Twenty20 tournament, to be hosted by India, and we dared to believe we could move beyond recent disappointments, find some form at the right moment and, at last, win an official ICC limited-overs tournament. We may have lacked depth and experience in the longer format, but, at the very least, we had a puncher's chance in T20 cricket.

The Australians made a detour on their way to the tournament and arrived in South Africa to play three warm-up T20 internationals; we won in Durban, but then lost in Cape Town and Johannesburg. Even so, our starting XI looked strong enough, combining talent with T20 experience, and lined up as: Amla, De Kock, De Villiers, Du Plessis (captain), Duminy, Miller, Morris, Abbott, Steyn, Rabada and Tahir.

We travelled to India and prepared to compete with England, West Indies, Sri Lanka and Afghanistan in Group 1, with the top two teams in the pool advancing to the semifinals.

Our opening match, against England in Mumbai, was going according to plan when we batted first and scored 229 for four in our 20 overs. We should then have closed out the win, but England got off to a flier. Our fielding was average at times and Joe Root led his team to a notable win with two balls to spare.

Playing with no margin for error, we faced an improving Afghanistan at the same venue, scored 209 in 20 overs and withstood an early onslaught from Mohammad Shahzad, the Afghan captain. Imran was again our most economical bowler, and Chris Morris took four wickets, as we won by 37 runs. Back on track, still fighting, we needed to win our third group match against the West Indies in Nagpur.

The pitch was low and slow, and 150 would have been par. Sent in to bat first, we needed to be calm and smart. Instead, there was a run out off the third ball, everything became a little frantic and, in the blink of an eye, we found ourselves in serious trouble at 47 for five. Quinton,

David Wiese and Chris Morris kept battling, helping us scrap to a barely adequate total of 122 for eight in our 20 overs.

Even so, we made the West Indians work hard to get the runs. Imran Tahir bowled magnificently again, conceding only 13 runs in his four overs. He was well supported by David Wiese and Aaron Phangiso, who each yielded only 19 runs and, defying the odds, chasing everything, urging each other on, we somehow stayed in the game.

The West Indians needed 20 off the last two overs, and then nine runs off the last over to be bowled by KG Rabada. I remember thinking that if we could just find a way to nick a win from this situation, it would give us the confidence to go far in the tournament.

Carlos Brathwaite was facing and he swung at the first delivery of the over … It was a slower ball, and he missed. Nine runs were needed off five balls. Brathwaite took guard again and swung … and connected, just as Grant Elliott had connected in Auckland a year before, and the ball soared for six. The contest ended there. The West Indies scored the last three runs and won with two balls to spare.

Our elimination was confirmed when England squeaked to victory over Sri Lanka the following day, which meant our emphatic victory over Sri Lanka in our last group match was meaningless.

The margins had been tiny, as usual, but again we had come short in a tournament which we could have won and, on this occasion, Faf was the captain and it was his turn to attend the post-match press conference and endure the familiar routine of explaining our disappointment, saying there were no excuses and dealing with the C-word. There was nothing new to say, and nothing new to think.

After a week at home, Danielle and I, and the little one, all flew back to India, where I joined the Royal Challengers Bangalore squad for the ninth edition of the Indian Premier League. My schedule was tough but, as a young family, we had made a decision to stay together. Living out of a hotel room was never going to be ideal, but it was a whole lot better than being apart.

It had been a stressful period: limited-overs success and the 3–0 Test series defeat in India, the 2–1 Test series lost at home to England followed by some limited-overs success, and then our failure to reach the last four of the ICC World Twenty20 ... and I looked forward to being revived by RCB in particular and by India in general.

In 2016, as in the five previous IPL tournaments, our team was known for three top-order batsmen – Kohli, Gayle and De Villiers – and an inexperienced bowling attack; this apparent imbalance was exacerbated when key bowlers Mitchell Starc and new signing Samuel Badree had to withdraw, injured, just before the tournament.

So we started our campaign, unsure about our ability to contain top-class opposing batsmen and believing that, whatever happened when we were fielding, we would just have to score more runs.

We started as we meant to go on, batting first and scoring 227 for four against Sunrisers Hyderabad. Virat Kohli and I added 157 for the second wicket, and I was pleased to be back at the Chinnaswamy, pleased to be hitting the ball cleanly, pleased to be contributing 82 runs to what unfolded as an encouraging victory.

Virat was in the form of his life, placing the ball brilliantly, driving magnificently through and over the covers, efficiently clipping anything fractionally off line through the leg side, brutally pulling anything remotely short to or over the boundary between square leg and long-on. His abundance of skill and talent was wrapped in a raw passion to score runs, and more runs, and a vein-busting determination to win.

IPL 9 would become a platform for what, in my assessment, was one of the most sustained periods of consistent brilliance in the history of our game. In the 14 group matches played by RCB, Virat scored an unimaginable and almost certainly unrepeatable 919 runs, including four centuries and six 50s at a strike rate of 151.70.

Through the power of his will and the genius of his batting, Virat literally dragged us, his teammates, through the group phase, into the top two in the league and on to the play-offs.

It was anything but a smooth ride. Our opening win was followed by five defeats in the next six matches as our bowlers struggled to execute their plans. As a team, we were struggling to defend anything and, barely halfway through the tournament, we were facing early elimination and needing to win, and win, and win again.

Virat kept batting and batting, and we beat Rising Pune Supergiants at the Chinnaswamy, and then squeaked to a one-run win at Kings XI Punjab, suffered a defeat at home to Mumbai Indians, and eventually found ourselves needing to win each of our last four group matches to have any chance of progressing.

Momentum is a powerful force in Twenty20 tournaments and, driven on by our growing self-belief, we overcame Gujarat Lions at home, won against Kolkata Knight Riders in Kolkata, beat Kings XI Punjab at home and then, carefully, won a low-scoring match away at Delhi Daredevils to clinch our qualification.

Everything seemed to be falling into place. The complex play-off format meant that we had earned two chances to secure a place in the IPL final, and the first arrived in the form of a qualifier against the Gujarat Lions, a match to be played at a predetermined 'neutral' venue ... the Chinnaswamy Stadium in Bengaluru.

It was odd to see our home stadium dressed in neutral signage, but there was nothing neutral about the crowd and our bowlers performed exceptionally well to restrict Gujarat to 158 in their 20 overs. We launched our chase in a reasonably confident frame of mind but, as if to prove that anything really can happen in T20 cricket, we found ourselves in a crisis at 29 for five in the sixth over.

I had managed to survive and, together with Stuart Binny, was content to take singles and twos, and to punish anything short or loose. We began to fight our way back into the game and took 14 off one over after Virat sent out a message that there was rain around. With a little luck – one six cleared the fielder on the boundary by a few inches – we reached our target with an over and a half to spare. I finished unbeaten on 79 runs from 47 balls, and was happy to have made a difference for the team when we had seemed down and out in a vital match.

The final of IPL 9 was played at the Chinnaswamy Stadium in Bengaluru on Sunday 29 May, and our opponents were Sunrisers Hyderabad, brilliantly captained by David Warner. The Australian opener won the toss, seized the initiative by deciding to bat first, and led from the front as he scored 69 from only 38 balls. We regained some control in the middle of the innings but it was another big-hitting Australian, Ben Cutting, who cut loose in the closing overs.

It was our stadium, our crowd and, we dearly hoped, our big night, but we conceded 52 runs from the last three overs and were left to chase a target of 209 to win the game and take the title.

Virat had asked me to say a few words to the team before the match and I had urged everyone to believe that, whatever happened in the game, whatever challenges we would face, however difficult it got, we would prevail and get there in the end. As we prepared to start our chase, we really did need to keep believing.

Chris Gayle gave us exactly the start we needed, Virat was settling into his rhythm again, and we seemed on track at 112 without loss at the end of the tenth over. Then Chris was caught at third man for 76 in the 11th over, Virat was unfortunate to play on in the 13th over and I skied a drive and was caught at deep mid-off in the 14th over.

We fought hard to stay in the game, to a point where we needed 18 runs off the last over, but the Sunrisers bowlers had proved themselves to be the most effective attack in the competition, and they held their nerve and deservedly closed out a victory by eight runs.

Our dressing room was very quiet afterwards. We had come back from nowhere, and fought our way through to a home final in front of our own supporters at the Chinnaswamy, and fallen short. We walked around the field at the end, thanking our supporters, and it was heart-rending to see the disappointment on so many sad faces.

We didn't get back to our hotel until after one o'clock in the morning and there was not much time to rest and reflect because I was booked to leave Bengaluru at seven o'clock the following morning, flying to London and then on to join the Proteas in the Caribbean.

As I settled into my seat on another long-haul flight, sitting beside my wife Danielle who was cradling our young son, I considered just how ridiculously fortunate I have been and continue to be.

How fortunate to be raised by unconditionally loving parents and brothers ... to have such loyal friends and family ... to have married such an incredible and loving wife ... to have been embraced by such wonderful parents-in-law ... to have a beautiful son ... to have made a living by doing something I would have been happy to do for fun.

Looking back on all these years, I feel so enormously grateful to so many people ... to teachers and coaches, to friends and teammates at school ... to everybody at the Titans and Royal Challengers Bangalore ... to each and every person who has shared with me the great honour of being a Protea and representing our country on the cricket field: to the national coaches and selectors, to the officials and staff of Cricket South Africa who work so selflessly to make it possible for people like me to do what we do and take too much of the credit ... to each of the members of the professional team who continue to guide me off the field ... to everyone anywhere in the world who has come to watch the cricket and, by so doing, has made it possible for me to live a life far beyond any of my dreams ... last, but not least, to the talented people at Pan Macmillan, notably Terry Morris and Andrea Nattrass, for the opportunity to write this book.

The flight flew by and, in a quiet moment, my mind switched back to a brief conversation with Virat Kohli during the IPL.

I had arrived at breakfast one morning and sat down beside my friend, the player of the tournament, who was already at the table.

'So I was wondering,' I said, out of the blue, 'how long do you think you're going to keep playing cricket?'

Virat's face broke into a beaming smile, his eyes alight.

'I'm going to play forever,' he replied.

'If only that were possible,' I smiled, 'if only that were possible.'

STATISTICS

AS AT 31 MARCH 2016

COMPILED BY ANDREW SAMSON

Key

M – Matches

INNS – Innings

NO – Not Out

RUNS – Runs scored

HS – High Score

AVG – Average

SR – Strike Rate

100 – 100 runs scored

50 – 50 runs scored

CT – Catches

ST – Stumpings

UNB – Unbeaten

TEST CAREER

By series

SERIES	VENUE	SEASON	M	INNS	NO	RUNS
V ENGLAND	South Africa	2004/05	5	10	1	362
V ZIMBABWE	South Africa	2004/05	2	2	0	145
V WEST INDIES	West Indies	2004/05	4	7	0	460
V AUSTRALIA	Australia	2005/06	3	6	0	152
V AUSTRALIA	South Africa	2005/06	3	6	0	127
V NEW ZEALAND	South Africa	2005/06	3	5	0	144
V SRI LANKA	Sri Lanka	2006	2	4	0	217
V INDIA	South Africa	2006/07	3	6	0	102
V PAKISTAN	South Africa	2006/07	3	6	1	48
V PAKISTAN	Pakistan	2007/08	2	4	1	131
V NEW ZEALAND	South Africa	2007/08	2	2	0	66
V WEST INDIES	South Africa	2007/08	3	5	1	247
V BANGLADESH	Bangladesh	2007/08	2	3	1	66
V INDIA	India	2007/08	3	5	1	304
V ENGLAND	England	2008	4	6	0	384
V BANGLADESH	South Africa	2008/09	2	2	0	3
V AUSTRALIA	Australia	2008/09	3	5	1	243
V AUSTRALIA	South Africa	2008/09	3	5	1	357
V ENGLAND	South Africa	2009/10	4	7	0	276
V INDIA	India	2009/10	2	3	0	68
V WEST INDIES	West Indies	2010	3	6	4	330
V PAKISTAN	UAE	2010/11	2	3	1	308
V INDIA	South Africa	2010/11	3	5	0	201
V AUSTRALIA	South Africa	2011/12	2	3	0	145
V SRI LANKA	South Africa	2011/12	3	4	1	353
V NEW ZEALAND	New Zealand	2011/12	3	5	0	218
V ENGLAND	England	2012	3	4	0	161
V AUSTRALIA	Australia	2012/13	3	6	1	276
V NEW ZEALAND	South Africa	2012/13	2	2	0	118
V PAKISTAN	South Africa	2012/13	3	5	1	352
V PAKISTAN	UAE	2013/14	2	3	0	273
V INDIA	South Africa	2013/14	2	3	0	190
V AUSTRALIA	South Africa	2013/14	3	6	0	341
V SRI LANKA	Sri Lanka	2014	2	4	0	121
V ZIMBABWE	Zimbabwe	2014	1	1	0	7
V WEST INDIES	South Africa	2014/15	3	3	0	310
V INDIA	India	2015/16	4	7	0	258
V ENGLAND	South Africa	2015/16	4	7	0	210
TOTALS			106	176	16	8074

HS	AVG	SR	100	50	CT	ST
109	40.22	58.38	1	2	13	1
98	72.50	75.91	0	1	2	0
178	65.71	50.77	2	1	1	0
68	25.33	40.75	0	2	0	0
50	21.16	39.93	0	1	6	0
97	28.80	56.03	0	1	5	0
95	54.25	69.10	0	2	2	0
47	17.00	42.50	0	0	5	0
15	9.60	38.09	0	0	7	0
77	43.66	67.17	0	1	0	0
33	33.00	50.38	0	0	6	0
103	61.75	60.39	1	2	1	0
46	33.00	42.03	0	0	2	0
217*	76.00	61.04	1	0	4	0
174	64.00	48.18	1	1	5	0
3	1.50	17.64	0	0	3	0
106	60.75	43.16	1	2	6	0
163	89.25	60.00	2	1	7	0
64	39.42	54.33	0	3	5	0
53	22.66	48.22	0	1	2	0
135*	165.00	48.81	1	2	4	0
278*	154.00	66.09	1	0	2	0
129	40.20	62.22	1	0	5	0
73	48.33	59.91	0	2	4	0
160*	117.66	63.03	1	2	0	0
83	43.60	71.00	0	2	2	0
47	40.25	53.84	0	0	9	0
169	55.20	43.87	1	0	8	1
67	59.00	56.19	0	2	9	0
121	88.00	61.32	2	1	17	0
164	91.00	53.84	1	1	5	1
103	63.33	62.09	1	1	14	0
116	56.83	44.05	1	1	8	0
51	30.25	44.48	0	1	7	0
7	7.00	20.58	0	0	1	0
152	103.33	68.28	2	0	7	1
85	36.85	42.43	0	2	4	0
88	30.00	49.41	0	1	9	1
278*	**50.46**	**53.74**	**21**	**39**	**197**	**5**

• De Villiers has hit 934 fours and 57 sixes in his Test career.

• He has taken two Test wickets for 104 runs (avg. 52.00) in 34 overs, with a best of 2–49 v West Indies at St John's in 2005.

• As a fielder and wicketkeeper, he has been involved in executing 11 run outs.

Against each opponent

AGAINST	M	INNS	NO	RUNS	HS	AVG	SR	100	50	CT	ST
AUSTRALIA	20	37	3	1641	169	48.26	46.96	5	9	39	1
BANGLADESH	4	5	1	69	46	17.25	39.65	0	0	5	0
ENGLAND	20	34	1	1393	174	42.21	52.58	2	7	41	2
INDIA	17	29	1	1123	217*	40.10	53.07	3	4	34	0
NEW ZEALAND	10	14	0	546	97	39.00	60.33	0	5	22	0
PAKISTAN	12	21	4	1112	278*	65.41	59.52	4	3	31	1
SRI LANKA	7	12	1	691	160*	62.81	60.29	1	5	9	0
WEST INDIES	13	21	5	1347	178	84.18	55.09	6	5	13	1
ZIMBABWE	3	3	0	152	98	50.66	67.55	0	1	3	0

In each country

COUNTRY	M	INNS	NO	RUNS	HS	AVG	SR	100	50	CT	ST
AUSTRALIA	9	17	2	671	169	44.73	42.87	2	4	14	1
BANGLADESH	2	3	1	66	46	33.00	42.03	0	0	2	0
ENGLAND	7	10	0	545	174	54.50	49.72	1	1	14	0
INDIA	9	15	1	630	217*	45.00	50.52	1	3	10	0
NEW ZEALAND	3	5	0	218	83	43.60	71.00	0	2	2	0
PAKISTAN	2	4	1	131	77	43.66	67.17	0	1	0	0
SOUTH AFRICA	58	94	6	4097	163	46.55	56.27	12	21	133	3
SRI LANKA	4	8	0	338	95	42.25	57.67	0	3	9	0
UNITED ARAB EMIRATES	4	6	1	581	278*	116.20	59.71	2	1	7	1
WEST INDIES	7	13	4	790	178	87.77	49.93	3	3	5	0
ZIMBABWE	1	1	0	7	7	7.00	20.58	0	0	1	0
HOME	58	94	6	4097	163	46.55	56.27	12	21	133	3
AWAY	48	82	10	3977	278*	55.23	51.36	9	18	64	2
AS KEEPER	24	39	3	2067	169	57.41	53.02	7	7	89	5
AS PLAYER	82	137	13	6007	278*	48.44	54.00	14	32	108	0

At specific venues (minimum three matches)

VENUE	M	INNS	NO	RUNS	HS	AVG	SR	100	50	CT	ST
CAPE TOWN	17	26	2	1117	163	46.54	57.22	3	4	34	2
CENTURION	13	19	0	1157	152	60.89	63.60	4	5	20	0
JOHANNESBURG	11	20	2	689	104*	38.27	55.47	3	3	38	0
DURBAN	10	18	2	747	103*	46.68	50.37	1	6	28	1
PORT ELIZABETH	6	10	0	384	116	38.40	49.93	1	3	12	0
PERTH	3	6	1	422	169	84.40	62.24	2	2	8	1
NOTE:											
ABU DHABI	2	4	1	412	278*	137.33	60.58	1	1	4	0

Test centuries

START DATE	AGAINST	VENUE	SCORE	MINS	BALLS	FOURS	SIXES
21/01/2005	England	Centurion	109	276	169	11	1
21/04/2005	West Indies	Bridgetown	178	555	352	15	1
29/04/2005	West Indies	St John's	114	251	173	13	1
10/01/2008	West Indies	Durban	103*	160	109	15	1
03/04/2008	India	Ahmedabad	217*	480	333	17	2
18/07/2008	England	Leeds	174	512	381	19	0
17/12/2008	Australia	Perth	106*	276	186	9	0
26/02/2009	Australia	Johannesburg	104*	285	185	9	1
19/03/2009	Australia	Cape Town	163	313	196	12	7
18/06/2010	West Indies	Basseterre	135*	274	168	13	6
20/11/2010	Pakistan	Abu Dhabi	278*	601	418	23	6
16/12/2010	India	Centurion	129	149	112	12	5
03/01/2012	Sri Lanka	Cape Town	160*	301	205	19	2
30/11/2012	Australia	Perth	169	225	184	21	3
01/02/2013	Pakistan	Johannesburg	103*	157	117	11	0
22/02/2013	Pakistan	Centurion	121	326	215	15	0
23/10/2013	Pakistan	Dubai	164	374	274	17	1
18/12/2013	India	Johannesburg	103	240	168	12	0
20/02/2014	Australia	Port Elizabeth	116	322	232	14	1
17/12/2014	West Indies	Centurion	152	318	235	16	2
02/01/2015	West Indies	Cape Town	148	324	194	15	1

Double-century partnerships

WKT	PART	WITH	AGAINST	VENUE	YEAR
3	227	JH Kallis	England	Centurion	2005
1	217	GC Smith	Zimbabwe	Cape Town	2005
1	245	GC Smith	West Indies	St John's	2005
5	256	JH Kallis	India	Ahmedabad	2008
5	212	AG Prince	England	Leeds	2008
4	224	JH Kallis	India	Centurion	2010
5	338	GC Smith	Pakistan	Dubai	2013*
5	205	F du Plessis	India	Johannesburg	2013
4	308	HM Amla	West Indies	Centurion	2014*

* These are the South African records for the wicket. He also holds the 10th wicket record for South Africa.

10	107*	M Morkel	Pakistan	Abu Dhabi	2010/11

Against specific bowlers

BOWLER	RUNS	BALLS	FOURS	SIXES	WKTS	AVG	SR
SCJ BROAD	163	349	22	0	10	16.30	46.70
PM SIDDLE	273	595	42	1	6	45.50	45.88
MG JOHNSON	259	537	26	1	5	51.80	48.23
S SREESANTH	103	237	15	0	5	20.60	43.45
RA JADEJA	113	202	15	0	4	28.25	55.94
MS PANESAR	92	187	10	0	4	23.00	49.19
RD KING	48	142	4	0	4	12.00	33.80
SK WARNE	34	87	2	0	4	8.50	39.08
JM ANDERSON	210	427	28	0	3	70.00	49.18
SJ BENN	184	360	12	3	3	61.33	51.11
B LEE	159	297	23	0	3	53.00	53.53
Z KHAN	114	221	16	0	3	38.00	51.58
DJ BRAVO	105	240	13	0	3	35.00	43.75
CS MARTIN	102	140	16	0	3	34.00	72.85
MJ HOGGARD	87	158	12	1	3	29.00	55.06
M MURALITHARAN	69	106	7	0	3	23.00	65.09
A MISHRA	37	62	5	0	3	12.33	59.67
JEC FRANKLIN	33	32	4	0	3	11.00	103.12
MOHAMMAD ASIF	26	78	2	0	3	8.66	33.33
SR CLARK	21	67	2	0	3	7.00	31.34
SHAKIB AL HASAN	17	18	2	1	3	5.66	94.44
HARBHAJAN SINGH	207	394	14	3	2	103.50	52.53
ABDUR REHMAN	138	260	5	4	2	69.00	53.07
JE TAYLOR	133	203	21	0	2	66.50	65.51
I SHARMA	115	227	15	0	2	57.50	50.66
A FLINTOFF	104	259	15	0	2	52.00	40.15
HMRKB HERATH	102	299	7	1	2	51.00	34.11
R ASHWIN	101	272	9	1	2	50.50	37.13
GP SWANN	98	207	7	1	2	49.00	47.34
NM LYON	229	421	23	5	1	229.00	54.39
DBL POWELL	159	276	23	0	1	159.00	57.60
DL VETTORI	80	212	5	0	1	80.00	37.73
SAEED AJMAL	166	385	12	1	0	–	43.11
S SHILLINGFORD	129	202	9	4	0	–	63.86

This list includes all bowlers from whom De Villiers has faced 200 or more balls or has been dismissed by at least three times. It is ordered by wickets, then runs.

Most Test runs for South Africa

NAME	M	INNS	NO	RUNS	HS	AVG	SR	100	50
JH KALLIS	165	278	39	13206	224	55.25	45.98	45	58
GC SMITH	116	203	13	9253	277	48.70	59.70	27	38
AB DE VILLIERS	106	176	16	8074	278*	50.46	53.74	21	39
HM AMLA	92	156	13	7358	311*	51.45	50.05	25	29
G KIRSTEN	101	176	15	7289	275	45.27	43.45	21	34
HH GIBBS	90	154	7	6167	228	41.95	50.25	14	26
MV BOUCHER	146	204	24	5498	125	30.54	50.18	5	35

Highest Test scores for South Africa

SCORE	MINS	BALLS	FOURS	SIXES	NAME	AGAINST	VENUE	START DATE
311 *	790	529	35	0	HM Amla	England	The Oval	19/07/2012
278 *	601	418	23	6	AB de Villiers	Pakistan	Abu Dhabi	20/11/2010
277	540	373	35	0	GC Smith	England	Birmingham	24/07/2003
275 *	658	490	27	2	DJ Cullinan	New Zealand	Auckland	27/02/1999
275	878	642	26	0	G Kirsten	England	Durban	26/12/1999
274	417	401	43	0	RG Pollock	Australia	Durban	05/02/1970

Most innings before first duck in Test career

INNS	NAME	TEAM	FROM	UNTIL
78	AB de Villiers	South Africa	17/12/2004	19/11/2008
75	PA de Silva	Sri Lanka	23/08/1984	11/10/1994
58	CH Lloyd	West Indies	13/12/1966	02/02/1974
58	LRPL Taylor	New Zealand	08/11/2007	01/12/2011
54	JM Anderson	England	22/05/2003	07/08/2009
51	AK Davidson	Australia	11/06/1953	06/07/1961
51	GO Jones	England	10/04/2004	01/12/2006

Players with at least two stumpings and at least two wickets in Tests

NAME	TEAM	M	RUNS	AVG	CT	ST	WKTS	AVG
RJ CHRISTIANI	WI	22	896	26.35	19	2	3	36.00
AB DE VILLIERS	SA	106	8074	50.46	197	5	2	52.00
CL WALCOTT	WI	44	3798	56.68	53	11	11	37.09

Most consecutive Test appearances from debut

NAME	TEAM	FROM	UNTIL	TESTS
BB McCULLUM	New Zealand	10/03/2004	20/02/2016	101
AB DE VILLIERS	South Africa	17/12/2004	02/01/2015	98
AC GILCHRIST	Australia	05/11/1999	24/01/2008	96
RS DRAVID	India	20/06/1996	10/12/2005	93
SR TENDULKAR	India	15/11/1989	15/06/2001	84

LIMITED-OVERS INTERNATIONAL CAREER

By year

YEAR	M	INNS	NO	RUNS	HS	AVG	SR	100	50	CT	ST
2005	14	14	0	221	39	15.78	66.76	0	0	4	0
2006	12	12	1	466	92*	42.36	84.88	0	3	6	0
2007	33	32	5	1209	146	44.77	92.29	3	8	20	0
2008	17	14	2	434	77	36.16	78.33	0	3	15	0
2009	17	17	3	762	121	54.42	92.81	1	6	12	0
2010	16	16	4	964	114*	80.33	102.11	5	4	22	1
2011	10	10	1	467	134	51.88	104.94	2	2	7	1
2012	13	12	6	645	125*	107.50	108.58	2	3	23	1
2013	27	26	3	1163	128	50.56	97.07	3	7	25	0
2014	16	16	4	879	136*	73.25	114.45	2	6	8	0
2015	20	18	3	1193	162*	79.53	137.91	5	5	17	2
2016	5	5	2	218	101*	72.66	96.46	1	1	5	0
TOTALS											
FOR SOUTH AFRICA	195	187	34	8471	162*	55.36	100.36	24	47	159	5
FOR AFRICA	5	5	0	150	70	30.00	90.90	0	1	5	0
ALL	200	192	34	8621	162*	54.56	100.18	24	48	164	5

By competition

COMPETITION	M	INNS	NO	RUNS	HS	AVG	SR	100	50	CT	ST
WORLD CUP	23	22	3	1207	162*	63.52	117.29	4	6	12	0
ICC CHAMPIONS TROPHY	10	10	1	378	70*	42.00	84.37	0	3	7	0
OTHER MATCHES	167	160	30	7036	149	54.12	98.70	20	39	145	5

De Villiers has hit 763 fours and 184 sixes in his limited-overs international career.

He has taken seven limited-overs international wickets for 202 runs (avg. 28.85, RPO 6.31) in 32 overs, with a best of 2–15 v United Arab Emirates in Wellington in 2015.

'As a fielder and wicketkeeper, he has been involved in executing 42 run outs.

Against each opponent

AGAINST	M	INNS	NO	RUNS	HS	AVG	SR	100	50	CT	ST
ASIA	5	5	0	150	70	30.00	90.90	0	1	5	0
AUSTRALIA	23	23	4	1189	136*	62.57	99.74	1	10	16	0
BANGLA-DESH	6	5	2	213	69*	71.00	82.55	0	2	9	0
ENGLAND	26	24	3	738	121	35.14	84.34	2	2	25	0
INDIA	28	28	4	1279	119	53.29	111.21	6	5	15	1
IRELAND	3	3	0	64	40	21.33	136.17	0	0	1	0
KENYA	2	2	0	39	28	19.50	100.00	0	0	1	0
NETHER-LANDS	3	2	0	134	134	67.00	134.00	1	0	1	0
NEW ZEALAND	20	20	7	729	106*	56.07	94.67	1	5	9	1
PAKISTAN	31	30	7	1423	128	61.86	91.39	3	10	29	1
SCOTLAND	1	1	0	62	62	62.00	137.77	0	1	1	0
SRI LANKA	17	16	2	756	125*	54.00	101.61	2	5	14	0
UNITED ARAB EMIRATES	1	1	0	99	99	99.00	120.73	0	1	1	0
WEST INDIES	21	19	3	1219	162*	76.18	113.29	5	4	20	2
ZIMBABWE	13	13	2	527	109	47.90	104.35	3	2	17	0

In each country

COUNTRY	M	INNS	NO	RUNS	HS	AVG	SR	100	50	CT	ST
AUSTRALIA	12	11	2	678	162*	75.33	118.11	1	5	7	0
BANGLA-DESH	4	3	1	144	69*	72.00	76.19	0	1	9	0
ENGLAND	14	12	1	363	75*	33.00	82.68	0	2	16	0
INDIA	20	20	4	1125	134	70.31	113.98	7	3	11	0
IRELAND	4	4	0	79	40	19.75	69.91	0	0	1	0
NETHER-LANDS	1	0	0	0	–	–	–	0	0	1	0
NEW ZEALAND	10	10	6	571	106*	142.75	111.08	1	4	11	1
PAKISTAN	5	5	2	173	103*	57.66	88.26	1	0	2	0
SOUTH AFRICA	86	83	13	3628	149	51.82	99.34	8	23	64	3
SRI LANKA	8	8	0	349	108	43.62	99.71	1	2	6	0
UNITED ARAB EMIRATES	10	10	1	402	115*	44.66	81.54	1	2	16	1
WEST INDIES	17	17	1	702	146	43.87	97.63	2	4	10	0
ZIMBABWE	9	9	3	407	136*	67.83	107.38	2	2	10	0
HOME	86	83	13	3628	149	51.82	99.34	8	23	64	3
AWAY	72	68	16	3161	146	60.78	101.41	11	16	66	1
NEUTRAL	42	41	5	1832	162*	50.88	99.78	5	9	34	1

At specific venues (minimum four matches)

VENUE	M	INNS	NO	RUNS	HS	AVG	SR	100	50	CT	ST
CENTURION	18	18	5	593	109	45.61	88.24	1	3	11	0
PORT ELIZABETH	14	13	0	434	84	33.38	90.79	0	4	8	1
DURBAN	13	13	0	632	87	48.61	85.29	0	6	8	1
CAPE TOWN	11	11	2	481	121	53.44	99.79	2	2	8	0
JOHANNES-BURG	10	9	2	646	149	92.28	133.19	3	2	7	0
BLOEM-FONTEIN	6	6	1	164	65	32.80	91.11	0	1	6	0
HARARE	6	6	3	322	136*	107.33	115.82	2	1	9	0
CARDIFF	4	2	0	107	70	53.50	110.30	0	1	2	0
COLOMBO-RPS	4	4	0	161	75	40.25	101.89	0	2	1	0
ABU DHABI	4	4	0	144	51	36.00	81.81	0	1	5	0
DUBAI	4	4	0	139	61	34.75	68.47	0	1	8	1
CHENNAI	4	4	0	220	112	55.00	98.21	1	1	5	0
BELFAST	4	4	0	79	40	19.75	69.91	0	0	1	0
BENONI	4	4	2	309	109	154.50	107.29	1	3	3	0
AS CAPTAIN	81	77	18	4098	162*	69.45	112.24	13	22	78	3
AS PLAYER	119	115	16	4523	146	45.68	91.30	11	26	86	2
AS KEEPER	59	55	13	2833	149	67.45	99.47	9	17	93	5
AS PLAYER	141	137	21	5788	162*	49.89	100.53	15	31	71	0

Double-century partnerships

WKT	PART	WITH	AGAINST	VENUE	YEAR
3	219	JP Duminy	Zimbabwe	Benoni	2010
3	221	HM Amla	Netherlands	Mohali	2011
3	238	HM Amla	Pakistan	Johannesburg	2013
3	206	F du Plessis	Australia	Harare	2014

Limited-overs international centuries

DATE	AGAINST	VENUE	SCORE	MINS	BALLS	FOURS	SIXES
10/04/2007	West Indies#	St George's	146	195	130	12	5
26/08/2007	Zimbabwe	Harare	107	131	89	8	6
18/10/2007	Pakistan	Lahore	103*	125	95	9	3
27/11/2009	England	Cape Town	121	118	85	14	0
24/02/2010	India	Gwalior	114*	154	101	13	2
27/02/2010	India	Ahmedabad	102*	76	59	11	3
22/05/2010	West Indies	North Sound	102	145	101	5	2
17/10/2010	Zimbabwe	Potchefstroom	101*	103	72	5	5
22/10/2010	Zimbabwe	Benoni	109	119	99	5	5
24/02/2011	West Indies#	Delhi	107*	149	105	8	2
03/03/2011	Netherlands#	Mohali	134	126	98	13	4
22/01/2012	Sri Lanka	Johannesburg	125*	144	98	10	4
25/02/2012	New Zealand	Wellington	106*	151	106	3	4
17/03/2013	Pakistan	Johannesburg	128	148	108	12	3
11/11/2013	Pakistan	Sharjah	115*	148	102	10	3
11/12/2013	India	Centurion	109	133	101	6	5
12/07/2014	Sri Lanka	Hambantota	108	101	71	11	4
27/08/2014	Australia	Harare	136*	173	106	11	2
18/01/2015	West Indies	Johannesburg	149	59	44	9	16
27/02/2015	West Indies#	Sydney	162*	103	66	17	8
11/10/2015	India	Kanpur	104*	116	73	5	6
22/10/2015	India	Chennai	112	128	107	10	2
25/10/2015	India	Mumbai	119	98	61	3	11
14/02/2016	England	Cape Town	101*	152	97	11	1

World Cup matches
* not out

Against specific bowlers

This list includes all bowlers from whom De Villiers has faced 100 or more balls or has been dismissed by at least three times. It is ordered by wickets, then runs.

BOWLER	RUNS	BALLS	FOURS	SIXES	WKTS	AVG	SR
SAEED AJMAL	174	204	15	3	6	29.00	85.29
SHAHID AFRIDI	227	274	11	4	5	45.40	82.84
BAW MENDIS	91	91	6	2	4	22.75	100.00
MG JOHNSON	147	140	17	1	3	49.00	105.00
TM DILSHAN	98	92	7	3	3	32.66	106.52
KD MILLS	63	94	8	0	3	21.00	67.02
RA JADEJA	100	102	9	1	2	50.00	98.03
MOHAMMAD ASIF	84	113	15	0	2	42.00	74.33
NW BRACKEN	73	103	6	1	2	36.50	70.87
MOHAMMAD HAFEEZ	151	160	8	4	1	151.00	94.37
HARBHAJAN SINGH	139	127	10	4	1	139.00	109.44
DJG SAMMY	110	141	4	0	1	110.00	78.01
HMRKB HERATH	101	116	6	2	1	101.00	87.06
MOHAMMAD IRFAN	72	103	6	0	1	72.00	69.90
P UTSEYA	139	122	8	7	0	–	113.93
WAHAB RIAZ	130	129	12	3	0	–	100.77
DJ BRAVO	107	105	9	1	0	–	101.90
Z KHAN	91	112	12	1	0	–	81.25
NOTE:							
JO HOLDER	138	50	12	12	0	–	276.00

Fastest limited-overs international 50s

BALLS	SCORE	NAME	TEAM	AGAINST	VENUE	YEAR
16	149	AB de Villiers	South Africa	West Indies	Johannesburg	2015
17	76	ST Jayasuriya	Sri Lanka	Pakistan	Singapore	1996
17	68	MDKJ Perera	Sri Lanka	Pakistan	Pallekele	2015
17	93*	MJ Guptill	New Zealand	Sri Lanka	Christchurch	2015/16

Fastest limited-overs international 100s

BALLS	SCORE	NAME	TEAM	AGAINST	VENUE	YEAR
31	149	AB de Villiers	South Africa	West Indies	Johannesburg	2015
36	131*	CJ Anderson	New Zealand	West Indies	Queenstown	2014
37	102	Shahid Afridi	Pakistan	Sri Lanka	Nairobi	1996
44	147*	MV Boucher	South Africa	Zimbabwe	Potchefstroom	2006
45	117	BC Lara	West Indies	Bangladesh	Dhaka	1999
45	102	Shahid Afridi	Pakistan	India	Kanpur	2005

Fastest limited-overs international 150s

BALLS	SCORE	NAME	TEAM	AGAINST	VENUE	YEAR
64	162*	AB de Villiers	South Africa	West Indies	Sydney	2015
83	185*	SR Watson	Australia	Bangladesh	Mirpur	2011
92	170*	L Ronchi	New Zealand	Sri Lanka	Dunedin	2015

Fewest innings to reach 8000 limited-overs international runs

NAME	TEAM	M	INNS	NO	RUNS	HS	AVG	100	50
AB de Villiers	SA	190	182	31	8045	162*	53.27	20	47
SC Ganguly	Ind	208	200	15	8044	183	43.48	19	48
SR Tendulkar	Ind	217	210	21	8038	143	42.52	22	43

Fewest innings to reach 3000 limited-overs international runs as captain

NAME	TEAM	M	INNS	NO	RUNS	HS	AVG	100	50
AB de Villiers	SA	63	60	14	3153	162*	68.54	9	17
MS Dhoni	Ind	80	70	19	3037	124	59.54	4	22
SC Ganguly	Ind	75	74	6	3010	144	44.26	8	18
GC Smith	SA	85	83	5	3051	134*	39.11	6	19
Misbah-ul-Haq	Pak	87	83	16	3003	96*	44.82	0	27

1 000 limited-overs international runs as captain and wicketkeeper in same match

NAME	TEAM	M	INNS	NO	RUNS	HS	AVG	SR	100	50
MS Dhoni	Ind	191	166	48	6441	139*	54.58	86.85	6	46
KC Sangakkara	SL	45	43	6	1756	111	47.45	84.30	1	14
AB de Villiers	**SA**	31	28	7	1433	149	68.23	107.02	4	8
A Flower	Zim	46	44	2	1077	76	25.64	68.07	0	10

Highest limited-overs international partnership averages (minimum 2 500 runs)

PAIR	TEAM	INNS	UNB	RUNS	BEST	AVG	100	50
HM Amla and AB de Villiers	**SA**	37	2	2851	238	81.45	11	8
MS Dhoni and SK Raina	Ind	72	11	3569	196*	58.50	9	18
TM Dilshan and KC Sangakkara	SL	108	6	5475	210*	53.67	20	19
DL Haynes and CG Greenidge	WI	103	4	5206	192*	52.58	15	25
ML Hayden and RT Ponting	Aus	73	6	3519	219	52.52	10	15

Note: Amla and De Villiers partnerships have been scored at 6.57 runs per over.

Most limited-overs internationals before taking first wicket

NAME	TEAM	M
Mohammad Yousuf	Pak	236
AB de Villiers	**SA**	170
MS Dhoni	Ind	145
L Vincent	NZ	100

Most limited-overs international runs for South Africa

NAME	M	INNS	NO	RUNS	HS	AVG	SR	100	50
JH Kallis	323	309	53	11550	139	45.11	73.12	17	86
AB de Villiers	195	187	34	8471	162*	55.36	100.36	24	47
HH Gibbs	248	240	16	8094	175	36.13	83.24	21	37
GC Smith	196	193	10	6989	141	38.19	80.86	10	47
G Kirsten	185	185	19	6798	188*	40.95	71.98	13	45
HM Amla	131	128	9	6204	159	52.13	89.06	22	29
JN Rhodes	245	220	51	5935	121	35.11	81.05	2	33
WJ Cronjé	188	175	31	5565	112	38.64	76.49	2	39

Best strike rates in limited-overs international for South Africa

NAME	M	INNS	NO	RUNS	HS	AVG	SR	100	50
AB de Villiers	195	187	34	8471	162*	55.36	100.36	24	47
L Klusener	171	137	50	3576	103*	41.10	89.89	2	19
HM Amla	131	128	9	6204	159	52.13	89.06	22	29
SM Pollock	294	196	70	3193	90	25.34	85.67	0	13
MV Boucher	290	216	57	4523	147*	28.44	84.65	1	25

Players with at least five stumpings and at least five wickets in limited-overs internationals

NAME	TEAM	M	RUNS	AVG	CT	ST	WKTS	AVG
JC Adams	WI	127	2204	28.62	68	5	43	34.86
AB de Villiers	SA	200	8621	54.56	164	5	7	28.85
BRM Taylor	Zim	167	5258	34.82	98	20	9	45.11
HP Tillakaratne	SL	200	3789	29.60	89	6	6	23.50

TWENTY20 INTERNATIONAL CAREER

COMPETITION	M	INNS	NO	RUNS	HS	AVG	SR	100	50	CT	ST
ICC WORLD TWENTY20	30	29	5	717	79*	29.87	143.4	0	5	30	2
OTHER MATCHES	41	39	5	651	71	19.14	121.22	0	3	31	5
TOTALS	71	68	10	1368	79*	23.58	131.91	0	8	61	7

De Villiers has hit 116 fours and 48 sixes in his Twenty20 international career.
He has not bowled in Twenty20 internationals.
As a fielder and wicketkeeper, he has been involved in executing 12 run outs.

Against each opponent

AGAINST	M	INNS	NO	RUNS	HS	AVG	SR	100	50	CT	ST
AFGHANISTAN	2	2	0	81	64	40.50	162.00	0	1	2	0
AUSTRALIA	8	8	1	52	21	7.42	86.66	0	0	5	1
BANGLADESH	4	4	1	92	40	30.66	113.58	0	0	5	1
ENGLAND	12	12	2	244	71	24.40	167.12	0	2	5	1
INDIA	9	9	0	208	63	23.11	131.64	0	2	8	0
NETHERLANDS	1	1	0	21	21	21.00	100.00	0	0	0	0
NEW ZEALAND	10	10	3	244	52*	34.85	116.74	0	1	10	0
PAKISTAN	10	8	0	144	53	18.00	122.03	0	1	7	2
SCOTLAND	1	1	1	79	79*	–	232.35	0	1	0	0
SRI LANKA	6	6	2	105	30	26.25	145.83	0	0	6	0
WEST INDIES	7	7	0	98	25	14.00	111.36	0	0	9	2
ZIMBABWE	1	0	0	0	–	–	–	0	0	4	0

In each country

COUNTRY	M	INNS	NO	RUNS	HS	AVG	SR	100	50	CT	ST
AUSTRALIA	1	1	0	0	0	0.00	0.00	0	0	2	0
BANGLADESH	7	7	1	171	69*	28.50	143.69	0	1	7	0
ENGLAND	9	9	1	199	79*	24.87	149.62	0	2	5	0
INDIA	6	6	1	180	64	36.00	157.89	0	2	3	0
NEW ZEALAND	3	3	1	76	39*	38.00	100.00	0	0	3	0
SOUTH AFRICA	26	25	4	423	71	20.14	135.57	0	2	21	3
SRI LANKA	8	7	1	120	30	20.00	121.21	0	0	11	2
UNITED ARAB EMIRATES	4	3	0	16	11	5.33	66.66	0	0	0	0
WEST INDIES	7	7	1	183	53	30.50	117.30	0	1	9	2
HOME	26	25	4	423	71	20.14	135.57	0	2	21	3
AWAY	18	18	2	303	51	18.93	110.98	0	1	17	2
NEUTRAL	27	25	4	642	79*	30.57	142.03	0	5	23	2

CAREER SUMMARY

Career record

COMPETITION	M	INNS	NO	RUNS	HS	AVG	SR	100	50	CT	ST
Test	106	176	16	8074	278*	50.46	53.74	21	39	197	5
Franchise First-class	15	28	1	1217	151	45.07	61.74	2	10	35	1
Other First-class	11	17	4	670	100	51.53	71.04	1	4	16	0
All First-class	**132**	**221**	**21**	**9961**	**278***	**49.80**	**55.53**	**24**	**53**	**248**	**6**
Limited-overs international	200	192	34	8621	162*	54.56	100.18	24	48	164	5
Franchise one-day	25	24	2	1100	107	50.00	86.07	2	8	21	0
Other List A limited overs	7	7	1	237	113*	39.50	89.77	1	1	5	0
All limited overs	**232**	**223**	**37**	**9958**	**162***	**53.53**	**98.13**	**27**	**57**	**190**	**5**
Twenty20 international	71	68	10	1368	79*	23.58	131.91	0	8	61	7
Franchise Twenty20	13	12	1	359	91*	32.63	143.60	0	2	9	2
Indian Premier League	104	93	23	2570	133*	36.71	144.87	2	15	56	7
Other Twenty20	6	6	1	172	77	34.40	163.80	0	1	6	0
All Twenty20	**194**	**179**	**35**	**4469**	**133***	**31.03**	**141.15**	**2**	**26**	**132**	**16**

First-class centuries (outside of Tests)

START DATE	FOR	AGAINST	VENUE	SCORE	MINS	BALLS	FOURS	SIXES
14/10/2004	Titans	Western Province Boland	Benoni	151	352	246	18	2
21/10/2004	Titans	Warriors	East London	124	228	182	17	1
25/07/2008	South Africa A	Bangladesh A	Worcester	100	171	139	7	2

List A limited-overs centuries (outside of internationals)

DATE	TEAM	AGAINST	VENUE	RUNS	MINS	BALLS	FOURS	SIXES
03/12/2004	Titans	Western Province Boland	Centurion	102	163	130	11	1
16/10/2007	South Africa A	Pakistan Board XI	Lahore	113*		95	9	1
09/12/2012	Titans	Cape Cobras	Cape Town	107	155	124	11	0

Twenty20 centuries

DATE	TEAM	AGAINST	VENUE	RUNS	MINS	BALLS	FOURS	SIXES
23/04/2009	Delhi Daredevils	Chennai Super Kings	Durban	105*		54	5	6
10/05/2015	Royal Challengers Bangalore	Mumbai Indians	Mumbai	133*		59	19	4

Bowling

De Villiers has taken two first-class wickets for 138 runs (avg. 69.00) in 39 overs, with a best of 2–49 for South Africa v West Indies at St John's in 2005.

He has taken seven limited-overs wickets for 202 runs (avg. 28.85, RPO 6.31) in 32 overs, with a best of 2–15 for South Africa v United Arab Emirates in Wellington in 2015.

He has not bowled in Twenty20 matches.

Captaincies

COMPETITION	PLAYED	WON	LOST	TIED	D/NR	% WON
Tests	2	1	1	0	0	50.00
Limited-overs international	81	47	30	1	3	60.25
Twenty20 international	15	7	7	0	1	46.66

Note: % won calculation excludes 'no results'.

ACKNOWLEDGEMENTS

Songs

Lyrics from David Gray's 'Please Forgive Me' on pages 141, 143, 145 and 146 reproduced with the kind permission of David Gray and iht Records/Mondo Management.

Lyrics from David Gray's 'This Year's Love' on page 230 reproduced with the kind permission of David Gray and iht Records/Mondo Management.

Lyrics from Elvis Blue's 'Lighthouse' on page 234 reproduced with the kind permission of Elvis Blue.

Lyrics from Toto's 'Africa' on page 150 reproduced with the kind permission of Toto, Sheer Publishing and Sony.

Lyrics from Johnny Clegg's 'Asimbonanga' on page 151 reproduced with the kind permission of Johnny Clegg and Rhythm Safari.

Photographs

All personal photographs supplied by AB de Villiers and family.

SECTION 1

PAGE 6, TOP: Mirpur, Bangladesh. 12 March 2008. AB de Villiers in action during the second ODI match between Bangladesh and South Africa held at the Shere Bangla National Stadium. Photo by Duif du Toit/Gallo Images.

PAGE 6, BOTTOM: Johannesburg, South Africa. 3 February 2008. AB de Villiers in the field during the fifth ODI between South Africa and West Indies held at the Liberty Life Wanderers in Johannesburg, South Africa. Photo by Duif du Toit/Gallo Images.

PAGE 7: Lahore, Pakistan. 18 October 2007. AB de Villiers during the first ODI match between Pakistan and South Africa held at the Gaddafi Stadium in Lahore, Pakistan. Photo by Lee Warne/Gallo Images.

PAGE 8, TOP: Ahmedabad, India. 4 April 2008. AB de Villiers celebrates his 200 runs during day one of the second Test match between India and South Africa held at the Sardar Patel Gujarat Stadium in Motera, Ahmedabad, India. Photo by Duif du Toit/Gallo Images.

PAGE 8, BOTTOM: Durban, South Africa. 26 December 2013. AB de Villiers and Graeme Smith of South Africa walk off for bad light during day one of the second Test match between South Africa and India at the Sahara Stadium Kingsmead. Photo by Duif du Toit/Gallo Images.

PAGE 9: Johannesburg, South Africa. 4 February 2013. AB de Villiers and Graeme Smith of South Africa appeal during day four of the first Test match between South Africa and Pakistan at the Bidvest Wanderers Stadium. Photo by Duif du Toit/Gallo Images.

PAGE 10: Melbourne, Australia. 26 December 2008. Makhaya Ntini celebrates with AB de Villiers and JP Duminy after getting the wicket of Brad Haddin during day one of the second Test between Australia and South Africa at the MCG. Photo by Tertius Pickard/Gallo Images.

PAGE 11, TOP: Ahmedabad, India. 3 April 2008. Jacques Kallis and AB de Villiers at the end of play with an unbroken partnership of 100 runs during day one of the second Test match between India and South Africa held at the Sardar Patel Gujarat Stadium in Motera. Photo by Duif du Toit/Gallo Images.

PAGE 11, BOTTOM: Johannesburg, South Africa. 13 January 2010. AB de Villiers and Mark Boucher waiting to bat during the South African cricket team training and press conference session at the Bidvest Wanderers Stadium. Photo by Duif du Toit/Gallo Images.

PAGE 12, TOP: London, England. 8 August 2008. AB de Villiers of South Africa makes a diving catch to stop a ball played by Steve Harmison of England during day two of the fourth npower Test match between England and South Africa at The Oval. Photo by Tom Shaw/Getty Images.

PAGE 12, BOTTOM: London, England. 11 August 2008. The South African team celebrates winning the series during the final day of the fourth npower Test match between England and South Africa at The Oval. Photo by Richard Heathcote/Getty Images.

SECTION 2

PAGE 1, TOP: Durban, South Africa. 23 April 2009. AB de Villiers celebrates his century during the IPL T20 match between Chennai Super Kings and Delhi Daredevils from Sahara Park. AB de Villiers is the first South African to reach his century in the year's IPL tournament. Photo by Anesh Debiky/Gallo Images.

PAGE 1, BOTTOM: Bangalore, India. 23 September 2011. Royal Challengers Bangalore player AB de Villiers plays a shot against the

Warriors during the Champions League Cricket Twenty20 League Group B match at the M. Chinnaswamy Stadium. AFP Photo/ Manjunath Kiran.

PAGE 2, TOP: Bangalore, India. 22 May 2011. Royal Challengers Bangalore bowler Virat Kohli (R) celebrates with teammate AB de Villiers after taking the wicket of Chennai Super Kings batsman Wriddhiman Saha as other Chennai Super Kings batsman Mahendra Singh Dhoni (L) looks on during the IPL Twenty20 match between Chennai Super Kings and Royal Challengers Bangalore at the M. Chinnaswamy Stadium. AFP Photo/Dibyangshu Sarkar.

PAGE 2, bottom: Dharamsala, India. 2 October 2016. AB de Villiers of South Africa during the India and South Africa first Twenty20 International (T20) of their three-match series, at the Himachal Pradesh Cricket Association Stadium (HPCA) in Dharamsala. Photo by Pankaj Nangia/India Today Group/Getty Images.

PAGE 3: Bangalore, India. 17 April 2012. Royal Challengers Bangalore batsman AB de Villiers celebrates as he runs towards the pavilion after winning the IPL Twenty20 cricket match against Pune Warriors (PW) at the M. Chinnaswamy Stadium in Bangalore. RCB scored 186 runs against a target of 182 set by PW. AFP Photo/Manjunath Kiran.

PAGE 7, TOP: Wellington, New Zealand. 12 March 2015. Hashim Amla (L) and AB de Villiers of South Africa are all smiles after winning the 2015 ICC Cricket World Cup match between South Africa and the United Arab Emirates at the Wellington Regional Stadium. Photo by Hagen Hopkins/Getty Images.

PAGE 7, BOTTOM LEFT: Auckland, New Zealand. 24 March 2015. Dale Steyn (R) and AB de Villiers of South Africa chat in the last over during the 2015 Cricket World Cup semifinal match between New Zealand and South Africa at Eden Park. Photo by Anthony Au-Yeung-IDI/IDI via Getty Images.

PAGE 7, BOTTOM RIGHT: Auckland, New Zealand. 24 March 2015. AB de Villiers of South Africa faces the media at the press conference after the 2015 Cricket World Cup semifinal match between New Zealand and South Africa at Eden Park. Photo by Anthony Au-Yeung-IDI/IDI via Getty Images.

PAGE 8, bottom: Bengaluru, India. 14 November 2015. South Africa cricket team player AB de Villiers taking a short run during the second Test match between India and South Africa at the M. Chinnaswamy Stadium. Photo by Ajay Aggarwal/Hindustan Times via Getty Images.

PAGE 9: Cape Town, South Africa. 4 January 2016. AB de Villiers of South Africa bats as Jonny Bairstow of England keeps wicket during day three of the second Test at the PPC Newlands Stadium. Photo by Julian Finney/Getty Images.

PAGE 10: Cape Town, South Africa. 3 January 2016. Hashim Amla of South Africa celebrates his 50 with AB de Villiers during day two of the second Test match between South Africa and England at the PPC Newlands Stadium. Photo by Carl Fourie/Gallo Images.

PAGE 11, BOTTOM: Johannesburg, South Africa. 15 January 2016. AB de Villiers fielding during the Test match between the Proteas and England at the Bidvest Wanderers Stadium. Photo by Anne Laing.

PAGE 12, TOP: Johannesburg, South Africa. 18 January 2015. AB de Villiers of South Africa celebrates his 100 runs off 31 balls during the second Momentum ODI between South Africa and West Indies at the Bidvest Wanderers Stadium. Photo by Duif du Toit/Gallo Images.

PAGE 12, BOTTOM: Nagpur, India. 25 March 2016. AB de Villiers of South Africa in action during the ICC World Twenty20 India 2016 Group 1 match between South Africa and West Indies at the Vidarbha Cricket Association Stadium.

INDEX